Smoke Signals

Leisure, Consumption and Culture

General Editor: Rudy Koshar, *University of Wisconsin at Madison*

Leisure regimes in Europe (and North America) in the last two centuries have brought far-reaching changes in consumption patterns and consumer cultures. The past twenty years have seen the evolution of scholarship on consumption from a wide range of disciplines but historical research on the subject is unevenly developed for late modern Europe, just as the historiography of leisure practices is limited to certain periods and places. This series encourages scholarship on how leisure and consumer culture evolved with respect to an array of identities. It relates leisure and consumption to the symbolic systems with which tourists, shoppers, fans, spectators, and hobbyists have created meaning, and to the structures of power that have shaped such consumer behaviour. It treats consumption in general and leisure practices in particular as complex processes involving knowledge, negotiation, and the active formation of individual and collective selves.

Smoke Signals

Women, Smoking and Visual Culture in Britain

Penny Tinkler

⊘ BERG

Oxford • New York

English edition
First published in 2006 by
Berg
Editorial offices:
First Floor, Angel Court, 81 St Clements Street, Oxford OX4 1AW, UK
175 Fifth Avenue, New York, NY 10010, USA

Berg is the imprint of Oxford International Publishers Ltd.

Library of Congress Cataloging-in-Publication Data

Tinkler, Penny.
    Smoke signals : women, smoking and visual culture in Britain / Penny Tinkler.—
English ed.
        p. cm.—(Leisure, consumption, and culture)
    Includes bibliographical references and index.
    ISBN-13: 978-1-84520-267-5 (pbk.)
    ISBN-10: 1-84520-267-8 (pbk.)
    ISBN-13: 978-1-84520-266-8 (cloth)
    ISBN-10: 1-84520-266-X (cloth)
    1. Women—Tobacco use—Great Britain—History. 2. Women—Great Britain—
Social conditions—19th century. 3. Women—Great Britain—Social conditions—20th
century. 4. Mass media and culture—Great Britain—History. I. Title.

    HV5746.T56 2006
    364.1'4—dc22

                                                                        2006019890

British Library Cataloguing-in-Publication Data

A catalogue record for this book is available from the British Library.

        ISBN-13   978 1 84520 266 8 (Cloth)
                       978 1 84520 267 5 (Paper)

        ISBN-10   1 84520 266 X (Cloth)
                       1 84520 267 8 (Paper)

Typeset by JS Typesetting Ltd, Porthcawl, Mid Glamorgan
Printed in the United Kingdom by Biddles Ltd, King's Lynn

www.bergpublishers.com

For my parents, Joy and Frank Tinkler

Contents

List of Illustrations

Acknowledgements

My research on women and smoking has extended over many years. Earlier versions of some material in this book were originally published elsewhere. Chapters 4 and 5 draw on two articles. Material from '"Red Tips for Hot Lips": advertising cigarettes for young women in Britain, 1920–1970', *Women's History Review* 10 (2001), pp. 249–72, is reproduced with permission from Taylor & Francis; and material from 'Rebellion, Modernity and Romance: Smoking as a Gendered Practice in Popular Young Women's Magazines, Britain 1918–1939', *Women's Studies International Forum* 24 (2001), pp. 1–12, with the permission of Elsevier. Material from 'Refinement and Respectable Consumption: the Acceptable Face of Women's Smoking in Britain, 1918–1970', *Gender & History* 15 (2003), pp. 342–60, is reproduced in Chapter 6 with the permission of Blackwell Publishing.

Since beginning work on this project I have received help and support from many people. I am especially grateful to: Audrey Linkman for information and insights on photography, including feedback on Chapter 7; Cheryl Warsh for fruitful collaboration on several smoking articles and for reflections on Chapter 3; Virginia Berridge for helpful feedback on Chapter 8; and Penny Summerfield for constructive comment at the book proposal stage. Special thanks also go to Marcus Collins, David Doughan, Judy Giles and Lisa Z. Sigel for generously sharing thoughts and references, and to Richard Howard for seeking out pictures of women smokers. For references and images I am also grateful to Julie Anderson, Rosemary Betterton, Helle Bertramsen, Anne Charlton, Laura Doan, Carol Dyhouse, Rosemary Elliot, Hilary Graham, Fiona Hackney, Catherine Horwood, David Morgan, Lynda Nead, Tessa Stone, Ian Tyrrell, Jim Wood.

I would also like to thank the archivists, curators, librarians and administrative staff who assisted me in my research and in securing permission to reproduce images: the staff at the Imperial War Museum, especially Stephanie Clarke and Stephen Walton in the Department of Documents; Francis Dimond, The Royal Collection at Windsor Castle; Yvonne Edge, the Pankhurst Centre; the staff at the National Portrait Gallery Heinz Archive, especially Terence Pepper and Emma Butterfield; the staff, especially Natalia Illingsworth (formerly), at Bridgeman Art Library, London; Toni Booth, the National Museum of Photography, Film and Television; Vincent McKernan, the Greater Manchester County Record Office;

staff at The John Rylands University Library, especially Special Collections and Dorothy Clayton; staff at the British Library and the British Library Newspaper Library at Colindale, especially Christine Campbell and Stewart Gillies. Thanks also to the helpful staffs of the: Bristol Record Office; British Film Institute; Centre for North-West Regional Studies, Lancaster University; Girlguiding UK Archives; Manchester Central Library; Mass-Observation Archive at Sussex University; Nottingham Record Office; Women's Library.

In the course of researching this book, especially the chapter on portraiture, I have been touched by people's willingness to share their recollections and even their photographs with me. Warmest thanks go to Heather Barthelmas, Lucy Bland, Kits Browning, Marjorie Hughes, Richard Hutchison, Nigel Nicolson, Doug Rendell and Mary Shuttleworth.

Kathleen May and Fran Martin at Berg deserve special mention for keeping this book project on track; thanks also to George Pitcher for careful copyediting. On the home front, I would like to thank my Mum, Dad and friends for their ongoing support, especially Paula Shakespeare, Jan Lees, Mario Chin and Brenda and John Jackson. My greatest debt is, however, to Carolyn Jackson. Although working to complete her own book, *Lads and Ladettes in School*, Carolyn has been tireless in her support of me. Her careful and critical reading and rereading of chapters has been invaluable, as has her fresh perspective on images. I am deeply indebted to Carolyn for this amd much more.

Women, Smoking and Visual Culture, 1880–1980: An Introduction

Vesta Tilley, famous male impersonator of the late-Victorian and Edwardian music hall, enchanted and amused her audiences because she was a woman who, on stage or in front of the camera, *appeared* as a man in dress and behaviour (Fig. 1.1). Her performance hinged on a precise and unambiguous performance of masculinities. Hence the clothes, the poses and the props, including the cigarette, were all associated almost exclusively with men and masculinities. Her success hinged on her play with gender, and the stark contrast the audience assumed between her female gender and the masculinities she performed.[1] Key to Tilley's performance was the fact that women very rarely smoked (especially in public), while men routinely did. The smoking practices of a man would have been dull

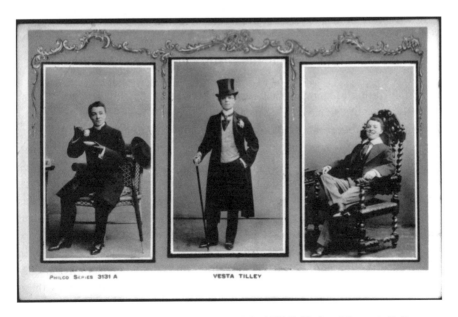

Figure 1.1   Postcard of Vesta Tilley, actress (NPG x33288). National Portrait Gallery, London.

viewing for a music-hall audience, while a woman who smoked in public would have provoked outrage. But when Vesta Tilley appeared on stage or in front of the camera dressed as a dandified gentleman with a cigarette between her teeth, she induced laughter.

At the time that Vesta Tilley performed, few women smoked, and even fewer dared to be seen smoking. Smoking did gain in popularity among certain groups of women from 1880, but in 1920 the proportion of women who smoked was too small to record.[2] Over the next three decades this changed dramatically. By 1949, 41 per cent of women aged sixteen years and over, from across the social-class spectrum, were smokers of manufactured cigarettes, but though cigarette smoking was established as a female practice it was still more common among men (63 per cent) than women.[3] By 1980, however, the proportion of men and women who smoked cigarettes was almost equal (42 and 39 per cent respectively).[4] The period between 1880 and 1980 also witnessed dramatic changes to the gender associations of smoking. While in the 1800s smoking was an activity associated almost exclusively with masculinities as demonstrated by Vesta Tilley, by 1950 cigarette smoking was widely perceived as compatible with a range of respectable femininities (cigars and pipes remaining firmly masculine in association). In spite of the emergence after 1950 of scientific evidence that smoking caused fatal diseases, it has been difficult to dispel the idea that smoking is compatible with femininity. The processes by which cigarette smoking was established, and then consolidated, as a female and feminine practice are the subject of this book.

A Visual Dimension to the History of Women's Smoking

The feminization of smoking that occurred between 1880 and 1980 was fundamentally, but not exclusively, a visual phenomenon. Visual themes are central to the history of women's smoking in three main ways. First, there were shifts in the visibility of women smoking, and changes in the implications for women from different social groups of being *seen* to smoke. Second, smoking practices were perceived and used by women as *visual statements* about status and identity. Women were aware of the power of appearances to communicate and smoking was a highly visual practice. Some even used photography to explore and experiment with the signifying possibilities of the cigarette. Third, during the twentieth century *visual images* of women smokers became increasingly prominent especially in print media, on film and, after 1950, on television. While the visual was widely utilized to promote women's smoking, visual imagery was also utilized by those who sought to discourage women from smoking. There was also another, and more peripheral, visual theme. Aside from taste and physical sensations, smoking offered women *visual pleasure*.

In this book I argue that visual culture is key to mapping and understanding the history of women's smoking in Britain. Visual culture provides a vital contribution to explanations of the gender dimensions of smoking history including the changing experiences and expectations of women, shifting constructions of femininity, and the gendering of smoking practices. Attention to the visual also heightens the explanatory potential of concepts which are central to the history of women's smoking and, more generally, to the history of women, such as femininity, respectability and modernity. The need for a visual dimension goes beyond the importance of looking at representations of women's smoking 1880–1980: it is essential to understanding how people saw images, themselves and others.

Though there is widespread acknowledgement of the importance of visual images for the history of women's smoking in the West,[5] there has been no detailed exploration of the relationship between women, smoking and visual culture in Britain or, indeed, elsewhere. Studies of specific visual media, notably fine art, tobacco packaging and erotica, provide valuable insights into aspects of the relationship between women, smoking and visual culture but these are not integrated into a broader exploration of the history of women's smoking and the place of the visual in this.[6] Recent studies by Matthew Hilton, and by Rosemary Elliot whose oral history study focuses exclusively on women, offer important insights into the gender dimensions of British smoking history, but they only briefly address visual images of women smokers and, more generally, the visual dimensions of the relationship between women and smoking.[7]

This book explores the changing social, economic, political, medical and technological contexts which provided the framework of opportunities and motivations for women to smoke; it also gives a central place to smoking in visual culture. Exploration of smoking in visual culture does not simply involve the study of visual images or objects 'which address the sense of sight to a significant extent',[8] it also takes account of 'the centrality of vision in everyday experience and the production of meaning'.[9] Visual images are essential features of this study and I use them in two main ways. First, I consider the visual images which contributed to the discourses framing women's understanding of smoking. By 'discourse' I mean 'a group of statements which structure the way a thing is thought, and the way we act on the basis of that thinking'.[10] The focus on the visual dimension of discourses is justified by, at a general level, the cultural dominance of the visual in late nineteenth- and twentieth-century Britain and, at the specific level, the proliferation after 1920 of images of women smoking. Christina Hughes identifies several features of discourse pertinent to this exploration of the history of women's smoking. A discourse can shape subjectivity, it can 'both authorize' some experiences and 'deauthorize' others.[11] As discourses are not static and change in relation to changing socio-economic conditions, so too do subjectivities. There are also multiple discourses at any one time. Often 'the individual is the

3

meeting point of many, sometimes conflicting, socially and historically defined discourses'[12] and this can result in complex and diverse subjective positions. Discourse is also not a straitjacket: women may take up dominant meanings, seek to resist them, or position themselves in a counter-discourse. Women may also seek to invent new discourses; this can happen when experience jars with, or is quite literally inconceivable within, available discourses. It is, however, not easy to reject dominant discourses. Drawing on Edholm, Hughes explains that: 'Even when we as individuals reject the subject positions offered in dominant images, or see them as irrelevant, it is still difficult, in the absence of many powerfully visualized alternatives, to escape their influence and impact'.[13]

The study of the visual images that contributed to discourses on women's smoking involves consideration of a range of public – especially media – images in terms of how they produced understandings of gender. To do this I explore whether, and to what extent, images of women smoking become part of everyday life and discourse for women. This necessitates attention to the accessibility of images, how and where they were displayed, seen and used by women. I also examine what Stuart Hall calls the 'preferred meanings' of these images.[14] As Ros Ballaster et al. explain: '[w]hile any one cultural text offers a multiplicity of meanings to its readers, ultimately not just any meaning can or will be drawn from it'; '[r]eadings are "structured in dominance" offering a pattern of "preferred" options in line with the "preferred" institutional, political and ideological order'.[15] This necessitates recognition of the socio-historical context of the image and its intended frame (advertisement, postcard, art work). It also requires attention to the location of the image (women's magazine, art gallery, street billboard) as 'places, with their particular ways of spectating, mediate the visual effects of those images'.[16] Of course, not all images were encountered in their intended frames and locations and this has implications for meaning. Additionally, 'preferred meanings' do not translate automatically into 'preferred readings': individuals may not recognize preferred meanings or they may reject, resist or rework them.[17] However, though there were exceptions, when women read texts in their intended contexts they usually recognised preferred meanings even if they subsequently resisted or rejected them.

The second way in which I use visual images is to shed light on how women used smoking in the construction of identities. This can illuminate aspects of women's engagement with discourses on smoking. For this I draw on women's photographs of themselves smoking. Women's portraits of themselves as smokers have so far been overlooked as a historical resource although, as this book demonstrates, they can be revealing. Working with photographic portraits requires attention to the content of the image (which needs to be read alongside prevailing discourses on women and on smoking). It also involves consideration of how the image was produced and the part the woman played in this process, and how the photograph was subsequently read and used by the woman.

Context is crucial for interpreting images of women smoking and teasing out their social and historical significance. The changing social, economic and cultural conditions of life for women are a crucial part of this context, and an important element of this is the place of the visual in women's experience. In the period 1880 to 1980 the visual dimensions of social and cultural life were inextricably related to processes of modernization and women's experience of modernity. 'Modernity' has been conceptualized in a confusing number of ways.[18] The notion that modernity is a quality of social experience, an approach promoted by Marshall Berman and subsequently adopted and developed by many cultural theorists, is the one used here.[19] As Alan O'Shea explains, modernity is lived out in the constantly shifting 'economic, political, social and cultural co-ordinates of modernization'; modernity is, therefore, 'the practical negotiation of one's life and one's identity within a complex and fast-changing world'.[20] Modernization began in the seventeenth century, but in Western societies the process has accelerated since 1880. This has involved 'massive transformations in economic and industrial structures, in forms of production and consumption, in demographic movements, in communications, in political forms, in the arts and intellectual thought, and in popular culture'.[21] A key feature of the Western experience of modernity is 'a preponderance of occasions for people to *see*, and *want* to see'.[22] The processes of modernization are, however, experienced differently, not least by national context. As Judy Giles notes, the 'British experience of modernity was fashioned from specific forms of class that were distinctive to Britain and had their roots in the past, from Britain's position as the first industrialized nation, from its wide-scale colonization that created an enormous world empire, and from its, often difficult, cultural relationship with the USA'.[23] Understanding the feminization of smoking, therefore, needs to be approached in the context of the processes and experiences of British modernity in which the visual assumed considerable importance in the cultural construction of social life. The next section of this chapter maps out the visual terrain of women's experience of British modernity before introducing the shape of this book.

Modernity and Visual Experience

Although a narrative of increased reliance on the visual is problematic because it marginalizes the experiences of blind and partially-sighted people, the visual did assume a central place in daily life and in the production and exchange of meaning for most people living in Britain from the 1850s: 'The modern world is very much a "seen" phenomenon.'[24] Even if the visual was not the only sensory dimension, it was often the one which people seemed most aware of. Victorian society, as Kate Flint demonstrates, offered an 'accelerated expansion of diverse opportunities for differing sorts of spectatorship' (the look, the gaze, the practices of observation, surveillance, visual pleasure);[25] this 'frenzy of the visible'[26] continued into the twentieth century. This process involved more than a proliferation of visual images, but also included new viewing opportunities, new positions from which to see and new ways of seeing. Experiences of space and time altered. Pleasures changed. Understandings of identity shifted. There emerged a heightened awareness of the communication potential of the visual and, following from this, acquisition of new and more refined visual literacies.

The ascendancy of the visual was facilitated by the expansion of cities from the 1800s. In the context of (sub)urban life, 'surface impressions' became increasingly important. As Mica Nava explains, amid the 'continuous flux and frequent encounters' of the city, 'signs and appearances acquire a new importance and substitute increasingly for traditional narratives of social and geographical belonging'.[27] While the railways brought increasing numbers of commuters and day-trippers into the cities, trains also offered 'new positions of spectatorship' and the speed of travel produced new visual experiences.[28] Consumer culture contributed to the dominance of the visual as 'spectacle and capitalism became indivisible'.[29] Visual image was key to the cultural framing of mass-produced goods and their transformation, through retailing practices and advertising strategies, into what sociologists have variously termed 'symbolic goods' or 'commodity signs'.[30] Advertisement 'turned the streets quite literally into environments to be read',[31] while sophisticated visual literacies were increasingly required to distinguish between commodities. The ascendancy of the visual was consolidated by its heightened status as a source of knowledge (exhibitions, museums, galleries, also empiricist forms of knowledge). Photography, invented in 1839, contributed to this and became a primary source of knowledge about the world, the self and, through advertising and marketing, commodities. While the expansion of the illustrated press – *Punch*, *The Illustrated London News*, *The Graphic*, *Pictorial Times*, and *The Sketch* – disseminated photographs and other images to the well off,[32] the carte de visite (a small photographic postcard patented in 1854) brought to the masses knowledge of the famous, the far-off and the familiar.

How people related to the visual and their opportunities for spectatorship were mediated by social class and gender. The idea of modern life as a visual spectacle has traditionally been conceived in masculine terms and in relation to specific types of public space: 'In standard accounts of modernity the key figures are all male – the *flâneur*, the dandy, the loner in the crowd – and the key spaces of modernity are also masculine – the nation-state, the workplace, the corporation, the city street.'[33] These androcentric accounts have recently been challenged.[34] At least from the 1880s, women were not excluded from the visual experiences of modernity in the public sphere. Women increasingly engaged in paid work, political action and education in urban centres, and also had unaccompanied access to exhibitions and galleries and participated, through their use of department stores, in the 'exploding culture of consumption and spectacle'.[35] Women's access to the visual terrain of modernity was not, however, restricted to public urban spaces. As Giles reveals, the visual was crucial to 'domestic modernity'[36] in the first half of the twentieth century. In the 'parlour and the suburb' housewives engaged in the visual work and pleasures of shopping (purchasing or just looking) and the perusal of magazines. Through visions of modern living offered by department stores and magazines, and also by the Ideal Home Exhibition, millions of suburban wives were touched by the processes of modernization and, moreover, could imagine themselves, indeed create themselves, as modern subjects.[37] Many of these modern visual experiences were, nevertheless, restricted to women of the middle and upper classes at the turn of the century. Indeed, most working-class women and men, even city dwellers, were positioned on the margins of the visual terrain of modernity until around the time of the First World War.

The dramatic growth of mass media in the first half of the twentieth century, alongside the further expansion of urban spaces and commodity culture, extended and consolidated the dominance of visual culture for women and men of all social classes. Photographs, cartoons and illustrations became increasingly prominent in the national press after 1900, and by the 1920s photographs were a regular feature of news reportage and advertisements; the *Daily Mail* featured a whole page of photographs as a regular entertainment feature. Within these features, as Bingham demonstrates, images of women became increasingly common, to the point that newspapers were visually feminized.[38] The spread of newspaper reading ensured that these pictures entered the lives of women and men from all walks of life. In 1910 the national dailies sold 4.5 million copies; by 1939 this had risen to 10.5 million, and 69 per cent of the population aged sixteen and over read a national newspaper and 82 per cent a national Sunday paper.[39] The women's press, which proliferated from the end of the nineteenth century and diversified to cater for all social-class groups, also contributed to the prominence of the visual. Women's magazines were not only increasingly commonplace in the lives of women but, as Sally Stein has observed of US magazines at this time, though still dominated by large chunks of text they were 'becoming a predominantly visual experience, constructing an audience of spectators'.[40] The increased priority given to images was first noticeable in elite publications. In the 1890s *The Lady* featured lots of illustrations while *The Princess* also included photographs. The stylish magazine *Vogue*, first published in Britain in 1916, relied heavily on photographs and illustrations. Magazines for women lower down the social scale were limited to illustrations, although by 1930 middle-class monthly magazines were filled with photographs and other visual images mainly in the form of advertisements. The development of colour gravure printing provided the necessary conditions for *Woman*, launched in 1937, to offer to the masses full-colour illustrations as well as photographs.

The advent of film had a dramatic impact on visual culture. Cinema-going was first established as a leisure pursuit for children, men and especially women, of the urban working class in the years just prior to the First World War, but by the late 1920s it was a cross-class pleasure.[41] The growing popularity of cinema is reflected in the expansion of provision: in Liverpool there were thirty-two cinemas in 1913 and ninety-six by 1939, while in Birmingham there were fifty-seven and 110 cinemas respectively.[42] In the 1950s the growth of television ownership began to alter the visual experience of domestic life and eroded the previously central place of cinema in the leisure of women and young people.[43] Although the first regular television programme service was broadcast in 1936 to viewers who lived within a 25-mile radius of London's Alexandra Palace, in 1948 television viewing was still an elite practice restricted to upper- and middle-class homes; there were roughly 45,000 licences in a population of roughly 50 million.[44] In the 1950s television viewing was an occasion, and it seems likely that the programmes and spot advertisements were watched with care. A study of middle-class television viewers reveals that a 'sense of public excitement ... accompanied the initial spectacle of TV' and that early TV viewing 'was often an occasion for large numbers to gather at friends' or relatives' houses'.[45] The formality of early viewing experience was accentuated by the location of the television, viewing was a 'more deliberate, self-conscious activity, often requiring a move into a separate room for those who were allowed to watch'.[46] This way of viewing changed as the television became integrated into everyday life for all social-class groups. The number of households possessing televisions increased rapidly and, in 1955, some 5 million licences were issued and, by the late 1960s, 16 million had been issued; by 1956, ownership or rental of a television was 'becoming a standard feature of every home'.[47]

The 'impact on women of being able to look cannot be overestimated'.[48] Exposed to the visual spectacles of modern life, women acquired new and complex visual skills which, as Nava points out,[49] equipped them with valuable cultural capital. Women became increasingly experienced at using the persuasive power of the visual, as revealed by the suffragettes' use of colour and spectacle in the period 1908–1914 and the use of photography by the Women's Police Service in 1919.[50] On a day-to-day basis, initially through their experience of department stores and magazines, and then the cinema, women acquired sophisticated visual literacies to decode and encode the 'new signs ... of status and individuality'.[51]

New kinds of spectatorship were afforded by the shift in the visual terrain of womanhood, including opportunities for scrutinizing others. In a culture where it was rude to stare, and still is, photographs allowed women to look closely. Carte de visites of famous people and, increasingly, of one's friends and family facilitated this from the 1860s, as did photographic portraits which appeared in papers, magazines and all manner of advertising and publicity materials after

1920. Cloaked in darkness, movies afforded women pleasurable opportunities for scrutinizing desirable others. In the interwar years when most working-class women made, rather than bought, fashions, women would regularly view and review movies to copy the fashions of Hollywood film stars such as Jean Harlow and Greta Garbo.[52] Hairstyles, make-up and mannerisms were also copied,[53] a process that required the explicit study of images and the development of refined skills of observation.

Photographs and film altered people's relationship to time (the apparent immediacy of the photograph belying its production in the past, often a distant one) and space. On the one hand these visual media offered glimpses of people far removed from everyday life. The four corners of the globe were, for example, accessible from a cinema seat in virtually all towns and cities by 1930, but the dominance of the American film industry ensured that it was the American way of life that was most frequently 'experienced' on screen. On the other hand, these visual media also offered close ups of people that were far more intimate than facilitated by ordinary social encounters. Sexual intimacies were seen at close quarters at the cinema while, with the establishment and dissemination of visual pornography around 1900, visual intimacy extended to parts of the body (most often a woman's) usually hidden from view: 'Cheap, mass-produced representations transformed dirty words into dirty pictures. Sexual ideas now relied on visual, rather than literary, cues'.[54]

Film, magazines, advertising, were all 'novel cultural mirrors'[55] in which women came to know others differently. Modern life also provided new ways of knowing oneself. Changes in the urban environment, such as the introduction of large windows and mirrors in department stores, contributed to a shift in women's visual self-knowledge as they scrutinized their images in full-length mirrors or caught glimpses of themselves as they went about their work and pleasures.

Photography is perhaps the most significant factor in changing the way people knew themselves, a phenomenon observed on both sides of the Atlantic.[56] In the 1840s, Mayhew discovered a photographer who claimed that some of his clients were unable to recognize themselves in a photograph and were therefore duped into purchasing a photographic portrait of someone else: 'The fact is, people don't know their own faces. Half of 'em have never looked in a glass half a dozen times in their life, and directly they see a pair of eyes and a nose, they fancy they are their own.'[57] Flint perceptively comments that even if this was a fabrication on the part of the photographer, the photographer's story conveys the novelty which could be involved for some people in 'fixing and objectifying an image of the self'.[58]

Following a period of rapid expansion in the late 1850s, commercial photographic studios were established in most large towns and cities. Manchester had 17 studios in 1855 and 34 by 1858, Edinburgh had 24 in 1858.[59] In 1931, according to one estimate, there were about 30 studios just in and around London's Bond Street.[60] The development of new photographic technology in the 1850s and 1870s enabled photographs to be made relatively cheaply, in multiples and 'while-you-wait'.[61] By 1900 all social classes used the services of commercial photographic studios. 'Club packages', often organized through the paid workplace from the 1870s, allowed poorer people to save for a portrait through weekly payments. Cheap, 'instant', but poor quality, photographs were also available from itinerant photographers who touted for trade at fairgrounds and on beaches.[62] The introduction of the Kodak camera in 1888, which by 1895 had dropped in price from five guineas to one, expanded photographic opportunities among the middle and upper classes; a process extended by the introduction in 1900 of the brownie camera which was portable and cost a mere five shillings.

Women experimented with different looks in front of the camera: they did this at home and at commercial studios. Titled women willingly posed in strange costumes to allow professional photographers to produce exhibition work.[63] Visual self-knowledge was not confined to the face and the clothed figure, some women desiring to know themselves in other ways. One example of a desire for new know-ledges of the self is the demand for nude portraiture. Madame Yevonde recalls that in the interwar years she was 'often asked by women sitters to take them in the nude'.[64] Whether home cameras were used to such effect is impossible to comment on.

By the twentieth century an increasing number of women had become conscious of their image, practised at critically assessing it, and concerned to exert control over it. The changing fortunes of photographic studios are revealing of women's image-consciousness. The use of photographic portraits as self-publicity is also evidence of this. Distributing professional photographs of oneself became a common practice from the late 1800s, a practice facilitated by the availability of cheap multiple copies. In the interwar years, Society women and those in literary, artistic and sporting circles often distributed signed photographs of themselves to friends and professional contacts. Interwar debutantes regarded photographic portraits as self-advertisement and were keen to sit for photographers in return for a complimentary free photograph and the knowledge that their portrait would most likely appear in the pages of a glossy magazine.[65]

Important outcomes of these changes were greater attention to appearances and new ways of thinking about self as under scrutiny. Women were increasingly schooled in the subtleties of looking and being looked at. Visual self-assessment was encouraged by the media. Advertisements targeted at women frequently deployed this line, emphasizing that women were always on view. Women's magazines also made an art of guiding readers in studying how others looked and in refashioning oneself; this feminine art was communicated widely as papers catering for teenaged girls and women from all social-class groups proliferated in the twentieth century.[66] Newspapers took these feminine lessons into the home on a daily basis as most of the popular papers introduced 'women's interest' features on beauty and fashions.

New opportunities for self-inspection contributed to changing understandings of selfhood. Appearance was elevated to being the key to identity. The importance of outward appearance as an indicator of identity occurred from the mid-nineteenth century, according to Sennett.[67] Flint notes of late-Victorian Britain that though there was an expansion of disciplines which claimed to read character from features of the body, there was simultaneously a recognition that identity was 'not innate, but performative'.[68] Focusing on fashion, Elizabeth Wilson also argues that from the 1850s the individual played an active role in visible identity construction: 'It was the beginnings of the idea of the Self as a Work of Art, the "personality" as something that extended to dress, scent and surroundings, all of which made an essential contribution to the formation of "self" – at least for women.'[69] The processes of self-monitoring and reflexive self-fashioning that Anthony Giddens identifies as features of late or high modernity clearly operated in the late Victorian period, especially for women of the upper and middle classes, and was well established for women across the social-class spectrum by the 1950s (although not always realizable).[70] Body planning, which was integral to the identity project,[71] was quite fundamentally a visual project and one tackled largely through consumption.

After 1880, smoking practices increasingly became part of the modern and highly visual project of constructing feminine identities. Images of women smoking were features of the visual terrain of modern life and contributed to how women understood what it was to be successful, feminine, modern, sexy, respectable, sophisticated and so on. But even before women smokers had a high-profile visual presence in interwar British society, smoking offered women a graphic vocabulary to say things about themselves and, indeed, to experiment with identities. Women became adept at using the significations of smoking not only to articulate identities, but to read others and to shape the meaning of social interactions. Smoking also served other purposes and was experienced most notably by many as a comfort and/or as a stimulant, but these purposes were inseparable from the visual significance of smoking. Particularly after 1920 with the proliferation of images of smoking in the mass media, women's understandings of smoking were inextricably bound up with these visual representations. Moreover, and this preceded the emergence of mass-media images of women smokers, even if women were not concerned to smoke for the sake of appearances they were still aware of the meanings attached to smoking and the significance of being seen to smoke. Issues relating to being seen to smoke were often important for whether women did smoke and, if they did, how and where.

11

Outline

The growing popularity of smoking among women between 1880 and 1950 is explored in Chapters 2 and 3. Together these chapters chart the changing social, economic, political and technological contexts that provided the framework of opportunities and motivations for women to smoke. They also explore explanations of why women smoked. Chapter 2 charts the emergence of smoking among women from 1880 through to 1919. While smoking increased among certain groups of women, and the practice attracted increased attention in the media, women were rarely seen smoking in public and visual images of women smokers were scarce. Chapter 3 focuses on the period from 1920 to 1950 during which the prevalence of women's smoking grew dramatically and, moreover, became established as a cross-class phenomenon. Shifts in smoking culture and the high visual profile of women smokers provided an important context in which interwar women decided whether or not to smoke. The ascendancy, during the Second World War, of the idea that smoking was a legitimate source of comfort for women as well as men encouraged an even greater number of women to take up the smoking habit and to do so in public.

Chapters 4–6 explore in detail the visual dimensions of the discourses that were central to the feminization of smoking between 1880 and 1950. This period, and especially the years between 1920 and 1950, was pivotal in the redefinition of smoking from a practice associated principally with men and masculinities to one also associated with women and femininities. Each chapter addresses a range of public – especially commercial – representations of women smokers including illustrations, advertising, portraits, cartoons and fashion features in the print media, as well as representations of women smokers in film, art and visual ephemera such as erotic postcards.

The association of smoking with modern and emancipated women is explored in Chapter 4. From an alignment with women's liberation in the late Victorian and Edwardian period, the notion of a woman's right to smoke gained heightened significance in the context of the interwar discourse of modernity. Indeed, in the interwar period smoking became a signifier of women's modernity and was aligned, in particular, with the modern companionate ideal of relationships with men and with modern looks. Smoking was, however, more than just a sign of modernity, the practice of smoking actually contributed to the making of modern women.

The discourse of the modern and emancipated smoker drew on two long-established sets of ideas, the association of smoking with men and masculinities and the association of smoking with female sexuality. The 'sexual promise' is the subject of Chapter 5. This chapter considers the equation, especially prior to 1915, of smoking with men's enjoyment of women's bodies, and it explores the sexualized images of women smokers that circulated prior to 1914. Although this sexual discourse on smoking was not dominant (the association of smoking with men and masculinities was still paramount), it was important in providing the foundations for the highly visible feminization of smoking that occurred after 1920; indeed the feminization of smoking was inextricably tied to its heterosexualization. By 1940, mainstream representations of women's smoking were firmly associated with sexual allure and sexual signalling.

When women smokers began to appear regularly in the interwar mainstream media they were invariably portrayed as respectable. This was due, in part, to the media preoccupation with attractive images of respectable women and the efforts of tobacco companies to cast aside the disreputable associations of women's relationship to tobacco. Chapter 6 explores the visual parameters of respectable smoking for women and argues that it is no coincidence that interwar women smokers were invariably portrayed as middle or upper class. At no point did working-class women appear routinely as smokers; respectability was always a class act.

After 1920 the photographic image, largely through the prominence of advertising and fashion promotions, became increasingly key to the visual presence of women smokers in the media. It was nevertheless unusual for women to appear smoking in their own photographs prior to 1940. To be photographed smoking was an extremely meaningful gesture for an interwar woman; prior to 1920 it was rare and radical. Chapter 7 considers whether portraits of women smoking can contribute to understanding women's relationship to smoking. Drawing on 'joke', 'casual' photographs and commissioned portraits from the period 1900–1940, this chapter explores the shifting photographic opportunities for women to appear smoking, and how some women used these opportunities to make visual statements about themselves.

The final chapter looks to the period between 1950 and 1980 when smoking was firmly established as a feminine practice. In the context of mounting scientific evidence of a link between smoking and fatal diseases, a key question is why women continued to smoke cigarettes even though men were increasingly quitting or changing to pipes and cigars. Three key factors are addressed: the tendency in the media and health-education campaigns to play down or sideline the dangers of smoking for women; the continued high visibility of smoking as a feminine practice; and the gender-specific stresses that women experienced and why they felt that cigarettes helped them cope. Although in abstract terms smoking seemingly became an unattractive option for women as well as for men, in visual terms smoking continued to look good. It was not until the 1960s that images of physically unattractive women smokers were seen in the media and these were the exception rather than the rule. Significantly, it was in this context that the working-class woman smoker became visible.

Notes

1. Maitland, *Vesta Tilley*, p. 24.

2. Wald, et al., *UK Smoking Statistics*, p. 13, Table 2.1.

3. Ibid., pp. 34–5, Tables 4.1.1, 4.1.2.

4. Ibid. The prevalence of smoking was still higher among men than women because a minority of men also smoked cigars and pipes.

5. On Britain: Hilton, *Smoking*; Elliot, 'Destructive but Sweet'. Also Tinkler: '"Red Tips for Hot Lips"'; 'Rebellion, Modernity and Romance'; 'Refinement and Respectable Consumption'; 'Smoking and Sapphic Modernities'. On the US: Ernster, 'Mixed Messages for Women'; Schudson, *Advertising*; Brandt, 'Recruiting Women Smokers': Greaves, *Smoke Screen*; Warsh, 'Smoke and Mirrors'; Tate, *Cigarette Wars*. On Australia: Tyrrell, *Deadly Enemies*; Tyrrell, 'The Limits of Persuasion'. See also Gilman and Xun, *Global History*.

6. Mitchell, 'The "New Woman" as Prometheus'; Mitchell, 'Images of Exotic Women'; Koetzle, *Seductive Smoke*; Kalmar, 'The Houkah'. See also, Hutcheon and Hutcheon, 'Smoking in Opera'; Isenberg, 'Cinematic Smoke'.

7. Hilton, *Smoking*; Elliot, 'Destructive but sweet'.

8. Walker and Chaplin, *Visual Culture*, p. 2.

9. Lister and Wells, 'Seeing Beyond Belief', p. 63.

10. Rose, *Visual Methodologies*, p. 136.

11. Hughes, *Women's Contemporary Lives*, p. 4.

12. Cited in Hughes, Ibid., p. 19.

13. Ibid., p. 11.

14. Hall, 'Encoding/Decoding', p. 134.

15. Ballaster et al., *Women's Worlds*, p. 29.

16. Rose, *Visual Methodologies*, p. 26.

17. On people's different responses to 'preferred meanings' see, for example, Hall, 'Encoding/Decoding', pp. 136–8; Ballaster et al., *Women's Worlds*, chapter 5.

18. Peter Osborne identifies three understandings of modernity: 'as a category of historical periodization, a quality of social experience, and as an (incomplete) project', the latter toward a rational moral and political order characterized by the triumph of science and reason over nature, religious mysticism and superstition. Cited in O'Shea, 'English Subjects of Modernity', p. 8.

19. For example, essays in Nava and O'Shea, *Modern Times*; Doan, *Fashioning Sapphism*; Giles, *Parlour and the Suburb*.

20. O'Shea, 'English Subjects of Modernity', p. 11.

21. Ibid., p. 13.

22. Bell, *Cultural Contradictions of Capitalism*, p. 106.

23. Giles, *Parlour and the Suburb*, p. 7.

24. Jenks, 'The Centrality of the Eye', p. 2.

25. Flint, *Victorians*, p. 2.

26. Jean-Louis Comolli, cited in Flint, *Victorians*, p. 3.

27. Nava, 'Modernity's Disavowal', p. 39.

28. Flint, *Victorians*, p. 8.

29. Richards, *Commodity Culture*, p. 16.

30. Laermans, 'Learning to Consume', p. 94; Leiss et al., *Social Communication in Advertising*.

31. Flint, *Victorians*, p. 5.

32. Ibid., p. 3.

33. Giles, *Parlour and the Suburb*, p. 9.

34. Nava, 'Modernity's Disavowal'. See also Felski, *Gender of Modernity*; Giles, *Parlour and the Suburb*; Rappaport, *Shopping*.

35. Nava, 'Modernity's Disavowal', p. 46.

36. Giles, *Parlour and the Suburb*, p. 11.

37. Ibid.

38. Bingham, *Gender, Modernity and the Popular Press*, p. 32.

39. Stevenson, *British Society*, pp. 402–3.

40. Stein, 'The graphic ordering of desire', p. 146.

41. Davies, 'Cinema and Broadcasting', pp. 269–71.

42. Ibid., p. 269. See also Richards, *Age of the Dream Palace*.

43. O'Sullivan, 'Television Memories', p. 161.

44. Corner, 'General Introduction', p. 3.

45. O'Sullivan, 'Television Memories', p. 164.

46. Ibid., p. 167.

47. Corner, 'General Introduction', pp. 4, 6.

48. Giles, *Parlour and the Suburb*, p. 109.

49. Nava, 'Modernity's Disavowal', p. 48.

50. Tickner, *Spectacle of Women*; Doan, *Fashioning Sapphism*.

51. Nava, 'Modernity's Disavowal', p. 47.

52. Alexander, 'Becoming a woman', pp. 263–4.

53. Jackson, *Middle Classes*; Stacey, *Star Gazing*.

54. Sigel, *Governing Pleasures*, p. 145.

55. Peiss, 'Making Faces', p. 143.

56. Peiss, *Hope in a Jar*, p. 45.

57. Cited in Flint, *Victorians*, p. 3.

58. Ibid., p. 3.

59. Linkman, *The Victorians*, note 28/2/32, available from author.

60. de Ville and Haden-Guest, *Society Photography*, p. 19.

61. Replacement of the daguerrotype by the cheap collodion positive made photography much cheaper and the stereostopic camera enabled production of multiple prints, see Linkman, *Victorians*.

62. Linkman, *Victorians*.

63. Yevonde, *In Camera*, p. 232.

64. Ibid., p. 243, see also p. 244.

65. de Ville and Haden-Guest, *Society Photography*, p. 20.

66. Tinkler, *Constructing Girlhood*; White, *Women's Magazines*.

67. Cited in O'Shea, 'English Subjects of Modernity', p. 23.

68. Flint, *Victorians*, p. 18.
69. Wilson, *Adorned in Dreams*, p. 123.
70. Giddens, *Modernity and Self-Identity*.
71. Ibid. See also, Shilling, *Body and Social Theory*.

2

Invisible Women Smokers, 1880–1919

In the 1840s, when Charles Dickens encountered an English mother and daughter travelling in Geneva who smoked cigarettes, he was astonished: 'for in all my experience of "ladies" of one kind and another, I never saw a woman – not a basket woman or a gypsy – smoke before!'[1] Women have used tobacco since it was first introduced to Britain in the sixteenth century; pipes were smoked by women until the 1700s when snuff became fashionable.[2] With the Industrial Revolution, which was accompanied by the separation of home and workplace and the ascendancy of the ideology of separate spheres, the genders became polarized in their relationship to tobacco. Tobacco use became defined as a masculine activity; correspondingly, it was defined as unfeminine and unrespectable for women. Some upper-class women did continue to use tobacco, so too did women of the *demi-monde* and, at the other end of the social spectrum, old and poor women. However, as evident from Dickens' astonishment, tobacco use was widely perceived as a male practice. It was unusual for women to smoke and even more unusual for women to be seen smoking. From the end of the nineteenth century this began to change. This chapter introduces the range of women that used tobacco products, and especially cigarettes, in the period 1880 to 1919, before considering why. Although by 1919 smoking was established among certain groups of women, particularly from the middle and upper classes, women smokers were rarely seen in public. The final part of this chapter addresses the issues which being seen to smoke posed for women.

The Re-emergence of the Woman Smoker

Signs emerged from the 1880s that the 'cigarette habit' was growing among women.[3] By the 1890s women's smoking was a hot topic. 'Female fumigators', according to J.D.Hunting in 1889, were on the increase;[4] a claim that was reiterated repeatedly in press reports and in the pages of *Punch* throughout the 1890s. Writing to the *Evening News* in 1897 a woman smoker declared, 'I know a great many smoking ladies; in fact, I do not know many who don't smoke.'[5] One source claimed that in 1898 one in ten women smoked.[6] These reports give a misleading impression of the extent of the practice because they invariably refer to specific groups of women and are probably exaggerated for the sake of the argument. Although they cannot, therefore, be read as precise measurements of the extent of smoking among women, they do indicate that in certain communities smoking was not uncommon and, moreover, that there was a growing awareness of women smokers. Claims about 'ladies' were, however, often ambiguous about social class. 'Smokeresses'[7] were noted across the social-class spectrum according to London tobacconists: 'smoking has been increasing among ladies for years past, and is increasing still. Of course it is principally practised among members of the demi-monde, but there are lady smokers in all ranks of society'.[8] The tobacco trade journal, *Tobacco Trade Review* (*TTR*), reiterated this in 1899 when it declared that it is 'an open secret that women of all grades in society ... are beginning to indulge in the cigarette'.[9] Although commentators pointed to evidence of smoking among women from across the social spectrum, the consensus was that the growth was particularly pronounced among the upper classes and certain sections of the middle class.

Upper- and Middle-class 'Smokeresses'

The Lady, a Society paper, declared in 1893 that 'more ladies smoke than ever before'.[10] Another Society journal, *The Princess*, reiterated these claims and reported that cigarettes were routinely offered to ladies after dinner and that the practice was pursued by such notables as the Empress of Russia and Princess Maud of Wales.[11] The veracity of these claims was confirmed by the *Westminster Gazette* which concluded that there 'was considerable foundation for the story'.[12] One Piccadilly tobacconist, the *Gazette* noted, 'frankly admitted that he did count a number of ladies among his regular customers' but, reflecting the continued stigma attached to women smoking, several tobacconists denied all knowledge that women smoked or even that 'ladies'' cigarettes existed.[13] Significantly, given the contentious nature of women's smoking, the Piccadilly retailer doubted that Princess Maud of Wales was a smoker. In 1898, the *Court Circular* offered further evidence that smoking was not uncommon among 'Society ladies'; 'young ladies' in Leeds and Liverpool were also reported to enjoy cigarettes.[14] Informal photographs of Queen Alexandra, Queen Consort of Edward VII, reveal that by the early 1900s she too had adopted the smoking habit.[15] Although reports suggest that women's smoking was principally an urban practice, there is also evidence of a rural following among upper- and middle-class women. In some country houses, according to Hunting in 1889, 'it is not uncommon thing for the ladies to join the gentlemen in the smoking-room, and to mingle the fumes of their dainty, mild-flavoured cigarettes with the more masculine cigar smoke'.[16] Although a country journal subsequently declared that 'habitual' smoking among female country folk was rare, it did acknowledge that some rural 'ladies' 'play at smoking … mild, scented cigarettes'.[17] In general, however, women's smoking appears to have been principally an urban phenomenon.

Middle-class women workers were also adopting the smoking habit by the late 1880s. Female art students and some 'literary' ladies had been identified by Hunting as smokers in 1889. By 1898, Edith Vance, secretary of the National Secular Society and a supporter of women's suffrage, declared confidently in a letter to the *Daily Mail* that 30 per cent of women workers smoked.[18] It is unlikely that Vance included working-class women in this figure: her statistic seems more probable for professional women workers. Nevertheless, though the *Daily Mail* declared that 'Miss Vance's admission is shocking' and her statistics 'fanciful', it admitted that 'it is certainly true that ladies smoke more than they used to'.[19] Occasional letters to magazines confirm that some young working women of the lower middle classes had succumbed to the cigarette habit, although this was often greeted with disapproval.[20] While it is not possible to offer precise measurement of the taking up of smoking among middle-class women workers, by 1914 smoking was sufficiently common in London that one employer, Thomas Disher (later to became Richmal Crompton's brother-in-law), expressly advertised for a secretary who *did not* drink or smoke.[21]

Middle-class women smokers were not exclusively from the ranks of the employed, since there is also evidence of smoking among 'genteel' feminine residents of London suburbs,[22] going on largely behind closed doors. One woman recalled her early smoking experiences for Mass Observation; her memory testifies to the existence of smoking among women and to the outrage it could provoke.

> I smoked when I was 14. That must have been 1888. I was taught by a kitchen maid under the table. My father was furious. Then I remember one day I was smoking in the bathroom. My father was going into Swansea. He smelt the smoke and said, 'You nasty, dirty little thing' … My mother said no lady would ever smoke![23]

Another Mass-Observation respondent described how:

> I remember before the 1914–18 war, mother drawing the curtains and locking the door to smoke a gold-tipped cigarette, then flinging the windows and door wide open to get rid of the smell. She used to wear a green silk kimono so that the smell shouldn't linger in her clothes.[24]

Madame Yevonde's mother similarly smoked in the privacy of her bedroom.[25]

There are no precise indicators of the level of smoking among women prior to 1921, as their consumption was too low to record. Increased provision for middle- and upper-class women smokers is, however, evidence of growth in tobacco use. Several women's clubs of the late Victorian and Edwardian years provided smoking spaces for the upper and middle classes.[26] Although these were urban clubs, many had 'country' members. Politically radical women who smoked were catered for at the Pioneer Club (1892), whose members included Eleanor Marx, Olive Schreiner, Mona Caird and Dora Montefiore. Smoking spaces were also provided for members of the aristocracy. The Empress Club, established in 1897, included a smoking gallery and smoking room for its membership; although men were admitted to the smoking room, the gallery was reserved for women. Smoking rooms were also provided for 'ladies of social position' at the New County Club, established in 1899 to offer members 'the comforts and convenience that men have found in their clubs for years'.[27] Women smokers of modest means were catered for at the Ichester Club. Rules prohibiting women from smoking in their clubs suggest that the practice of smoking was not uncommon. Smoking was banned at London's Alexandra Club, founded in 1884 'for ladies eligible to attend the Queen's Drawing Rooms', while 'smoking and card playing for money' were prohibited at the Ladies Park Club in Knightsbridge.[28] Such restrictions on smoking were, however, increasingly outmoded and by 1900 at least one west-end tea shop catered for women smokers.[29]

Reinforcing the impression of a growth in smoking among women, Edith Vance in a letter to the *Daily Mail* in 1898, complained that there were too few places where women could smoke comfortably. Vance called for a 'League of Women Smokers' to campaign for the right of women to smoke in public spaces:

> What is wanted is facility to indulge in a harmless and soothing habit when we most need it – at our work, on top the 'bus, in the railway carriage ... we might approach the railway companies on the question of providing smoking carriages for women, and restaurant keepers on permitting women to smoke after dinner – a right arbitrarily and illegally denied them.[30]

Vance claimed that more than 150 women responded in support of her campaign.[31] The response from railway companies revealed that while some women did smoke on trains, they often encountered hostility from men. The manager of the District Railway pointed out that

> women were perfectly free now to smoke in the ordinary smoking cars, and in the case of any annoyance or insult, to complain to the guard, but he had usually found that ladies were unwilling to appear in court, and so many railway offenders unfortunately got off free.[32]

The vulnerability of women smokers was reiterated in an 'ungallant' response from a representative of the London and North-Western Railway: 'At present the smoking carriages are free to both sexes; what men will say to women smokers we don't know.'[33]

Specially produced 'ladies'' cigarettes also testify to the growing importance of a female market for tobacco products. These cigarettes were advertised regularly in the tobacco trade press but did not appear in mainstream magazines and newspapers at this time. 'Floral Cigarettes', for example, boasted paper made from real flowers; reinforcing the feminine targeting, the advertisement featured a woman's head.[34] Sweet Cherry-Tipped cigarettes were promoted by a scantily clad woman with a cigarette in her mouth.[35] Select west-end tobacconists also promoted 'ladies'' cigarettes which were 'very dainty in appearance … having gold-tipped mouthpieces, while they exhale the sweet odours of violets and roses'.[36] Such retailing strategies were unusual outside London but by the late 1890s the trade press was keen to encourage tobacconists to change their practice and begin targeting women: 'The novelty of the experiment [targeting ladies] would be sure to arrest the attention of others besides ladies, and anyhow it is better to be a little in advance of the times than a little behind them.'[37] The sale of 'ladies'' cigarette cases was a further sign of the increased popularity of cigarettes among the affluent.[38] A good trade in telescopic cigarette holders, that could be attached to the chain women wore to hold their hand-muffs in position, was noted at Dunhill's Bond Street shop.[39] By 1913 popular newspapers heralded smoking coats for women as 'fashion's latest'. These 'novelties' were available from Selfridges and came in three styles, two of which were very feminine. But, 'for the woman who means business to the extent of carrying matches and cigarette case', presumably a woman who is not dependent on men for her tobacco, 'a severer type is recommended, cut like a pyjama coat, and eminently suitable for billiard-room wear.'[40]

'Ladies' cigarettes were not the only form of tobacco consumed by upper- and middle-class women at this time. Some tobacconists noted that women smoked the same cigarettes as men; 'we no longer manufacture a special brand for them. They prefer those which the men smoke. Several ladies have a standing order with me for 200 a week.'[41] Cigars were also popular with some women, although this seems to have been more unusual than cigarette smoking and far more radical. According to Havelock Ellis, in 1897, cigar smoking was a lesbian practice and one not shared by straight women, but there is little evidence to support either claim.[42] Occasionally a pipe is mentioned, as in the account of the London woman who smoked her briar from the safety of her carriage.[43]

Working-class 'Fumigators'

At the other end of the social spectrum cigarette smoking was associated with lower-class women on the margins of respectable society. Descriptions of chorus girls and other stage performers mention cigarettes,[44] as do accounts of prostitutes and 'wayward girls': 'Round the fire was a group of girls far gone in dissipation; good-looking girls most of them, but shameless; smoking cigarettes, boasting of drinks, or drinking'; 'In a very dirty hand she [a fourteen-year-old-girl suspected of soliciting] flourished a cigarette, waving it about a great deal to show the most scarlet of fingernails, which she had bitten down to the quick.'[45] According to a report in the tobacco trade press in 1898, young working-class women also featured among the growing pool of female cigarette smokers.[46] In large provincial towns, factory girls smoked small cigarettes called 'brownies' that were sold in packets of three for half a penny, and domestic servants who lived out also smoked. There is some evidence to support these claims. At least one middle-class woman, mentioned earlier, recalled being taught to smoke by a kitchen maid in this period,[47] and smoking was observed in some clubs for young women working in the cities.[48] Aside from these pockets of practice, cigarette smoking seems to have been rare – or at least almost invisible – among working-class women, especially in towns and small communities. Contemporary social surveys and autobiographies shed little light on women smoking cigarettes, reinforcing the impression that the practice was highly localized and/or hidden. The Preston, Lancaster and Barrow people interviewed by Elizabeth Roberts reveal that pre-1914 working-class women were rarely seen smoking cigarettes in these localities and that it was considered unrespectable for women to use any form of tobacco. Nevertheless, some of Roberts's working-class respondents did recall smoking surreptitiously. An apprentice dressmaker prior to marriage remembered how she and her sister, Muriel, progressed from smoking herbal cigarettes for their catarrh to Virginian cigarettes (this was on the advice of the female shop assistant who claimed that her doctor recommended them); but 'mother never knew that I smoked. When they did a bit of visiting ... Muriel an [sic] I used to go out in the garden and have a bit of a smoke.'[49]

Older forms of tobacco consumption also continued among women. Clay pipes were a long-established form of tobacco consumption among poor women in certain communities. Hippolyte Taine, in his notes on mid-nineteenth-century England, described women sorting through rubbish for rags and bones in the East End of London: 'One of them, old and wrinkled, had a short clay pipe in her mouth.'[50] Poor women in Northumberland and on the Scottish border also smoked pipes mid-nineteenth century, as did gypsies and elderly Irish women trading their wares in the streets of London.[51] By the end of the century this practice was still ongoing in some areas. The *Daily Mail*, in 1898, referred to 'country districts of the north, where old ladies sit at their doorsteps in the cool of a summer evening, puffing reflectively at well-seasoned clay pipes, which are both black and short'.[52] People who grew up in Preston and Barrow, interviewed by Roberts, also recalled women smoking clay pipes prior to 1914, although they were less sure about whether they had actually seen them: 'I know they did smoke but *I don't remember seeing* them'; 'I *think I remember* seeing an old woman smoking a pipe. I heard a lot about it' (my emphasis).[53] Occasional accounts of pipe smoking are also noted among southern city women. A London woman, charged in May 1913 with drunkenness, claimed that it was her pipe, which she had smoked for twenty years, which 'always makes me giddy!'[54] Snuff was another traditional form of tobacco enjoyed by some, mainly old and poor women. Dayus describes going to the cinema in pre-war Birmingham and sitting next to an 'old woman' who 'smelt of snuff': When the lights went down this woman

> took a paper bag out and I thought she had some sweets and might give one to me. But she dipped her thumb and forefinger into the bag and took out a pinch of snuff. She saw me looking at her and thrusting the bag under my nose invited me to take a pinch. I jumped up in fright and in the process knocked the snuff out of her hand. It went all over us. I began sneezing and couldn't stop; nor could several of our neighbours who'd shared in the shower.[55]

Snuff was also used by old women in Preston, Lancaster and Barrow. According to one man interviewed by Roberts, the five oldest women in Lancaster were regular users: 'Old Mrs Whittle about ninety-four, Mrs Beck another ninety odder (Snuffy Beck they called her) ... She used to cadge a ha'penny off me to make into a penny for a pennyworth of snuff.'[56] While snuff could be purchased in quantity, some retailers also sold it by the pinch thereby making if affordable for the poorest members of society.[57]

The First World War

On the eve of the war cigarette smoking was established among some sectors of the upper and middle classes but still unusual among working-class women. Although there are no figures that indicate the take up of smoking during the war, evidence suggests that with the outbreak of hostilities women's smoking continued and, among certain groups, it became more common. In letters to *Our Girls* in 1915 a reader from Tottenham bemoaned that smoking, 'is becoming very prevalent among women'; indeed, five of the twelve female letter-writers (there was also a letter from one man) admitted to smoking.[58] A number of the women and men from the North West, interviewed by Roberts, thought that women's smoking became more common around the time of the war.[59] On the homefront there were signs of increased smoking among women university students. At Girton College, for example, students were forbidden to smoke in 1914, a proscription that is in itself revealing of the taking up of smoking by middle- and upper-class women. During the war the ban was relaxed and, according to one ex-Girtonian, 'students could smoke in their own rooms after dinner. By the time I left, they could smoke in their rooms at any time. We also smoked when we went out to tea, or picnics, and, I think, at dances!'[60] Smoking was also evident among women engaged in war work. On the homefront, munitions workers were observed to smoke heavily;[61] smoking was also noted among women serving overseas as nurses, caterers and ambulance drivers. Muriel de Wend joined the First Aid Nursing Yeomanry (FANY) Motor Ambulance Convoy in France in 1916. In her letters home she referred to FANYs receiving a once-a-week ration of cigarettes and matches; they also received parcels of cigarettes from family, friends and well-wishers,[62] and enjoyed free cigarettes at formal gatherings such as the Whitsun Dinner.[63] Official photographs of women workers do not usually reveal women smoking even in their moments of relaxation,[64] but this absence appears to be a deliberate attempt to keep smoking out of the picture. Amateur photographs, such as those of Muriel de Wend, do confirm that smoking had a place in the routines and rituals of daily life for FANYs (see Chapter 7). An unusual set of photographs taken in 1919 by Imperial War Museum photographer Olive Edis also reveal that smoking was common among women of officer class serving in France. In a photo of three officers in a restroom at a VAD (Voluntary Aid Detachment) base, one woman smokes while writing and another while reading a newspaper.[65] A photograph of women officers in the Queen Mary Army Auxiliary Corps (QMAAC) portrays four of thirteen women enjoying cigarettes with their tea.[66]

Though the number of women who smoked increased during the war, it is difficult to know how far to attribute this growth to the conditions of war. 'Heavy' smoking was facilitated by the high wages that munitions girls could earn for the duration of the war,[67] but there is no evidence that the war caused these women to start smoking, and some may have been smokers before 1914. Serving overseas did provide a context in which some women took up smoking. Vera Brittain, for example, started smoking to keep insects at bay while serving as a VAD in Malta.[68] In other instances women probably smoked before the war but this may have been less frequent and less noticeable. No doubt some of the QMAAC officers merely transferred their smoking practice from their clubs to the officer's mess.

Why did Women Smoke? Opportunities and Motivations

Smoking grew in popularity among some groups of women between 1880 and 1919 despite continued opposition to the practice. Objections to female smoking often hinged on the practice representing a rejection of femininity and an appropriation of masculinity and male privilege. Women, according to this view, were imitating men and/or using cigarettes as a sign of their emancipation. Another type of objection was related to women smokers being the wrong type of women.

Women smokers were described as 'unrespectable', 'fast', 'common', 'degraded', 'dirty'. This language represented smoking as the practice of the hyper-sexual and, often synonymous with this, of the unrespectable working class – that is, lower-class women who reportedly lacked the qualities of respectable womanhood such as restraint (physical, sexual, emotional), modesty and refinement. Smoking was also deemed inconsistent with the fulfilment of traditional feminine roles, most notably the care of children (a view that persisted throughout the twentieth century). Objections were not restricted to debates in the press. Women smokers could also encounter physical and verbal harassment as suggested by responses to Edith Vance's campaign discussed earlier. Often objections to women smokers were rationalized by arguments that tobacco damaged health.[69] According to critics, smoking damaged a woman's constitution, especially her reproductive capacity and her nerves. Although the argument that smoking damaged nerves contradicted a more widely accepted view that nicotine had beneficial effects on the nervous system, critics of women smoking argued that women's nerves were fragile compared to men's and unable to withstand the effect of nicotine. (In general, the view that tobacco was good for nerves continued to be dominant; it achieved greater credibility during the First World War and after 1920 it became a frequently voiced justification for smoking among both men and women.) Given opposition to women's smoking, why did some women take to the habit?

There were several factors that provided the conditions for increasing numbers of women to smoke between 1880 and 1919. Prior to 1883 women smokers had to choose between pipes, cigars and hand-rolled cigarettes, either roll-your-own or shop-bought. Cigarettes were made with strong tobacco and the shop-bought variety were expensive. In the 1880s two technological developments altered the character of the tobacco trade in Britain and, following from this, they broadened the smoking opportunities of women as well as men. The advent of the bonsack machine revolutionized cigarette production when it was first introduced to Britain by Wills in 1883. Whereas a skilled woman could make several hand-made cigarettes a minute, the bonsack machine manufactured 300;[70] production went up, costs came down and cigarette sales rose.[71] In combination with mild forms of tobacco produced from new curing techniques, a relatively cheap, palatable and 'modern' cigarette emerged that was attractive to women as well as to men.

Arising from lower prices and new efforts to maximize sales, cigarettes became increasingly visible and accessible. Cigarettes were available through new outlets. For example, products by Wills, a Bristol-based tobacco company, were displayed and sold in more than 200 railway refreshment rooms around the country, and Wills's Autumn Gold cigarettes appeared for sale in automatic vending machines.[72] Wills's products were also available from the mid-1890s on P&O Steamships, at Gordon Hotels and at forty chalets, popular with the middle classes, run by the Cyclists' Chalet Company.[73] A transformation in packaging also contributed to the raised visual profile of cigarettes, as decorative boxes and enamelled airtight tins replaced the coarse paper or newspaper that many shopkeepers had previously used to package tobacco products.[74] Double Daffodil cigarettes, for example, were supplied in silver-edged boxes covered with basket patterned paper and fastened with a silver star.[75] Brightly coloured showcards and bill posters[76] also brought cigarettes into the public – and feminine – eye, as did extensive press advertising from around 1900.

Although the smoker was usually conceived as male, representations of women smokers gradually increased in number after 1880, thereby suggesting that women could and did smoke. Sporadically, women smokers were much talked about in newspapers and periodicals. Lively debate between Lady Colin Campbell (for) and Mrs Lynn Linton (against) about women smoking shed light on the topic for readers of *The English Illustrated Magazine* in 1893.[77] Literature also contributed to the raised profile of the woman smoker, especially the association between smoking and female emancipation as seen in *The Woman Who Did* by Grant Allen (1895) and *Ann Veronica* by H.G. Wells (1908).[78] Aside from textual references there were a few visual ones. Female smokers were in the limelight in theatre productions, most famously *Carmen*, which played at London's Gaiety Theatre in December 1890. Upper and middle-class women smokers were also seen increasingly in the pages of *Punch* from 1889 although, unlike representations of male smoking, this was not routine throughout the 1890s; moreover, compared to the attention that female bicyclists attracted, also the suffrage issue, coverage of smoking was sparse. After 1910, however, *Punch* increased dramatically its representation of women smokers, and cigarettes became visibly commonplace in the hands of respectable and feminine young ladies, who smoked at bridge parties, at home with friends and family, and in restaurants.[79] Cigarettes were no longer objects of satire or a sign of minority status in *Punch*. Summing up the shift in cigarette consumption, one cartoon depicted a house party at which all the women were smoking. The host turned to a male guest and offered him a cigarette, to which the guest replied 'No, thanks – I've chucked smoking – too effeminate, don't you know.'[80] *Punch* was, however, unusual in the space it afforded to women smokers and, moreover, in the visual representation of them. Women smokers may have been written about but they were not usually seen.

Tobacco advertising, which proliferated in newspapers from around 1900, raised the profile of the cigarette and male smoker, but it did little to raise the public profile of the woman smoker before 1919. The *Daily Express*, for instance, featured one or two cigarette and tobacco advertisements per issue in 1913 but these were usually masculine in focus and often located on the sports pages. On the eve of the First World War, women smokers were occasionally glimpsed in cigarette advertisements. An advert for Abdullah cigarettes, for example, covered the front page of the *Daily Mail* in July 1913, depicting both women and men smoking while engaged in a variety of holiday pleasures.[81] In 1913 a full-page advertisement for Boguslavsky's Russian Cigarettes offered a more subtle appeal to Society women in the pages of *The Sketch*. Entitled 'Forming a Lasting Relationship', a woman representing England is depicted accepting a cigarette from a bear representing Russia. At a time when it was not yet accepted practice to portray respectable women as smokers, this advertisement cleverly used the figure of woman as national symbol to justify portraying a lady selecting a cigarette. The small print in the advertisement did, however, make explicit that women could enjoy these cigarettes: 'There are Boguslavsky Cigarettes to suit all tastes; specially mild blends being made for lady smokers'.[82] Sporadic advertisements targeted at women continued in the elite press throughout the war. For example, women appeared smoking in a range of contexts in several full-page advertisements on the back page of the *Sketch*.[83]

Changes in male smoking practices had important implications for women's relationship to the cigarette. Elliot argues that the 'proliferation of [cigarette] smoking among men and, correspondingly, the increased visibility of the habit' produced the 'necessary climate for smoking to become more widespread among women'.[84] Schivelbusch similarly argues that the '*social* expansion of smoking' was linked to the '*spatial* expansion' of men's cigarette habit.[85] In the early nineteenth century, pipes, and then from 1840 cigars, were the manly ways to consume tobacco; prior to mid-century, cigarette smoking was regarded as coarse among men. As cigarettes gained in popularity among men so did their visibility for women. Whereas in 1890 cigarettes were smoked by a minority of men, by 1906 cigarette sales constituted a quarter of the total sales of pipe tobacco and cigarettes, and more than half by 1919.[86] The visibility of the cigarette was further heightened by shifts in where men could smoke. Whereas men's smoking had traditionally occurred away from the eyes of women, this began to change after 1860 as male smoking spaces expanded.[87] The First World War, Elliot argues, was 'pivotal': 'The growing popularity of cigarettes among the troops not only changed the status of smoking but involved women in the process of buying, packing and sending the necessity'.[88] There is no doubt that women's exposure to cigarettes was heightened by men's increased – and public – consumption of them. Wartime photographs reveal a very intimate dimension to women's exposure to cigarettes as they assisted wounded men to smoke in hospitals and convalescent homes.[89] However, men's smoking habits do not in themselves explain why women smoked. The significance for women of male smoking practices can only be gauged in the context of changes in the lives, experiences and expectations of women, and the meanings attached to the cigarette.

Although the ideology of separate spheres persisted up to 1914, in practice the boundaries were blurred and permeable for many women. Women increasingly used public space in the course of paid and voluntary work, leisure and political campaigning.[90] In the course of work activities and leisure, they also associated more with men than they had done in the past; the latter was facilitated by a reduction in chaperonage in some social circles and more companionate leisure.[91] They also mixed with other women as they worked, shopped, travelled, studied, socialized and campaigned. These changes brought women into areas such as stations and tobacconists, where cigarettes were displayed and sold. They also brought women into contact with both male and female smokers and opportunities – and sometimes encouragement – to try cigarettes. While for some smoking began with a solitary experiment, for others the habit began, and was consolidated, in company. Men initiated some women into smoking.[92] Women were also introduced to smoking by female friends and work colleagues. Ethel Mannin was 'initiated into the vice of smoking' around 1916–17 when working in an advertising agency: 'a girl in the office with whom I became friendly smoked, and she took me one evening after work to an underground tea place called The Cave where tea-for-two was served in alcoves, and the lighting was dim, and *women smoked*.' Mannin remembered the details of this first smoke: 'Monica gave me a De Reszke Turkish cigarette from a small packet, and there we two young girls viciously sat, with our pot of tea and our toasted scones, *smoking*, and in *public*.'[93] The conditions of war extended these opportunities as more women entered the paid workplace and/or the women's services. With more money to spend, the example of other smokers, and greater freedom from the prying eyes of disapproving parents or employers, the conditions were ripe for women to adopt the cigarette habit; that is, if they wanted to. So why were women motivated to smoke?

Motivations

In the context of changing lives some women felt that they had new needs and new rights. In some cases, women wished to signal that they had changed, or they wanted to visibly challenge the status quo.

Health benefits were one attraction of smoking cited by women. According to the *Lady* in 1893, 'many fashionable physicians have actually taken to recommending a cigarette or two after meals to numbers of their fair patients as a preventative of indigestion's awful pangs'.[94] This reason to smoke was adopted by women lower down the social scale as a lower-middle-class reader of *Our Girls* revealed in 1915: 'I have read that it aids digestion to smoke a cigarette after meals, and, from experience, I believe it does.'[95] Other medical benefits were also claimed for tobacco. A Harley Street physician was reported in the national press to argue that women caught colds more easily than men because they did not smoke.[96] Although health was the reason why some women turned to cigarettes, for others this argument probably served to justify a practice that was adopted, or at least continued, principally for other reasons.

Pleasure and stimulation were key motivations to smoke mentioned by a woman in a letter to the *Evening News* in 1897.

What can be more enjoyable than to be comfortably ensconced in a big armchair in a pretty cosy room, with a very few friends around you, discussing everything between heaven and earth while you puff your cigarette airily, lazily, dreamily, energetically, just as the theme discussed provokes you?

How easily the thoughts come, how well one talks, how confident one feels, while following the blue clouds floating upwards ...

Comfort was another attraction mentioned by this writer:

if one is alone before a cheery fire on a bleak, dreary day, with only the dainty little roll for a companion, what a trusty, soothing companion it is – never boring one, never touching just the wrong chord, but quietly insensibly calming one down, chasing away the depression once suffered from, whatever its cause may be, until one again puffs out pretty little rings contentedly with a cleared brow and lighter heart.[97]

The cigarette is described as a 'companion' that chases depression away, a concept that was to remain popular throughout the twentieth century (see Chapters 3 and 8). Although it is possible that this letter was manufactured to spark debate, the ideas expressed in it were reiterated in other accounts of why women smoked. Tobacco, according to Mrs Campbell in 1893, was a 'soother of overworked brains and nerves' and therefore most suitable for women, particularly as they coped with the demands of 'multitudinous modern developments and exigencies'.[98] This motivation for women to smoke was elevated during the First World War by the discourse on smoking and comfort which was popularized by press campaigns to supply troops with cigarettes and tobacco, and by the inclusion of tobacco products in military rations. In 1915 *Our Girls* tackled the topic of women smoking in 'Our Girls' Parliament', a regular feature on readers' views on topical issues.[99] Readers were advised to 'express their views as briefly as possible, and write on one side of the paper only'. Each letter published was attributed and the writer received a 'useful gift'. The letters appear quite genuine, even if they were edited carefully, and they do offer a range of perspectives on the topic. Sadie implied that she smoked because she was alone, possibly bored and/or lonely, and because it calmed her: 'My husband is at the Front, and I am in the house alone all day, and all night, too, and I smoke about half an ounce a day, but never in public. If I am in a pelting rage, or a tearful mood, nothing soothes me like a cigarette.' Consolation is also mentioned by other smokers. 'I think it is one of the most consoling things in the whole world, if one is in trouble, and wants to think hard', explained a

London reader, while a woman from Crouch End wrote that 'Nothing is more soothing than a nice cigarette'. While the cigarette may have been a comfort on the domestic front, it was also solace for women serving on the Front.

The fact that the virtues of tobacco were frequently extolled for men was picked up on by women. In the context of changes in women's lives, including war and exposure to the demands of modern living, and demands by some for equality with men, women claimed the right to benefit from the properties of tobacco. As Mrs Campbell reasoned in 1893, why should women be denied indulgence in a practice from which the vast majority of men derive pleasure.[100] Women, Hunting observed, were 'openly' asserting 'their right both to think *and smoke*'; it was men, she explained, who had previously excluded women from smoking culture: 'women were made non-smokers as they were made non-participators in many of men's privileges and pleasures, and women are becoming smokers because they no longer fear men's criticisms nor cherish their over-fanciful ideas concerning them'.[101] For women, the attraction of the modern cigarette was probably heightened by a degree of openness in its signification. On the one hand, cigarettes were a form of tobacco that women could claim was feminine and suitable for feminine consumption. Cigarettes were not widely smoked by men prior to the 1890s and were therefore not steeped in masculine tradition. Additionally, cigarettes were often derided by male pipe and cigar smokers as effeminate.[102] On the other hand, cigarettes were attractive to some women because, being tobacco products, they were associated with men, masculinity and male privilege and, from the 1890s, they quickly gained in popularity among men.

Cigarettes were used by women to make statements about identity and, especially, about gender and gender relations. The masculine meanings attached to tobacco consumption, which predated the popularity of cigarettes among men, were significant for some women's motivations to smoke; the increased visibility of cigarette smoking among men from the 1880s contributed to this masculine association. Drawing on the dominant masculine discourses of smoking, women could use the cigarette as a statement of rebellion against Victorian notions of womanhood, a means to construct and parade modern and emancipated feminine identities. The cigarette gave visual expression to changes in women's lives and thinking. Smoking could also be employed as a challenge to male privilege and an assertion of women's equality with men. As expressed by one contributor to *Our Girls*: 'if a man is privileged to smoke, I see no reason why a girl should not be.'[103] Opposition to women smoking often strengthened women's resolve to be defiant. In a battle between the Manchester University men's union 'Klaws' and the women's union, the women were 'harshly' criticized by the men for smoking in public. Undaunted, the women responded that 'Smoking is an instance of the many shocks that the free, independent and courageous women have in store for "Klaws"'.[104]

The importance of smoking as a statement of gender and gender relations was revealed, and indeed consolidated, by the popularity of smoking among the upper- and middle-class women who identified as New Women and/or supported the suffrage movement. A Mass-Observation correspondent recalled that 'I joined Christabel Pankhurst's W.S.P.V. [*sic*] for women's suffrage … the bravado part (of smoking) was very evident among the suffragettes!'[105] Endorsing smoking among feminists, the official weekly paper of the Women's Social and Political Union (WSPU), *Votes for Women*, carried cigarette advertisements. Pinoza cigarettes, made from finest tobacco blended with pine oil, were advertised in 1909, and advertisements for 'Smugglers Brand' cigarettes in 1910; by the summer of 1910 Vallora cigarettes were regularly promoted.[106] Following the high-profile launch in 1908 of the WSPU's colours (purple, white and green), and efforts by retailers to court suffragettes, 'Votes for Women' cigarettes were launched in August 1910 and advertised weekly in the WSPU's paper.[107] 'Votes for Women' cigarettes were also sold in the Women's Press Shop alongside 'Votes for Women' soap, marmalade, chocolate and sweet pea seeds; a 'Pethick' tobacco pouch was also on sale.[108]

Some of the ways in which women's cigarette smoking could be used to make statements feature in fictional representations. In the first volume of *Pilgrimage*, an autobiographical novel written from the vantage point of the First World War,[109] Dorothy Richardson describes how, in the 1890s, 'Miriam' takes up smoking. Although 'Miriam' is not synonymous with Dorothy Richardson, historians have found this novel useful because it illustrates key themes in the history of women's smoking, notably the furtiveness of women's early experiments with smoking and the association of this practice with modern and emancipated womanhood.[110] There are, however, other themes in this story which are also relevant to the history of women's smoking. Smoking is a rite of passage for 18-year-old Miriam, a complex interweaving of gender *and* age transitions. Most importantly, smoking signals Miriam's desire not just to be modern and emancipated, but to be *seen* to be so.

Miriam is first tempted to try a cigarette when rolling them for her father. The importance that Miriam attached to being physically able to smoke is underscored by her determination to succeed. She was, for instance, frustrated when she failed to light the cigarette on her first attempt: 'She struck another match angrily, urging herself to draw, and drew little panting breaths with the cigarette well in the flame. It smoked.'[111] Mastering the skill of smoking gave Miriam a 'sense of power. She had chosen to smoke and she was smoking.'[112] That she had not felt ill heightened her sense of achievement, particularly as she had consumed strong tobacco: 'Useless to tell any one. No one would believe she had not felt ill … She had smoked a whole cigarette of strong tobacco and liked it.'[113] This first experience turned in to a test of whether Miriam was able to handle tobacco like a man, hence her determination to succeed at smoking, and it confirmed that she was not constrained by Victorian conceptions of womanhood.

Miriam subsequently used smoking in a range of social settings to make statements about her gender and age. She smoked in a social gathering to display her modernity and assert her difference from the old-fashioned, and disapproving, women at the event: 'Miriam discharged a double stream of smoke violently through her nostrils – breaking out at last in a public defiance of the freemasonry of women. "I suppose I'm a new woman – I've said I am now, anyhow," she reflected ... "I'm not in their crowd, anyhow".'[114] Her next hurdle was to smoke in the company of her mother, 'She lit a cigarette with downcast lids and a wicked smile, throwing a triumphant possessive glance at her mother as it drew. The cigarette was divine. It was divine to smoke like this, countenanced and beloved – scandalous and beloved.'[115] Aside from gender defiance, smoking was also about growing up and, in relation to her mother, asserting her independence. Independence, as Dyhouse points out, was not a characteristic of feminine adolescent development or adulthood in the late Victorian and Edwardian period.[116] Miriam asserts herself in relation to her mother but, importantly, in relation to women en masse. The process (being independent) and the outcome (Miriam's unfeminine practice of smoking, especially in company) represent a double-headed challenge to feminine norms. As Miriam's experiences suggest, smoking was a potent visual symbol. Partly because of this, the conditions under which women could be *seen* smoking raised important issues for women.

Visibility

Smoking remained a private affair for most women prior to 1920; they indulged but did not always admit it and it was usually invisible to the public eye. In the garden, backyard or bedroom, or under the cloak of darkness, women kept their smoking practice out of public sight. As one woman explained: 'smoking was *unheard* of, and condemned if heard of' when she was at college in 1906, 'so I remember doing my smoking in the grounds after dark' (emphasis in original).[117] Some women smoked in the company of select family and friends. A west-end tobacconist countered the claim made by *The Princess* in 1893 about the routine character of women's smoking, declaring, 'I think it is an exaggeration ... to say that cigarettes are handed round after dinner as a usual thing. Ladies – and a very large number of them – undoubtedly do smoke; but they keep the fact as much as possible to themselves, and do it privately.'[118] Five years later, the *Court Circular* indicated that most Society lady smokers still kept their habit to themselves; she 'only rarely accepts the opportunity of smoking at her own club – Grosvenor, New Somerville, Empress, or Pioneer'.[119] Accounts from tobacconists suggest that by the early 1900s many women were no longer coy about their smoking: 'A few years ago gentlemen used to purchase mild cigarettes for ladies; ladies were far too bashful to come and purchase these themselves. Nowadays, the ladies have not the scruple in the matter. They just come in themselves and buy the cigarettes.'[120] Although more women were willing to concede that they smoked, and perhaps to smoke in restricted company, the practice was still not a public one.

Public acts of smoking were extremely unusual. According to one popular paper, one or two women smoked after dinner in fashionable west-end restaurants from as early as 1898.[121] Mass-Observation respondents also recall women smoking in Soho restaurants in Edwardian London, an impression reinforced by illustrations of restaurants and tearooms in contemporary books and magazines.[122] Outside the fashionable west end, such public acts of smoking were rare and this did not change until after the war. As Ethel Mannin recalled, 'it was ... quite some way into the Twenties before women smoked much in restaurants.'[123]

By 1914, the editor of *Girls' Friend* confidently proclaimed that, 'The time has gone by when the notion of a woman indulging in a cigarette filled most of us with something like genuine horror'.[124] In the same year, the social historian, Apperson, claimed that although many women who are well thought of did smoke, there were still many people who were 'shocked at the idea'.[125] Significantly, both statements refer to the 'notion' or 'idea' of women smoking, neither refer to the 'sight' or 'vision' of a woman smoking. On the eve of the First World War cigarette consumption was still restricted to specific groups and, although known about, it was not usually seen outside the upper classes and specific middle-class contexts. Although smoking increased among women during the war, this was still not widespread nor within sight of the general public. Before 1920, the only way that a respectable woman could smoke in the street without censure was when dressed as a man, as Vita Sackville West discovered when, in 1918, she dressed as a soldier and strolled around Mayfair: 'I stepped off the kerb, down Piccadilly, alone ... I walked along, smoking a cigarette, buying a newspaper off a little boy who called me "sir", and being accosted now and then by women.'[126]

Visibility was an important issue in relation to women's smoking and, quite often, a source of complex feelings and views. At one end of the spectrum were women who wanted to, or felt they should, smoke secretly; at the other extreme were a few women who wanted to parade their practice in public; occupying the middle ground were those who wanted to smoke and be seen by only a select group of people. This multiplicity of stances was characteristic of this first period in the feminization of smoking. Some of the reasons why visibility was problematic are illuminated in women's accounts.

Being seen smoking was an issue for an author of a letter in the *Evening News* mentioned earlier,[127] although it was important to her to be known to smoke. As her practices and preferences make clear, this woman located smoking within a particular form of modern femininity. She engaged in discussion with friends, suggesting an active and modern mind and relationships that are not characterized principally by the enactment of social niceties. Smoking is in itself a further and more radical sign of her emancipation, particularly when engaged in with friends and when the woman is practiced at blowing smoke rings. Although this woman's smoking practice challenges traditional constructions of femininity, she is determined that this should not be at the expense of a heterosexually attractive femininity. 'Pretty' smoke rings and 'pretty' puffing are aspects of cigarette smoking, but 'it is not a pretty sight to see a lady sucking away at a big cigar'. This woman claimed she never smoked 'in public places of any description, I don't think it is wrong, but personally I dislike it, that is all'. Although the writer insists that her dislike of public smoking is purely a personal preference, her comment is defensive. Moreover, in the context of a widespread disapproval of women smoking in public and, indeed, of the novelty of this, it seems likely that this woman is concerned to protect her appearance of respectability which hinges, principally, on what she is *seen* to do.

The visual relationship between smoking, femininity and respectability was also an issue for contributors to *Our Girls* in 1915.[128] Although the writers disagreed as to whether women should smoke (seven were decidedly against it and another was opposed to the 'ordinary' or working girl smoking), a view was shared by all but three readers that it didn't *look* 'nice' for a woman to smoke. Opponents of smoking stressed that it was 'unbecoming', 'manlike', 'degrading and common': 'No girl with any self-respect would be seen with a cigarette between her lips.' These descriptions relate to the symbolic association of smoking with men and masculinity and with hyper-sexualized and/or unrespectable working-class women. Most of the readers who were in favour of smoking made a different visual point. They emphasized the incompatibility of smoking with a feminine appearance, a problem that they circumvented by smoking in private and stressing the importance of moderation. As one London correspondent noted: 'In my opinion it is most unladylike to smoke in company; but in the seclusion of one's room I think it is one of the most consoling things in the whole world, if one is in trouble, and wants to think hard.' (This strategy had, for similar reasons, also been favoured by *The Lady* in the 1890s: 'it is to be sincerely hoped that ladies smoking ... will retire to the solitude of their boudoirs before "lighting up", and thus not tend by their example to encourage so unpleasant and eminently unfeminine practice.'[129]) A more liberal view was expressed by a young wife from Portsmouth: 'I consider it very bad form for a girl to smoke in public, but I see no harm in a girl smoking in her own home, or at a party where everyone else is smoking.' The significance of appearance re-emerged the following year in a discussion of 'everyday questions' which included 'Is smoking bad for girls?' The writer commented that the woman smoker 'never looks her best when she is doing so. I am not in the least prejudiced in the matter, and I think it silly to call it "fast" for a girl to puff a cigarette. But to me a girl looks unattractive with a cigarette between her lips, so if she must have one now and then, I prefer her to do the deed in private.'[130] Once again, moderate smoking was not unrespectable if pursued in private: the problem was the visual incompatibility of smoking with femininity which became an issue when a woman could be seen smoking, and particularly if seen in public.

Public smoking was considered an unfeminine and unrespectable practice. It was not just that smoking was associated with unrespectable women or women who sought to imitate men, but also that it was visibly inconsistent with looking feminine and respectable. Smoking drew attention to women and made a spectacle of them. This visibility was in itself unrespectable, as only women who traded on their bodies drew attention to themselves in public. The actual practice of smoking also appeared unfeminine and unrespectable because it disrupted the dignified facial and bodily composure that was fundamental to a feminine demeanour. The visual relationship between smoking, femininity and respectability had implications for whether and how women appeared as smokers in photographs, as will be seen in Chapter 7. It also became an important dimension of feminine modernity in the interwar years (Chapter 4).

Conclusion

Smoking among women began to re-emerge as a practice from around 1880. Whereas the pipe and then snuff had been the favoured ways of women consuming tobacco in the sixteenth and seventeenth centuries, in the late Victorian and Edwardian period the cigarette was preferred. Hilton argues that women's smoking was not seen as respectable until the First World War and therefore few women smoked: 'Beyond the smoking of pioneering new women and by those operating outside conventional respectability (prostitutes and actresses, old women in rural communities), there is little evidence of more widespread female tobacco consumption.'[131] While levels of smoking among women were undoubtedly low in real terms and relative to male consumption, smoking was not solely the practice of pioneering or unrespectable women: cigarettes in particular were tried and enjoyed by a growing number of women, especially from the upper echelons of society. While smoking was not widely seen as a respectable feminine practice, for some this was a definite attraction, while for others this was immaterial if their practice was unobserved. Moreover, by the eve of the First World War attitudes toward smoking were changing in some circles – mainly in the upper and upper-middle classes. Although women's smoking was not widespread, the significance of early women smokers and media discussion of them should not be underestimated in introducing women to the idea of smoking. Middle-class girls observed their mothers smoking in the confines of the home, friends shared cigarettes at home and in cafes and, in some circles, women smoked among fellow guests at dinner parties and among their club members. The war provided other contexts, especially overseas, in which women could smoke and be seen to smoke. For the most part, however, women's smoking was not a public practice and, although talked about in the media, it was not usually seen in it. This changed dramatically in the 1920s as women's smoking achieved a highly visual profile facilitated in large part by the media.

Notes

1. Apperson, *Social History of Smoking*, p. 219.
2. Ibid.; also Goodman, *Tobacco*.
3. *TTR*, 13 March 1880, p. 30. *Punch*, 8 August 1886, p. 66. Apperson, *Social History of Smoking*, p. 220.
4. Hunting, 'Women and Tobacco', pp. 218, 223.
5. *Evening News* (London), 7 January 1897, p. 1.
6. *TTR,* 1 April 1898, p. 164.
7. *The Princess*, 4 February 1893, p. 66.
8. *Westminster Gazette*, 20 February 1893, p. 9.
9. *TTR,* 1 February 1899, p. 45.
10. Reported in *TTR*, 1 January 1893, p. 2.
11. *The Princess*, 4 February 1893, p. 66.
12. *Westminster Gazette*, 20 February 1893, p. 9.
13. Ibid.
14. Cited in *TTR*, 1 April 1898, pp. 164, 165.
15. Thanks to Francis Dimond for this information. Queen Alexandra can be spotted holding a cigarette in a group photograph reproduced in 1908 in her *Giftbook,* a collection of Queen Alexandra's own snapshots of the Royal family. This was not a deliberate or overt smoking pose, the cigarette is hardly visible and the context was both private and informal. The photograph's inclusion in the published collection suggests that it was considered acceptable for upper-class ladies to smoke in private. It is significant that she is holding rather than actually smoking the cigarette. Affluent ladies can also be spotted smoking at Henley Regatta in 1914, see photograph in Laver, *Age of Optimism.*
16. Hunting, 'Women and Tobacco', p. 222.
17. Cited in *TTR*, 1 April 1898, p. 164.
18. *Daily Mail*, 9 March 1898, p. 3.
19. Ibid.
20. *Girls' Reader*, 30 July 1910, p. 380.
21. Cadogan, *Richmal Crompton*, p. 48.
22. *Daily Telegraph* cited in *TTR*, 1 April 1898, p. 163.

23. MOA FR 3192, p. 72.

24. Ibid.

25. Yevonde, *In Camera*, p. 139.

26. Gordan and Doughan, *British Women's Organisations*. Rappaport, *Shopping*, Chapter 3 discusses the popularity of 'female clubland'.

27. Gordan and Doughan, *British Women's Organisations*, p. 114.

28. Ibid., p. 12; *Every Woman's Yearbook*, 1909 and 1912.

29. Rappaport, *Shopping*, p. 102.

30. *Daily Mail*, 9 March 1898, p. 3.

31. *Daily Mail*, 12 March 1898, p. 3.

32. Ibid.

33. Ibid.

34. *TTR*, 1 January 1898, p. 17.

35. Ibid., p. 24.

36. *The Princess*, 4 February 1893, p. 66.

37. *TTR,* 1 February 1899, p. 46.

38. *TTR,* 1 April 1898, p. 163; *Daily Mirror* cited in *TTR* 1 September 1905, p. 334.

39. Dunhill, *Our Family Business*, p. 12-3.

40. *Daily Express*, 31 March 1913, p. 10.

41. *Daily Mirror,* cited in *TTR,* 1 Sept 1905, p. 334.

42. Cited in Jeffreys, *The Spinster and Her Enemies*, p. 106. There is evidence of cigar and pipe smoking, also tobacco chewing, among women who passed as men whether or not they were lesbian. See Oram and Turnball, *Lesbian History Sourcebook,* pp. 26, 30.

43. *TTR*, 1 April 1898, p. 163.

44. ERA Mrs M6B, p. 64.

45. Higgs, *Three Nights in Women's Lodging Houses,* p. 8, also p. 14; Cox, *Gender, Justice and Welfare*, p. 60.

46. *TTR*, 1 April, 1898, p. 163.

47. MOA FR 3192, p. 72.

48. National Archive (formerly PRO), ED 24/2110, Juvenile Organisations Committee, minutes of meeting, 1916-35, 14 March 1918. Thanks to Marcus Collins.

49. ERA Mrs H2B, p. 18, also p. 17.

50. Cited in Laver, *Age of Optimism*, p. 85.

51. Apperson, *Social History of Smoking,* pp. 215–17.

52. *Daily Mail*, 9 March 1898, p. 3.

53. ERA Mrs H2B, p. 18; Mr M2P, pp. 137-8.

54. Apperson, *Social History of Smoking*, p. 216.

55. Dayus**,** *Where There's Life*, pp. 87–8.

56. ERA Mr C1L, p. 41; see also Mr M2P.

57. ERA Mrs H2B, p. 136.

58. *Our Girls*, 27 November 1915, p. 623.

59. ERA Mrs P1L, Mrs N1L, Mr B1B, Mr H1L, Mr J1L.

60. MOA FR 3192, p. 68.

61. ERA Mrs N1L, p. 61; Mr W2L, p. 162.

62. IWM Documents, Muriel de Wend. Letter, 10 January 1917; *FANY Gazette*, July 1916, p. 5.

63. IWM Documents, Muriel de Wend. *FANY Gazette*, April 1917, p. 8.

64. Based on survey of images in IWM Photograph Archive.

65. IWM Photograph Archive, Q108106.

66. IWM Photograph Archive, Q8061.

67. Player's Archive, DDPL 7/19/2. *Yorkshire Post*, 21 April 1920, n.p.

68. Brittain, *Testament of Youth*, p. 354.

69. Goodman, *Tobacco*, shows that since the 1600s there had been debate about the effects of tobacco but by the 1800s there was much medical support for the therapeutic uses of nicotine including for 'disorders of the nervous system' (p. 117).

70. Hilton, *Smoking*, p. 83.

71. Alford, *Wills*, Chapter 8.

72. Ibid., p. 159.

73. Ibid., p. 214.

74. Ibid., pp. 160, 234.

75. Ibid., p. 160.

76. Ibid., pp. 213–14.

77. Campbell, 'A Plea for Tobacco'; Linton, 'A Counterblaste'.

78. See also American novels (cited in Tate, *Cigarette Wars*, p. 97). by Edith Wharton: *Age of Innocence* and *House of Mirth*, and also Marion Crawford's *Marion Darche*.

79. *Punch*, 25 May 1910, p. 383; 14 February 1912, p. 113; 20 August 1913, p. 165; 17 September 1913, p. 251; *Punch's Almanack,* 1914.

80. *Punch*, 22 February 1911, p. 136.

81. *Daily Mail*, 31 July 1913, front page.

82. *Sketch*, 21 May 1913, p. ix.

83. *Sketch*, 2 June 1915, p. 4; 30 June 1915, p. 4; 3 April 1918, p. 4. Some advertisements did not depict women smoking, but the text and occasional testimonials confirmed the appeal to women as well as to men, see *Sketch,* 29 May 1918, p. 4.

84. Elliot, 'Destructive but sweet', p. 88.

85. Schivelbusch, *Tastes of Paradise*, p. 125.

86. Hilton, *Smoking*, p. 85, Fig. 4.1.

87. Apperson, *Social History of Smoking*, ch xi.

88. Elliot, 'Destructive but Sweet', p. 88.

89. For example, IWM Photograph Archive, Q10666, Q10667; also cover of *War Budget*, 25 May 1916.

90. Nava, 'Modernity's Disavowal'; Rappaport, *Shopping*; Tickner, *Spectacle of Women*.

91. Collins, *Modern Love;* Rappaport, 'Travelling', pp. 34–5.

92. ERA Mrs P1L.

93. Mannin, *Young in the Twenties*, p. 72.

94. Cited in *TTR*, 1 January 1893, p. 2.

95. *Our Girls*, 27 November 1915, p. 623.

96. *Daily Express*, 31 March 1913, p. 10.

97. *Evening News* (London), 7 January 1897, p. 1.

98. Campbell, 'A Plea for Tobacco', pp. 81, 84.

99. *Our Girls*, 27 November 1915, p. 623.

100. Campbell, 'A Plea for Tobacco'.

101. Hunting, 'Women and Tobacco', pp. 222, 224.

102. Hilton, *Smoking*, p. 28.

103. *Our Girls*, 27 November 1915, p. 623.

104. Gregory, *In Memory of Burlington Street*, p. 82.

105. MOA FR 3192, p. 68.

106. *Votes for Women*, 19 November 1909, p. 128; 4 March 1910, p. 363; 29 April 1910, p. 498 and throughout May and June. Cigarette advertisements were not common in suffrage magazines: I discovered none in: *Englishwoman*, 1909-14, 1917–21; *Suffragette* 1912, 1918; *Suffragette News Sheet*, September–December 1916; *Time and Tide*, 1920.

107. For example, *Votes for Women*, 26 August 1910, p. 778.

108. Atkinson, *Suffragettes in Pictures,* pp. 12, 96. *Votes for Women*, 1 July 1910, p. 651.

109. Richardson, *Pilgrimage*. Vol. 1 is composed of three novels which were initially published separately – *Pointed Roofs (1915), Backwater* (1916), and *Honeycomb* (1917).

110. Hilton, *Smoking*; Elliot, 'Destructive but Sweet'.

111. Richardson, *Pilgrimage,* p. 209.

112. Ibid., pp. 209–10.

113. Ibid., p. 210.

114. Ibid., p. 436.

115. Ibid., p. 474.

116. Dyhouse, *Girls Growing Up.*

117. MOA FR 3192, p. 68.

118. *Westminster Gazette*, 20 February 1893, p. 9.

119. Cited in *TTR,* 1 April 1898, p. 164.

120. Cited in *TTR,* 1 September 1905, p. 334.

121. Cited in *TTR,* 1 April 1898, p. 164.

122. MOA FR 3192, p. 73; Tyau, *London through Chinese Eyes*, n.p; *Sketch*, 4 June 1913, p. 273.

123. Mannin, *Young in the Twenties*, p. 72.

124. *Girls' Friend*, 26 Sept 1914, p. 364.

125. Apperson, *Social History of Smoking*, p. 222.

126. Nicolson, *Portrait of a Marriage,* p. 22.

127. *Evening News*, 7 January 1897, p. 1.

128. *Our Girls*, 27 November 1915, p. 623.

129. Cited in *TTR*, 1 January 1893, p. 2.

130. *Our Girls*, 16 December 1916, p. 512.

131. Hilton, *Smoking*, p. 143.

3

The Feminization of Smoking, 1920–1950

This chapter maps out the history of women's smoking from 1920 to 1950. This period was key to the feminization of smoking in terms of both the proportion of women smoking and the redefinition of smoking as a feminine practice. Although the Second World War stands out as a landmark time in this process because of the dramatic growth in women's smoking that occurred, the foundations for this were established earlier. Therefore, the first part of the chapter addresses the interwar period. These years were characterized by the increased prevalence of women's smoking and shifts in the gender associations of cigarette consumption. The visibility of women smokers was key to this stage. The second part of the chapter looks at the 1940s, a period during which the feminization of smoking across all social classes was consolidated in the short term by women's experiences of war and in the longer term by the establishment of tobacco as a legitimate need for women.

Introducing the Interwar Woman Smoker

Government acknowledgement that women smoked first occurred in 1920 when the Chancellor, in his budget speech, identified women's smoking as a factor contributing to the increase in tobacco revenue: 'The actual increase in the consumption of tobacco has been unprecedented ... the increase in the main is due to an astonishing growth of consumption, which may be attributed to the continuous rise in wages, the return of our armies, and the growth of smoking among women'.[1] In the press coverage that followed, the manager of a Piccadilly tobacconist was quoted as saying that, 'many of our best customers are women ... They buy cigarettes in larger quantities, too, than do the men. A man buys a packet of ten or twenty, but a woman generally takes a box of a hundred or even a thousand.'[2] Bulk buying of cigarettes by women may not in all cases have been an indication that the purchasers were heavy smokers, but a sign that some women were still uncomfortable with public purchasing of cigarettes.[3] In her newspaper commentary on the budget, Lady Troubridge, partner of novelist Radclyffe Hall, suggested that women typically smoked a modest amount: 'The average woman smokes about six cigarettes a day.'[4] By 1920 a growing number of upper-class and professional women smoked, including writers Virginia Woolf, Vita Sackville-West and Richmal Crompton, as well as women's-rights campaigners Vera Brittain and Eleanor Rathbone.[5] However, Lady Troubridge's 'average woman' and the 'lady' customers of the Piccadilly tobacconist were clearly not representative of British womanhood in 1920; social class and regional differences in the adoption of smoking still prevailed. Citing the experience of Leeds tobacconists, the *Yorkshire Post* declared that: 'Ladies of a certain kind have indulged the habit for some years, and it may be quite true to say that in the limited circle of club habitués cigarette smoking is more common. But that the practice is making headway among women in general is disputed'.[6]

In the next two decades the number of women smokers did increase dramatically. One indicator of this was the steady rise in women's consumption of manufactured cigarettes.[7] Despite the Chancellor's comments, in 1920 annual consumption of cigarettes per woman aged 15 years and over was too low to record; this compared with 2,290 manufactured cigarettes per annum per man (roughly forty-four cigarettes a week), and men also smoked pipes, hand rolled cigarettes and cigars. By 1921 women's consumption had increased to thirteen manufactured cigarettes per annum and to 180 by 1930; this represented a fourteen-fold increase in women's consumption of manufactured cigarettes. In the 1930s women's consumption rose further, reaching 500 cigarettes per annum by 1939; this was equivalent to each woman aged 15 and older smoking nine cigarettes a week. On the eve of the Second World War women consumed nearly forty times as many cigarettes as they had done in 1921, although this still amounted to only 14 per cent of male consumption. These figures do not reveal how many women smoked, but they do suggest that by 1939 it was an increasingly common practice, particularly if, as contemporary surveys indicate, many women smokers consumed only a few cigarettes a day.

The most visible and talked-about new smokers of the 1920s were 'modern' young women, often Society girls or young working women from the middle classes.[8] Cigarettes, alongside the cocktail, were an integral part of social life for modern 'night-club girls'.[9] Parties provided opportunities for heavy smoking, and hostesses in London's West End complained that after parties, 'hundreds of cigarette-ends are to be seen trodden into the carpet, thrown behind cupboards and roughly hidden in plants'.[10] By the 1920s the establishment of social conventions around smoking testifies to its place in Society life: 'we always offered both Turkish and Virginian cigarettes when we entertained ... and we put out coloured matches for those who wished to smoke'.[11] 'The "gasper" habit' was also a daytime practice among young women in London, according to the *Daily Express*: 'They puff in the open air, in trains, in motor-omnibuses, and in the great London shops.'[12] To the horror of the managers of an Oxford Street department store, women also 'smoked in the crepe de Chine department, they smoked among the cretonnes, and they smoked while they examined jumpers'.[13] Newspaper photographs offered evidence of young women smoking in their leisure and lunch breaks. Visibility was not, however, an indicator of incidence. The fact that women's smoking was newsworthy in the mid-1920s suggests that it was still a novelty at least in some parts of the country, an impression reinforced by the efforts of the elite magazine *The Sketch* to convince its readers that the modern girl was not a myth.[14] Women's smoking was most fashionable and visible in the metropolis: the London base of national newspapers contributed to this impression.

In novels of the 1920s, such as later volumes of Galsworthy's *Forsyte Saga*, cigarette smoking was portrayed as 'ubiquitous' among middle-class women and 'almost a social necessity'.[15] Although fiction cannot be read simply as an indicator of smoking levels, such novels do suggest that it was regarded as a routine feature of upper- and middle-class women's lives. By the late 1930s cigarette smoking was commonplace among upper-class and middle-class women. A Mass-Observation study of smoking in 1937 received responses from fifty women, only ten of whom were non-smokers.[16] However, although the majority of women smoked, a quarter of these smoked only occasionally, usually in company or when offered a cigarette. Of the regular smokers, consumption varied enormously from one or two cigarettes a day, to twenty or more. An article by Dr Grinsing in *Modern Woman* reinforces the impression that middle-class women's smoking was not uncommon: 'We see them smoking everywhere – in trains, restaurants, at public meetings, even in the street.'[17] The pervasiveness of smoking among middle and upper-class women is humorously portrayed in a cartoon of a railway carriage in which all the women smoked while the solitary male did not.[18] The image, which appeared in *Men Only*, also revealed that the expansion in numerical and spatial terms of women's smoking was associated with the emasculation of men and their loss of space and status, a theme common in attacks on women's smoking (see Chapter 4). Significantly, in this cartoon, the man asked the ladies in the railway carriage for permission to *not* smoke.

As early as 1920 a woman's right to smoke had been acknowledged by the judiciary, as illustrated by a case brought to a magistrate's court by an irate husband. On return from a German Prisoner of War camp the man discovered that his wife had taken up smoking. He disapproved of his wife's habit and the feminine freedom this signified to him (an impression reinforced by his wife's refusal to quit smoking) and he promptly took the case to court. The magistrate, however, was not sympathetic to the husband's claims and dismissed the case commenting that, 'It is not an extraordinary thing to see women smoke nowadays ... Women now have the vote and more privileges and freedoms. They are as much a part of the Empire as man is.'[19] The magistrate's decision made explicit the alignment of smoking with women's new social and political rights. Disapproval of middle-class women smoking was, nevertheless, still evident even in the 1930s, especially among some older women and residents of smaller communities. (There was even more disapproval of working-class women smokers, discussed later.) Mass-Observation respondents recalled how: 'some of the elderly women would look rather disapprovingly at girls who smoked'; 'older people don't like it much in lower middle class circles'.[20] It was not only older people who objected to women smoking. Teenaged Angela Rodaway describes how she and her Bohemian friends tried to find ways not to conform; but while most of them drank, they did not smoke, 'because smoking was the more pernicious habit'.[21] More generally, as Mass Observation noted in 1949 'Prejudice against women smoking is, indeed, still far from being a thing of the past, and the Victorian emphasis on femininity is preserved in the hostility aroused if the woman smoker is doing something specifically feminine, nursing a child, pushing a perambulator or cooking.'[22] Presumably the masculine and modern significations of smoking were perceived as incompatible with the traditional feminine occupations of homemaking and mothering.

Hospital rules about who could smoke, and where, confirm that attitudes to smoking were dependent not only on gender considerations but also on class ones.[23] At the Chester Royal Infirmary, 'private patients, male and female, smoke when they wish except during doctors' visits'. However, male patients in ordinary wards were only allowed to smoke for thirty minutes after each meal; patients in female wards were not allowed to smoke at all. The hierarchy also applied to the hospital's staff. Doctors could smoke in the hospital corridors but not in the wards; nurses and sisters could 'smoke anywhere in the home, in or out of uniform but not in the grounds, nor in the hospital'; maids could only smoke in their own bedroom or sitting room (which was quite lenient compared to practice in other hospitals, which often barred maids from smoking at all). Working-class women were not expected or encouraged to smoke in the same way as their sisters higher up the social scale. A complex interweaving of issues of gender, class and respectability was one reason for this inequality.

Partly because working-class women's smoking was widely frowned upon prior to 1939, it is difficult to assess the extent of the practice. In general, cigarette smoking was not widespread among working-class women and not usually pursued in public. However, there is evidence that some working-class women smoked. In Bristol, among the women who worked in the Wills tobacco company, the Management Committee estimated that in 1927 'only about 20% of the girls smoke'.[24] This figure was produced in the context of a debate about whether to provide female employees with a cigarette allowance during holidays. At this time male employees received a weekly allowance which was doubled on holidays.

One committee member thought that a woman's allowance was an excellent form of propaganda, particularly as 'cigarette smoking among girls is on the increase'. However the Committee decided against the proposal because it concluded that most women were non-smokers. The politics of the debate suggests that the Committee's estimate of the extent of female smoking among its factory employees was a conservative one. Smoking was not confined to workers in the tobacco trade. A Liverpool woman interviewed by Sharon Messenger about factory life in the 1920s admitted that she and her fellow workers also smoked: 'They'd think you were a lunatic if you didn't smoke. They'd think you were barmy'.[25] Cigarettes also had a place in the leisure of some working-class domestics. As we have seen, hospital rules suggest that by the 1930s maids smoked in their rooms, but there is also evidence of this in private residences as one middle-class woman recalled: 'it became a habit for me to go into the housemaid's bedroom for quarter of an hour every Saturday evening, when she would invariably offer me a cigarette.'[26] Practical advice on smoking in magazines for working-class women, including the removal of cigarette stains, is further evidence of the increased uptake of the cigarette habit.[27]

By the late 1930s some working-class women smoked in public venues. Priestley describes a public whist drive in Birmingham attended by 'middle-aged decent working folk, with only a sprinkling of younger men and women. Nearly all the men smoked, and a fair proportion of the women'.[28] Bill Brandt's photos suggest that it was not uncommon to see young women smoking in bars in London's East End,[29] while Pearl Jephcott noted the 'slick, apparently assured, smoking, jitterbugging town girl of sixteen'.[30] The equation of smoking with youthful working-class feminine pleasures was primarily an urban phenomenon. One Preston woman interviewed by Elizabeth Roberts recalled how, with her friend, she used to get dressed up and go to the arcade where she sat in a cane chair at a glass-topped table smoking cigarettes in a long-green holder, 'or whatever colour dress I was wearing, I had a holder to match'. 'We thought we were really "bloods"', she remembered.[31]

The Preston woman admitted she was unusual among her peers in smoking at this time. Her assessment is consistent with other sources. The absence of references to teenaged girls smoking in the numerous studies of interwar youth testifies to this. So too do the recollections of other northern women interviewed by Roberts. Elliot also found that smoking was uncommon among working-class women growing up in central Scotland because of 'the prevailing standards of working class respectability ... which governed women's lives. Appearance, social mores and church authority were key factors.'[32] In Scotland, as in many other areas of the country, some working-class women did smoke clandestinely but the general view was that only 'a cheap class' of working-class woman would smoke in public; overt smoking was considered a respectable feminine pastime only for

Society folk. In general, smoking was still not widespread, visible or respectable among working-class women on the eve of the Second World War particularly outside large, urban communities. While young women may have imagined that the cigarette assured them a place among the chic and glamorous, many people disagreed.

Cigarettes were the most popular smoke among interwar women. In the 1920s 'ladies'' cigarettes were sold in tobacconists and promoted in elite women's magazines. These included 'multi-coloured cigarettes' which, in 1927, became the height of fashion:

> Many modern women, of course, have their own special cigarettes as to monogram and tip, but the notion of the cigarette paper to tone with the latest colours of the season is new, and these cigarettes have to be made to order. The gold tip, with in some cases monogram to match, remains, but the cigarette itself is wrapped in blue, green, mauve, begonia red, and so on to accord with the daytime or evening frock worn.[33]

Scented 'ladies'' cigarettes were also advertised in elite magazines, for example Perfumed Moments:

> The daintiest and most elegant cigarette ever offered to My Lady. A perfumed **silver tipped** cigarette hand made from carefully selected highest grade Virginian Tobacco. Perfumed by a special process giving a subtle and exquisite aroma … this process enables us to perfume our cigarettes to individual taste. When ordering name your favourite perfume and your cigarettes will be delicately scented to your fancy.[34]

Other 'ladies'' brands available from select tobacconists included Jazz, Miss Mayfair and Miss Blanche cigarettes.[35] 'Ladies'' cigarettes were usually produced by small manufacturers but these became less common by 1930, although there were exceptions such as De Reszke Minors 'Red Tips for Red Lips', launched in the late 1930s, which boasted the inclusion of a red tip, 'the brilliant notion that prevents lipstick from showing on a cigarette'.[36] In general, the large British tobacco companies did not favour producing cigarettes especially for women. Wills, for example, discussed the possibility of producing a ladies' cigarette on several occasions between 1926 and 1930 but were unconvinced of its viability.[37] 'Rainbow', a mild Virginian cigarette, was even 'worked up' but not pursued.[38] By the late 1920s, however, these companies were convinced of the potential of the female market and they began to target women with mainstream brands. Women were sold, and indeed smoked, the same cigarettes as men, including Player's Medium, Player's Weights, Craven A, Gold Flake, De Reske Minors, Senior Service, Embassy, Woodbines, Churchman's No.1 and Capstan; Turkish brands were particularly popular with middle-class women.[39] Advertisers did suggest that certain variants of a brand were particularly suitable for women, notably 'mild' and cork-tipped cigarettes.

Traditional forms of tobacco use were still in evidence among older working-class women. Snuff continued to be sold into the 1940s and was advertised sporadically in the tobacco trade press, but it was rarely promoted in the popular press after 1920.[40] Snuff nevertheless continued to have a small female following. Joyce Storey recalls her first meeting with her future mother-in-law, Minnie Alice, who was a regular user of snuff: 'She rummaged in a big black bag and produced a small silver box filled with snuff ... She offered me the box with an encouraging, "Take a pinch, kid!"'[41] Snuff was usually associated with the less respectable members of society although writers occasionally favoured it because 'it stimulates their minds'.[42] Clay pipes also continued to be smoked by some older working-class women. The *Manchester Evening News*, for example, reported in 1920 on an 'Old Woman's Last Pipe'.[43] Though clay pipes, often blackened by use, were principally a working-class smoke, small pipes did become fashionable for a while among upper- and middle-class women. Cartoons in *Punch* which portrayed women sporting large pipes were, however, less an indication of women's actual smoking practices in the 1920s than an expression of anxieties about the limits of 'modern' ways and the implications of these for gender and gender relations.[44] In the context of the ongoing feminization of the cigarette, the briar pipe was strongly promoted as a sign of masculinity.[45] According to Mary Dunhill, those 'concerned with trendy fashion and a new kind of emancipation, went for diminutive pipes specially designed for women, some ornamented with rubies, diamonds and sapphires'.[46] These 'tiny pipes', 'suitable for ladies', were displayed at the Tobacco Trade Exhibition at Olympia in 1927.[47] Radclyffe Hall, according to Dunhill, 'was one of many who helped revive women's interest in pipe smoking'.[48] Another public pipe smoker was the artist Gluck who also smoked cigars, as did Virginia Woolf and Joe Carstairs.[49] Pipe and cigar smoking were not, however, as popular or high-profile as cigarette smoking, and it is difficult to gauge the extent of these practices. Only very occasionally did a fashion feature portray a woman with a pipe, while cigars are even harder to discern in the press. During the Second World War, however, when cigarettes were often hard to come by on the domestic front, Mass Observation discovered that nearly a quarter of the 103 women it surveyed claimed they could become pipe smokers. As one woman explained: 'A month ago, when cigarettes were unobtainable, I smoked a pipe. I was not very successful with it, but I have little doubt that if cigarettes were not to be had but pipe tobacco easy to come by I should acquire the habit of smoking 2 or 3 pipes a day.'[50]

By 1939 women's smoking had become commonplace, especially among the upper and middle classes in both private and social contexts. While smoking was uncommon among working-class women generally, some older working-class women continued to use traditional forms of tobacco, while cigarettes were adopted – sometimes publicly, sometimes surreptitiously – by a minority of mainly young working-class women. Although the Second World War was an important catalyst in promoting the mass, and public, take-up of smoking among women, the foundations for it were already well established before this. Opportunities to smoke were increasingly available to upper-class and middle-class women prior to 1920, and these expanded in the interwar years. At a general level, greater freedom in many areas of life and the rejection of constraining conceptions of Victorian femininity and feminine roles enabled the take-up of smoking by women across the social classes but especially the middle classes. Paid employment contributed to this as, unlike their Edwardian counterparts, most interwar women engaged in paid work, at least prior to marriage.[51] The expansion of clerical, retail and factory work, and the decline in live-in domestic service, meant that middle- and working-class women increasingly worked outside the home. Facilitated by the conditions of employment and their wages, women had more freedom and more opportunities for sociability. These conditions exposed women to opportunities to smoke and, once started, the habit was often continued after marriage and after the customary withdrawal of a woman from the labour market. Money was an important factor in supporting the cigarette habit. Working-class women who smoked when single and employed often gave up smoking when living on a shoe-string budget and caring for a family.[52] But an independent income was not always essential. Women often smoked for quite some time before they purchased their own cigarettes because they would be provided with them by other smokers. Moreover, a married woman would often purchase cigarettes from housekeeping if finances and her husband allowed.[53] While these changes provided opportunities for women to smoke there are also other factors that explain the interwar growth of smoking among leisured 'ladies', suburban housewives and women in paid employment.

Why did Women Smoke in the Interwar Years?

A taste for tobacco and an ability to smoke 'properly' did not come easily for many smokers. Mass-Observation respondents of both genders frequently described having to 'persevere' with cigarettes. Gay Taylor remembered how she 'began to practise it as a habit about nineteen. Did not like it at all but persevered with my father's cigarettes (stolen) until I could produce at least an appearance of enjoyment.'[54] Miss Bridgen recalled 'buying a packet and practising secretly in my bedroom', and that it took her a month to 'acquire a taste for regular smoking'.[55] In more graphic terms, Miss Rowland, a 25-year-old stenographer, detailed the difficulties she encountered when she began smoking at college 'because other people did': 'Thought it more bother than it was worth. Difficult not to get smoke in eyes. Makes you feel awful if you swallow it. Used to get bits in her mouth. Thought she would get over these difficulties ... Gradually got more used to it and liked it better.'[56] Given that for many smoking was a 'distinctly unpleasant' experience,[57] why were so many women determined to smoke? There is no one reason, although changes in British smoking culture, especially the ascendancy of the cigarette, played an important part in the feminization of smoking.

Cigarette Culture

Cigarette smoking had by the 1920s begun to infiltrate all aspects of daily life. Women were surrounded at home, in the workplace and in their leisure by men smoking pipes and, in particular, cigarettes.[58] The proliferation of visual media through which smoking was represented was also key to this infiltration. New promotion strategies by the tobacco companies from the late 1920s contributed significantly to this process, in particular the extension of cigarette-smoking culture into middle- and working-class lives.

Women's exposure to cigarettes increased with the proliferation of tobacco sales outlets. Automatic cigarette machines appeared in 'good type public houses', also in hotels and restaurants.[59] Colourful displays of cigarette packets, sometimes with cigarette cards protruding, appeared in stationers' windows.[60] Women encountered cigarettes for sale when they shopped in dairies, herbalists and news-agents, or borrowed books from 'twopenny libraries', many of which were attached to tobacconists.[61] By the 1930s cigarettes were also available from top branches of Woolworths and department stores.

Advertising in shop windows, the street and railway stations raised the profile of cigarettes and smoking as did the increased use of floodlighting from the early 1930s and the use of neon signs.[62] Even the sky was used to promote cigarettes as when De Reszke arranged for a plane to fly several times over Arsenal Football ground trailing an advertisement.[63] Film shows promoted Woodbine cigarettes in clubs and department stores, including Lewis's in Manchester which had shows at mid-day and at 4pm in January 1934: 'At the former there were about 500–600 people present ... and at the latter about 200 people,... Women were predominant at both showings.'[64] Short films promoting cigarettes were shown at local cinemas, and smokers were increasingly prominent in the main performance.[65] Ironically, cigarette smoke often obscured the screen, as Doug Rendell recalled: 'smokers to the left, right, front and back ... many a time I've brushed off ash from my trousers. The projector lamp lit up the smoke, reaching the screen with difficulty'.[66] Local and national newspapers regularly featured cigarette advertisements: in 1937, 80 per cent of advertising expenditure was spent on the press.[67] Until the late 1920s, however, these advertisements rarely featured women, and most consolidated the masculinity of smoking practices.

Tobacco-related products became increasingly visible in all areas of life. Dummy cigarettes were tucked into handbags on sale in select clothes stores.[68] More commonly, sponsorship, advertising and branding initiatives contributed to the location of tobacco, especially cigarettes, at the heart of domestic life and leisure. The Wills tobacco company were involved in the Housing and Health Exhibition in Glasgow 1929,[69] and bookmarks promoting Wills' cigarettes appeared in homes in 1933.[70] Coupon schemes, reintroduced in Britain by Carreras in 1925,[71] were one of the most successful forms of domestic infiltration: by the time coupon brands were banned in 1933, they accounted for a third of UK cigarette sales.[72] Coupon brands raised awareness of tobacco products and created an ostensibly useful role for cigarettes in the domestic economy. They also co-opted women into promoting cigarettes even if they did not smoke, and in this way they implicated women in smoking culture. An advertisement for Carreras Black Cat cigarettes featured a woman displaying the non-ladder stockings that her boyfriend's or husband's coupons had secured:

> Molly told me about them first; I admired a pair she was wearing and couldn't believe her when she said she got them for coupons from Black Cat Cigarettes. So I asked Dick to smoke 'Black Cats' (the silly boy was always changing his cigarettes) so as to get me a pair. He just grumbled – but he tried 'Black Cats', and now he swears by them and will smoke nothing else. I'm perfectly satisfied too.[73]

In another instance, coupons used to promote Wills' Four Aces cigarettes could be exchanged for pullovers for men, women and children. Leaflets promoting the cigarettes and the scheme were distributed in working-class districts in 1933, and eight million leaflets were also distributed at football matches played by Arsenal, Aston Villa, Chelsea, Portsmouth and Sheffield Wednesday.[74] The success of coupon schemes was frequently alluded to by Mass-Observation respondents. Mrs Grant, for instance, was extremely positive about the Black Cat scheme even though she was a non-smoker: 'I have a very good ironing board, which I find most useful ... My husband is still using a thermos flask, which was another free gift'.[75] A 'hawk-eye camera' was the gift that another Mass-Observation respondent acquired by smoking Black Cat cigarettes.[76]

Cigarette cards, introduced in the 1890s, became a common fixture of interwar home life, especially for children and their carers.[77] Children's painting books, issued by Player's around Christmas 1929, were another scheme that extended cigarettes into the core of family life.[78] So too was the 'Woodbine Model Farm' which Wills were extremely pleased with because the toy offered 'a good way of bringing the brand to the notice of both the parents and the children, as the former often have to assist in building up the farm'.[79] The association of cigarettes with children ensured that future generations were exposed to smoking promotions and also that women, in their role as carers, encountered smoking as a safe and homely practice. Cigarettes were associated with the Boys' Scout Movement when Wills purchased advertising space in a number of newspapers for the Scouts to use. At the bottom of each advertisement appeared the words: 'placed at the disposal of the Boys' Scouts association by the courtesy of the manufacturers of "Capstan" cigarettes'.[80] The link between smoking and healthy, responsible boyhood was even made explicit in some advertising. A colourful full-page advert for Navy Cut cigarettes, prominently placed on the back page of *The Sketch* in 1925, featured a painting of a little boy, sat on the floor with discarded toys around him and a packet of Player's cigarettes upended on the floor. The boy had several cigarettes in his hand as he looked up at the reader. The parallel between the care invested in tobacco production and the care expended in raising children is implied by the text, while the purity of the product that this child has stumbled upon and the tradition it represents are made explicit.

> The name Player on a packet of cigarettes guarantees the quality and purity of the contents. It is more than a name – it is a reputation and a tradition. Far-reaching resources have secured for Player's the very cream of the world's tobacco crop, the choicest growths of Virginia leaf – cured and matured under ideal conditions with the skill and knowledge born of wide and varied experience.[81]

Tradition is emphasized in the passing down of good smoking habits from father – the picture is entitled 'Daddy's favourite' – to son. While this advertisement and other boy-centred promotion strategies confirmed the masculinity of smoking, they also stressed its harmlessness and located it in the female sphere of domestic responsibilities. The links with children contributed to the image of smoking as safe and respectable.

The notion that smoking was consistent with healthy living was reinforced by medical support for moderate tobacco use: 'In moderation, smoking probably does no harm whatever to the normally healthy man or woman. It even has good effects.'[82] Medical approval was also cited in cigarette advertisements: 'As a doctor I cannot recommend any brand, but personally I smoke Craven 'A'.'[83] In another advertisement a woman smoker explains that, 'Everytime I light a Craven "A" I thank my doctor for recommending them! He knows, and I know, that they don't harm the throat.'[84] Concerns about the dangers of smoking were aired in the press, but this was a marginalized discourse.[85] Moreover, anxious reports on the modern young woman smoking suggested that it was her behaviour rather than her health that was perceived as the greater problem. In general, the dominant view was that excessive consumption was problematic and doctors did advise some smokers to cut down or quit.[86] 'When smoked in excess', explained Dr Webb-Johnson, cigarettes have 'evil effects': 'They are bad for the digestive tract, for the eyes ... These seductive but deadly articles affect the heart ... they also have a toxic effect on the nerve cells.'[87] Moderate smoking was, in contrast, widely seen as acceptable, even as beneficial. Even sources that mentioned health risks often proffered ways for smokers to continue their habit rather than abstain. A 'nicotine neutralizer' was one solution offered to readers of the *Daily Express*: 'thousands of smokers enjoy complete immunity from Nicotine poisoning. One pastille eaten last thing neutralizes a whole day's smoking.'[88] Cigarette adverts often mentioned the health problems of smoking but, naturally, they circumvented these.[89]

Women encountered cigarettes not just in their dealings with men who smoked, but in their children's play, their daily reading material, when shopping or using urban spaces, when travelling by rail or underground, in relation to clothes, in cinemas and other leisure venues. In all these contexts smoking was for the most part presented as harmless and sometimes beneficial if pursued in moderation. A culture of smoking became the norm for all people.

Visibility of Women Smokers

Within the expanding and increasingly pervasive culture of cigarette smoking in interwar Britain, women smokers became more visible in the flesh and in representation. This provided the necessary context for smoking to increase among women and it facilitated the emergence of several discourses on women's smoking. The visibility of women as smokers in advertising and other media was key to the feminization of the cigarette and the redefinition of smoking as a feminine practice.

Women smokers were increasingly visible in the flesh with shifts in protocols about where women could smoke. Commentators on the 1920s frequently point to public displays of smoking by women, but there remained a regional and urban dimension to this exposure. Moreover, although some women's smoking did become visible and acceptable in certain public settings, the rules governing the propriety of smoking were complex. In 1920, women's smoking was observed in some London restaurants, but Graves and Hodge cite a report in *The New Statesman* that a young woman had her cigarette knocked out of her mouth by an 'irate elderly waiter'; apparently, 'bourgeois restaurants were stricter in preserving the old proprieties than more fashionable eating-houses'.[90] Lady Troubridge opined that 'I do not think it is good form for young girls to smoke in public, but older women may do so with propriety'.[91] Presumably Troubridge meant that only the assumed sexual propriety of older women provided immunity from the traditional assumption that a woman who smoked in public was sexually immoral; the risks for young smokers were heightened by the tremendous importance attached to an unblemished sexual reputation. The complexity of social rules governing women's smoking were also commented on by the *New Statesman* reporter who observed that while 'women could smoke without exciting interest in the restaurant-car of a train, it was still improper for them to smoke on the tops of buses'.[92] Presumably, it was inappropriate for a woman to smoke on the top of a bus because this was open to the street; a woman would therefore be perceived as parading herself. Objections to this stemmed from traditional assumptions that only prostitutes behaved in this way. Certainly it was not respectable or usual to see women smoking in the street in 1920. Indeed, the sight of a woman smoking in the streets made headlines in London's *Evening News*: 'When Bond Street Stared: The bold woman who had a cigarette during her stroll.'[93]

In London at least, some of the stigma against displays of women's smoking in public spaces, including streets, seem to have shifted by the mid 1920s. In 1925 the *Daily Express* noted that the 'out-of-door smoking girl is seen about a great deal'.[94] According to both a policeman and a reporter, there were 'women with cigarettes in Bond-street, in St James's Park, and on the top of omnibuses'.[95] This observation was consistent with the recollections of a worker at the Rothman's tobacconists who recalled a sudden shift in attitudes toward public smoking among his affluent female customers:

we used to get women coming in sometimes asking for cigarettes. About the end of the war they were pretty bashful about the whole matter still, and if I should ask them to try one just to see what it was like, they would take a dainty puff at it, say that they liked it or not as the case may be, and if they did put it out and take the rest of the box. But round about 1920 in next to no time at all all this changed. They would still take a puff but instead of putting the cigarette out they would walk out of the shop as large as life not worrying at all.[96]

In general, however, even in 1937, middle-class women and men still did not think it acceptable for women to smoke in the street, even in London.[97]

Photographs reproduced in the press of women smoking were another way in which actual women smokers achieved visibility. Miss Norah Clark appeared on the back page of the *Daily Mail* astride her horse, 'enjoying a cigarette at a meet of the Bray Harriers near Dublin'.[98] A photograph of '[t]hree city workers' lighting their cigarettes appeared in the *Daily Express*, as did one of young women smoking while sunbathing at Chiswick swimming baths.[99] Even if some of these photographs were staged, they contributed to the impression of an increased number of women smokers and, of course, to their visibility.[100] In the context of ambivalence about women smoking in public, these photographs raise interesting questions about the status of public images. A woman's smoking could have occurred in the confines of a home or a specific leisure context, but when this practice was photographed and displayed on the back page of a national paper was it still a private act of smoking? Was the visibility that a woman smoker achieved through the publication of her photograph more acceptable than if she were spotted smoking in the streets? The status of appearing smoking in a publicly available photograph seems to have been unclear at this time. Some women were happy to be photographed smoking and for the images to be used in public contexts. Miss Angela Joyce, who held the title of Miss England, suggested to Wills in 1928 that they use her photograph to promote their cigarettes. The offer was declined although no explanation was minuted.[101] Other women known to have smoked in 1920 did not permit public photographs of themselves smoking until the 1930s.

As press reports and photographs of smokers suggest, media representations constituted an important dimension of the growing visibility of women smokers. Press visibility contributed to a proliferation of meanings about smoking and the emergence of acceptable forms of feminine smoking. Press coverage magnified the exposure of actual women smokers and it brought them to the attention of those who lived in communities where smoking was not practised by women, at least not in public. This coverage was particularly important given regional differences in the visibility of women smokers in the flesh and in local papers. A book on fashion drawing for trainee draughtswomen articulates and explains these regional differences in approaches to women smoking: 'Some papers feature the haute vie type, smart but not "smarty". Others prefer the refined type, yet permit or encourage her to smoke a cigarette so that their readers may feel at home with her; and there is the quite definitely "cheeky" type.' For provincial work, draughtswomen were advised that a 'less advanced type' of figure is used: 'The provinces like to think themselves rather Puritans in these matters, and a cigarette-smoking female in some Midland papers would probably create a sensation.'[102]

Aside from photographs and reports of actual women smokers, national print media also paraded images of women smokers in fashion features, illustrations for fiction and articles, advertisements for non-tobacco products and, increasingly, cigarette advertising. The visibility of women smokers was enhanced considerably by explicit targeting of women in cigarette advertisements; initially these appeared in elite publications, then in the national press and middle-class women's magazines.[103] From 1920, readers of elite publications such as *Vogue* and *Eve*, and the Society paper *The Sketch*, regularly encountered representations of women smokers. Even if these papers were not read, the appearance of cigarette advertisements on the back cover would have ensured the visibility of women smokers. In 1920 *Eve* contained one or two cigarette advertisements per weekly issue, occasionally on the back cover, and in many of these women smoked, or it was suggested that they enjoyed cigarettes.[104] For example, in a sample of thirteen issues of *Eve* from 1920, only four had no images of women smoking whatsoever (in advertising, illustrations or portraits). *The Sketch* similarly featured several cigarette advertisements per weekly issue in 1920, usually one of which explicitly targeted women. Adverts for Muratti 'Ariston' cigarettes featured a woman, as did the colour advertisements for De Reske cigarettes which appeared roughly once a month on the back page.[105] There were also advertisements for Kenilworth cigarettes which stressed the secrecy that still surrounded most women's smoking: 'One Cigarette – somewhere where everyone won't see – but mind it's a Kenilworth.'[106] By the late 1920s women smokers were a common feature in these papers. They appeared in advertisements for underwear, 'slumberwear' and day wear.[107] Cigarette advertisements were, however, the medium in which women smokers most commonly appeared. A typical issue of the *Sketch* on 9 July 1930 contained two cigarette advertisements that focused solely on a woman smoker and a third, targeted at both genders, which portrayed a woman water-skiing on a packet of cigarettes. De Reske advertisements, which targeted women as well as men, appeared on the back cover of two of the four July issues.

Domestic servants may have been exposed in the course of their work to representations of women smokers featured in elite papers but, for the majority of people, it was not until the late 1920s that women smokers became visible in day-to-day reading material. In 1920 cigarette advertisements in the national press were mostly male in orientation and frequently located on the sports page; they rarely targeted women, although the appeal of some was ambiguous. Advertisements for Morris's blend, for instance, were clever in that they did not explicitly target women although the advertisement featured a packet on which was a picture of harem women smoking.[108] (This type of packaging contributed to the circulation of a racialized sexual discourse on women's smoking, discussed in Chapter 5.) Five years later, newspaper advertising of cigarettes still remained overwhelmingly male. Of ten advertisements in the *Daily Express* of 4 March 1925, only one depicted a woman, although she was not presented as a smoker, and three other advertisements were gender-neutral in that they featured only a cigarette packet; the remainder of the advertisements explicitly targeted men. Occasional advertisements for brands produced by small tobacco companies, for example Sarony cigarettes, did address women explicitly,[109] but often a week would pass without a glimpse of a female smoking.

Producers of the mainstream cigarette brands were slower than some of the smaller companies to sell cigarettes to women. Player's began to target women explicitly in 1925 with advertisements for Bachelor cigarettes, although these did not always depict women smoking.[110] By 1927 Wills, the largest UK tobacco company, followed suit using their current brands, initially Gold Flake and, from 1929, Three Castles Medium and Capstan cigarettes. Signs of change in the focus of newspaper advertising were apparent by 1928 but most cigarette advertisements remained male focused or, at minimum, gender-neutral in presentation. A typical

November 1928 issue of the *Daily Express* featured eight tobacco advertisements, five promoting cigarettes or cigars to men, three gender-neutral.[111] Across the whole month, however, women were targeted explicitly in seven cigarette advertisements.[112] Moreover, advertisements which addressed women did so with high-profile and often colourful images of women smoking, often accompanied by testimonials from titled and/or Society smokers such as Dame Clara Butt.[113] By 1930, the woman smoker had become a regular feature in cigarette advertising in national newspapers. Of twenty-four issues of the *Daily Express* noted in January 1930, eleven featured cigarette advertisements which explicitly targeted women smokers, and fifteen featured advertisements that were woman-centred or neutral. (Comparable figures for advertisements targeted at men were fourteen and nineteen respectively.) The high visibility continued until the outbreak of war. In July 1939 women smokers appeared in one or two cigarette advertisements a day in most daily newspapers from the *Daily Mirror* to the *Times*. The visibility of women smokers did vary between papers and while advertisements in the *Sunday Express* frequently embraced women, the *News of the World* featured less female-focused ones and placed more cigarette advertisements in the sports sections of the paper.

By 1930, women smokers were also increasingly seen in the pages of women's magazines. Whereas in 1920 this type of advertising had been limited to elite women's papers, by the 1930s they appeared also in papers for working-class and middle-class women. Capstan cigarettes were the first of the Wills' brands to be promoted in women's magazines in 1929, and by 1933 advertisements appeared in eight monthly magazines (mainly middle-class) and two weeklies (mainly working-class).[114] By 1939, the weekly mass-circulation *Woman* typically featured two, and on occasions three, advertisements per issue. It was not only advertisements that paraded women smokers. A shopping feature in *Miss Modern*, strategically placed adjacent to a Bachelors' cigarette advertisement, enthusiastically promoted these cigarettes to readers: 'Smokers please note! We have found just the very kind of cigarette to delight the bachelor girl. It is made up of attractive little boxes of ten and twenty – they fit so snugly into the handbag – so much neater and smarter than the packet variety. They have cork tips, which many girls prefer nowadays.'[115]

Cinema provided another medium in which cigarette culture was promoted in the interwar years. In American film the woman smoker became commonplace by 1930 and heroines, more so than female villains, brandished cigarettes.[116] The visibility of women smokers was heightened from the mid-1920s by the proliferation of film coverage in the print media. A photograph of Gloria Swanson holding a cigarette appeared on the back page of the *Daily Mail* promoting her latest film *The Love of Sunya*, while glamorous actress Tallulah Bankhead posed with a cigarette and her new husband in the *Daily Express*.[117] Consolidating the links between cigarette culture and the glamorous life of screen and stage celebrities, stars of film, and before them, of theatre, lent their names to the promotion of cigarettes.

In 1919 stage stars, including Peggy Kurton 'who played with great success in "The Officer's Mess"', Kyrle Bellew in *Scandal*, and Fay Compton in the leading part in *Caesar's Wife*, appeared in elite magazines promoting the pleasures of cigarettes.[118] In the 1930s, film stars such as Florence Desmond, Peggy Wood and Gracie Fields extolled the virtues of cigarettes to millions of women through the pages of national newspapers and leading women's magazines.[119]

The role of the media, and especially cigarette advertising, in encouraging women to start smoking is contentious. It is widely accepted that British and North American women did start to smoke prior to advertisements which targeted them. As we saw in Chapter 2, British women started smoking in the lateVictorian period, but it was not until the eve of the First World War that advertisements, mostly in the elite press, targeted women specifically. It was not until the late 1920s that a broader spectrum of women were targeted by cigarette companies through mass-advertising campaigns, by which time women's smoking was an established minority practice.

Accepting this, some argue that cigarette advertising was still influential even before it began to target women explicitly. Brandt claims that, even prior to advertisements for women, American cigarette advertising 'indirectly sought women smokers through images that emphasized the sociability and allure of the cigarette'.[120] There is no evidence of intentional targeting of women among the big British companies prior to the mid-1920s, although during the early 1920s smaller companies ran advertising campaigns that did embrace British women indirectly. Leaving aside the question of whether the tobacco industry deliberately sought to attract women, Brandt still makes a valid point about the possible influence of advertisements not overtly directed at women. Warsh similarly argues that North-American advertisements explicitly and exclusively targeted at men could still be significant for the increase of smoking among women: 'Cigarette advertising could have shaped women's views of what was masculine and therefore what would be an attractive aspiration for "new women".'[121] In relation to the British experience it does seem likely that, irrespective of whether women were targeted explicitly, cigarette advertisements contributed to the high-profile image of smoking and to discourses on smoking that could be attractive to women. But how important was cigarette advertising in general and, more specifically, advertising targeted at women?

Precise measurement of the effects of tobacco advertising on women or its impact relative to other media is 'unresolvable since the complex culture of tobacco consumption precludes any analysis in simple terms of cause and effect'.[122] As Chapman argues, in relation to isolating and assessing the influence of advertising in the 1980s, '[u]nlike the effects of nicotine, advertising cannot be dosed and its effects observed physiologically'.[123] It is, however, widely established that cigarette advertising contributes to a culture in which smoking is normalized and has a positive image. 'Whether advertising initiates consumer trends or only reinforces them ... [i]t is impossible to ignore their wider role in providing people a general education in goods.'[124] When advertisements started targeting women as smokers they *contributed to* a culture of smoking, to the impression that women were doing it, and to the proliferation of discourses on smoking that were meaningful and attractive to women. Other visual representations of women smokers also contributed to the impression that women smoked and to the formation of discourses on the attractions of smoking.

In a study of smoking in the US, Schudson argues that news coverage 'helped in the first instance to legitimate smoking among women', that advertising merely reinforced and naturalized this practice.[125] In Britain, newspaper reportage also played an important part in raising the profile of the earliest women smokers and, once photographs of smokers began appearing in the press after 1919, this profile was often a visual one. The importance of example should not be underestimated, and it was certainly recognized by tobacco companies which often constructed cigarette promotions around the image and reputations of well-known or titled women. Fashion promotions in elite magazines and in newspapers[126] also featured women smoking prior to the mass targeting of women by cigarette companies.

Film was also influential. Social commentators and historians often point to the influence of the cinema on British popular culture in the interwar years. According to Jackson, '[t]here is plenty of contemporary evidence that film stars (the Americans being far more numerous and influential than British) operated as role models' for middle-class women.[127] Working-class women were similarly influenced.[128] Lipstick and the small rosebud 'bee-sting' or 'cupid's bow' became popular on and off screen in the 1920s, and when, in the 1930s, Hollywood 'decreed' a large full mouth, 'this was widely copied'.[129] In the 1930s, styles of stockings also toed the line, and there was a 'beret-trend' following Greta Garbo's appearance in one. The activities of film stars, 'their clothes, their appearance, their manners, their love-making, their homes and general lifestyle all went to structure the dreams and even the behaviour of the upwardly mobile young'.[130] Unfortunately, Jackson and Alexander do not address the influence on women of filmic representations of smoking. Hilton, however, argues that the cinema did influence attitudes to women's smoking and far more so than advertising, but he provides scant evidence to support this claim.[131] Specific evidence of effect may be lacking, but from the late 1920s film undoubtedly contributed to the visibility of attractive women smokers. Moreover, popular women's magazines strongly encouraged readers to look to the screen for feminine inspiration.[132]

Cigarettes and a culture of smoking gradually infiltrated all areas of daily life, establishing the normalcy of smoking, and within this culture women increasingly gained a visible presence. The visibility of women smokers in real life was important in certain communities and contexts but media visibility was often more important, especially outside large urban centres. Images of women smokers contributed to a proliferation of discourses on smoking which aligned it with modernity, emancipation, sophistication, class and fashion. In combination with other aspects of cigarette culture, smoking was also understood as a means to enable women to cope. (These discourses will be explored in detail in subsequent chapters.) The importance of these discourses for women related, in part, to the conditions and experiences of interwar women's lives: their paid employment, leisure, domestic arrangements, social interactions and, in particular, their relations with men. Cigarettes appeared as an aid to managing modern lives, expressing modern identities and crafting complex statements about gender, class, sexuality and generation. That smoking should be increasingly perceived in this way, and valued for these contributions, stemmed from the importance of visual culture and visual forms of communication in the twentieth century.

The 'Act of Smoking': A Meaningful and Comforting Practice

Brenda Pool spoke for many women, and indeed men, when she explained to Mass Observation, 'I didn't take a liking to the actual tobacco for some time – just to the act of smoking.'[133] The 'act of smoking' had by the 1920s achieved prominence in British visual culture and, what's more, was increasingly encountered as a feminine act and a very meaningful one at that. The communication potential of the cigarette is a crucial part of its attractions according to Klein: 'Smoking cigarettes bodies forth an implicit language of gestures and acts that we have all learned subliminally to translate and that movie directors have used with conscious cunning, with the explicit intention of defining character and advancing plot.'[134] The interwar period was when the language of smoking became established as common parlance.

The importance attached to the language of smoking stemmed from the increased significance of the visual as a means of communication (discussed in Chapter 1). By the 1920s people relied more heavily than in the past on reading visual cues and on producing them, and were also more adept at both. There are several interrelated reasons for the new importance attached to the visual. It was due in part to the conditions of modern, especially urban, life where people were forced to rely on impressions in making judgements about people rather than on their experience of people or their reputations. It was also due to the emergence and accessibility of new visual technologies and media – film, photography, magazines and newspapers illustrated with photographs, illuminated outdoor advertising. These media produced a proliferation of visual forms that people had to interpret. In a related way, many of these new visual forms made it possible to study more closely how people appeared; women could scrutinize photographs of film stars or, indeed, of themselves. This encouraged increased self-awareness and scrutiny of how one looked to others. Some of the new visual media (magazine and newspaper advice columns on good grooming, etc.) provided explicit or implicit guidance on this.

But why is this important? Image was a crucial aspect of smoking both for those women who enjoyed it, and for those who disliked it but persisted with it anyway. Even motor-boat racer Joe (Marion) Carstairs, who regularly appeared in public with a cigarette, admitted privately that she smoked 'merely for effect; she never inhaled'.[135] Frequently, Mass-Observation accounts of why middle-class women started to smoke emphasize the importance of the visual dimensions of smoking, its 'effect', 'appearance', 'impression', particularly in the initial stages.[136] The 'act' of smoking was of immense personal and social significance and, in the context of shifting gender and age relations and a heightened awareness of generation, interwar women saw in smoking practices a means to say things about themselves. So although some women started smoking in private, it was with a view to developing their smoking skills such that they could be accomplished public smokers: the woman wanted to be seen as a smoker or at least known to smoke and therefore imagined as one. Women consciously exploited the visuality of smoking to make identity statements. In some social circles they even recorded their smoking in amateur photos and in commissioned portraits (discussed in Chapter 7).

Many women wanted to look like 'the type who smoked'. Emily Corradine described for Mass Observation how 'some people are most shocked to see one smoke or never imagine I'd do such a thing and so they don't offer – I get great fun out of this', 'but, poor me: why should *I* be an exception – my looks must be horribly deceptive or my reputation ridiculously unreal.'[137] So what did Emily hope to convey by smoking? By the 1930s smoking was widely perceived as an attractive and respectable feminine practice. Smoking cigarettes, apart from being fashionable in certain social circles, was also perceived as a defining feature of modern and emancipated womanhood. According to Ethel Mannin, herself a 'modern girl' of the 1920s, 'ladies ... all smoked, conscientiously, as the outward and visible sign of sex equality.'[138] In the 1930s, Ms Worden did not enjoy smoking but she continued 'because it was smart to do so – a sign of woman's emancipation'.[139] Appearing 'posh', fashionable, sophisticated, glamorous, even 'fast', were also attractions mentioned by many of Mass-Observation's women respondents. Brenda Poole 'liked the look of people smoking: I thought it gave them poise'.[140] Smoking also facilitated other useful impressions. As one woman explained: 'I felt that I looked less conspicuous as a wallflower when I had a cigarette in my hand.'[141] Whether this woman achieved an air of calm indifference is not clear – the important point is that she 'felt' that she looked less like a wallflower. This self-image drew on discourses about the social sophistication and competence of women smokers. To look like a non-smoker suggested that one was old-fashioned in looks, ideas and ways; that one was not a modern, emancipated, 'classy' and 'worldly' woman. The emergence of a discourse on non-smokers which cast them as less attractive because they did not smoke probably contributed to the negative image of the non-smoking woman in some social circles. Mass Observation's middle-class women respondents frequently comment that there was little real envy of non-smokers: although this referred particularly to men, it also included women.[142] Theodora Bosanquet, for example, admitted that she used to think of non-smokers as 'likely teetotallers' and 'priggish', and she observed that 'people congratulate non-smokers but often with a faint suggestion that a man or a woman who doesn't smoke is rather a kill-joy'. No wonder that Emily Corradine had mixed feelings about her ability to shock people by smoking.

The attractive and respectable associations of female smoking were, however, class-specific. Though the working-class Preston woman, mentioned earlier, who sported a cigarette in a green holder perceived that her smoking asserted her adulthood, modernity, style and glamour, many would have questioned her self-assessment. Smoking had a complex relationship to modernity, glamour and respectability for working-class women as discussed in Chapter 6.

Sociability was also frequently cited by women as a motivation to smoke, but this too was largely a matter of impression management. What did sharing a smoke say about a person and a social situation that was sufficiently important to encourage women to smoke even when they disliked the taste of cigarettes? Accompanying someone in a smoke was considered polite, especially in social situations. This etiquette, whatever its origins, was widely promoted in media representations of smoking, including cigarette advertisements targeted at both men and women. Moreover, the kind of cigarette offered was presented, and perceived, as highly important. Smoking also signified commonality. Mrs Noble and Mrs Cobb, for instance, 'started to smoke because everybody did it'; they were 'determined to be the same as other people'.[143] For these women, smoking in company could indicate a shared identity, such as being modern and emancipated. It could also signal that they shared the same need for tobacco as their companions, a need that arose perhaps from coping with the demands of modern life. Smoking could also indicate acceptance into a group. For some lesbians the exchange of tobacco products with men, especially cigars, was perceived – and utilized – as a symbol of their acceptance by men.[144] In some cases, women's comments suggest that they used smoking to assert their right to a place in a community that was not automatically given, as in women's insistence on their equal status with men in a community of adults. Smokers also described the sharing of cigarettes as a means of bridging social distance, of creating commonality prior to some form of social or professional exchange between people; it was, as Miss Bridgens explains, 'a *sign* that they meet on equal terms' (my emphasis).

I myself offer cigarettes when I want to talk on equal terms to charwomen or window cleaners or icecream vendors. I've noticed that business men offer each other cigarettes when they first meet to discuss a proposition … if a man comes to sell you a vacuum cleaner you don't offer him a cigarette but if he makes you a proposition on which you both stand to make money you begin by exchanging fags.[145]

Mrs Bosanquet similarly observed the use of cigarettes for this purpose: 'a man who is a lower class than you will use a cigarette to step over the caste hedge'.[146]

The visual and social significance of smoking was usually overlaid by other motivations, which were not static but changed over time and context. For example, the reasons women started to smoke were often different to the reasons which governed why they continued the practice and how much they smoked. Comfort and coping emerge as important reasons why some women started and/or continued to smoke. Mrs Corbett, a working-class woman, began to buy cigarettes regularly 'some time after marriage to drown unhappy thoughts, and keep from crying'.[147] Cigarettes were described as 'friends' by journalist Lyn Evans, who began smoking when she left home to live in 'digs': a 'packet of cigarettes kept me company in a lonely room. There was a friendly atmosphere about the smoke.'[148] As Mass Observation noted, 'it is the frequently expressed idea that the cigarette provides a soothing antidote to nervous tension, irritability, depression, boredom and worry. In other words they have the same effect as the *aspirin*'.[149] Habit and, in some cases dependence, were also noted in letters to women's magazines, and were mentioned by roughly a quarter of the women smokers surveyed in 1937 by Mass Observation.[150] The cost of smoking and dislike of being 'enslaved' by the habit were sometimes cited as disadvantages by Mass-Observation respondents but these were not sufficient to cast smoking in a negative light. Most women smokers, even those concerned about money and habits, did not advocate abstention. 'Enslaved' was the way Gay Taylor described herself and, typical of others who saw themselves in this way, she wrote: 'I would rather be able to smoke moderately and not feel myself a slave to it'.[151] Health issues sometimes underpinned smokers' concerns – that these were generally disregarded[152] is unsurprising given that tobacco use was condoned widely by the medical establishment as an aid to coping (see Chapter 6). In the context of wartime pressures, 'need' was to achieve particular prominence.

The 1940s

The Second World War contributed to the increased incidence of women's smoking across the social classes. Zweig's survey, conducted in the late 1940s, found that many women started to smoke during the war. Annual consumption of manufactured cigarettes per woman more than doubled between 1940 and 1945 from eleven cigarettes a week to twenty-four.[153] In 1945 one-third of women aged 20 years and over were smokers but, although they constituted a significant section of the smoking public, their consumption was still only 28 per cent of men's.[154] In the immediate postwar years women's consumption dropped a little but still remained higher than prewar. By 1949, 41 per cent of women aged 16 years and over were smokers of manufactured cigarettes (compared with 63 per cent of men).[155]

The presence of women smokers in the media dropped significantly with the advent of war; newspapers shrank in size, and space for advertising was reduced accordingly. Cigarette advertising became less common during the hostilities,[156] and also became more masculine. The *Daily Mirror* ran only one cigarette advertisement over a six-day period in July 1943 and this was linked to a Cigarette Appeal for men.[157] The *Daily Express* featured only two cigarette advertisements in six days, one of which was for duty-free cigarettes for the Forces.[158] *Sketch,* a Society paper, was still being produced on a weekly basis in 1943 with some advertising but not for cigarettes. Women's magazines similarly dropped cigarette advertisements during the war, a policy they continued into the immediate postwar years. Despite the lack of cigarette advertising during the war, women smokers continued to be visible. They featured in advertisements for other products, especially clothes, in government information advertisements,[159] and in film. Women smokers were also commonly encountered in the course of daily life, although public displays of smoking were not always perceived as respectable: taboos still existed against women smoking in the streets and also in uniform (see Chapter 6).

The wartime growth in women's smoking was precipitated by the conditions and experiences of war. Increased numbers of women entered paid employment and had both the money and the opportunity to engage in sociable smoking.[160] Mary Shuttleworth recalls that cigarette smoking was ubiquitous in the Lancaster factory where she worked making crank cases for fighter aeroplanes. Mary was teased by her workmates for refusing to smoke: 'they gave me stripes on my arm using chalk ... like a soldier's stripes ... for not smoking'.[161] Women were under greater stress as they coped with the dislocation of war – evacuation, bombing, fragmented families, uncertainty, injuries and loss. But why should women turn to smoking? Many were already smokers. As we have seen, there were regular smokers, those who smoked on occasion for show and sociability, also those who smoked surreptitiously. In wartime these women smoked more and more publicly as they had new or different motivations to smoke and as they gained new or different satisfactions from smoking. Whereas pre-1939 upper- and middle-class women increasingly felt that it was appropriate to smoke, if only for show and sociability, in the conditions of wartime a broader spectrum of women, including working-class women, were encouraged to take up the habit for social reasons and to assist in coping. These women did so because women's smoking was widespread, visible and, importantly, perceived as legitimate and therefore as respectable.

The expansion of women's smoking during the 1940s can be explained in large part by the establishment of tobacco consumption as a legitimate need for women as well as for men. Tobacco's role as a means of coping with wartime pressures had been widely established during the First World War, and with the approach of the Second World War this association re-emerged. Recognition that tobacco was a need for women as well as for men was evident in government initiatives to ensure that troops serving overseas received supplies of tobacco, and in the re-launch of the Overseas League's Tobacco Fund. Men were the principal recipients of these supplies but women's needs were also acknowledged. Following the budgets of 1942 and 1943, when heavy duties were levied on tobacco products, service women and men were allowed to purchase cigarettes and tobacco at pre-budget prices through NAAFI (Navy, Army and Air Force Institute) and other canteens.[162] Government also intervened to permit canteens in factories having more than 200 employees to sell tobacco products, and some munitions factories offered a cigarette ration as an incentive to productivity.[163] However, in the context of tobacco shortages, women were sometimes accused of using up valuable supplies, and some tobacconists allegedly refused to sell cigarettes to women.[164]

Despite shortages of cigarettes on the domestic front, the conditions of wartime were an important factor in smoking by women. Valerie Avery describes how young mothers 'celebrated' after surviving bomb raids: 'Thank you, Christ, for saving us this night. Now for a fag.'[165] Comfort and coping were key reasons why women from across the social-class spectrum started to smoke or increased their consumption. 'It is obvious', concluded Mass Observation, 'that the stress & strains of war have increased people's smoking'.[166] One woman described how her 'consumption has gone up over 100%. It started in September last during the Blitz. I found smoking kept me from getting jittery. I got fidgety & unstrung and found a cigarette seemed to help me.'[167] According to Mass Observation, 'the *widespread belief in the sedative effect* of cigarettes meant that many people turned to smoking spontaneously as a relief from wartime tension, and also that non-smokers in shelters and ARP [Air Raid Precaution] posts as well as in the Front Line found themselves *constantly offered cigarettes* and *encouraged to smoke*.'[168]

In the immediate postwar years the legitimacy of women's tobacco use was consolidated. In the context of widespread concern about the effects of higher tobacco prices on the elderly with limited means, a Tobacco Duty Relief scheme, otherwise known as 'pensioner's tobacco', was introduced by government. Details, set out in the national papers, explained that elderly smokers and snuff takers, both women and men, could apply at the Post Office for tokens to be used in part payment against tobacco products.[169] The acceptability of women's smoking was also evident in other contexts. A journal for paraplegics, for example, celebrated an invention by Bunty Noon which enabled a disabled woman to assert her right to smoke. As the article explained: 'Pat Theobald wanted to smoke. But without the use of her hands it was a tricky business ... almost impossible. People *would* complain about ash on the bed or holes in the sheets. It was all very disheartening. After all why shouldn't she smoke?'[170] The postwar years were, however, characterized by shortages of tobacco. This prompted the government in 1947 to encourage the public to smoke fewer cigarettes, the Chancellor even advising people to 'smoke your cigarettes to the butts ... it may even be good for your health'.[171] Women may have been acknowledged as smokers, but amid shortages of cigarettes some questioned whether women were as entitled to smoke as men. According to Ann Blythe in *Woman*, a London newspaper had devoted a leader to 'the chain-smoking ladies of London' who were robbing working men of their hard-earned comfort.[172] In response to the frequently voiced criticism that women smoked merely for effect, Blythe pointed to the importance of appearances for both sexes, especially when young: 'the boy because he thinks he looks manly, the girl because it is rather daring'. This was not, she insisted, the motivation for 'older people who pay 3s 6d for 20 out of hard-earned income'. Need was the motivation and, 'In spite of what men will say, a girl can enjoy and *need* tobacco as much as her brother, and it is just as hard for her to live without it.'

Whereas discussion of women smokers pre-1939 had referred almost exclusively to the middle and upper classes, by the time that Blythe was writing the smoking community also embraced working-class women. In their study of life and leisure in England and Wales in 1947, Rowntree and Lavers were surprised to discover the importance of smoking in everyday life of women as well as that of men across the classes and age groups. Unfortunately the study's methodology prohibits an accurate assessment of the significance of class, and smoking details are not entered for all women aged over 20 years. However, on the basis of seventy-six cases where smoking information was recorded on women aged over 20 years, it emerges that 65 per cent were smokers, and nine of the ten women aged 20 or under were smokers. One-third of the women were moderate smokers, and a quarter were heavy or chain smokers; in both categories working-class women were well represented. Zweig's interviews with 445 people, including 244 women workers and forty-seven full-time housewives, confirms the picture of smoking as a feminine practice among the middle and working classes; 40 per cent of the women workers he surveyed were smokers.[173]

Disposable income was highly important in women's determining whether they would smoke, and this was related either to their husband's income or to their own ability to earn an independent income. In Rowntree and Lavers' study, moderate smoking (regular, up to ten cigarettes a day) was popular among full-time housewives, especially those married to professional men (managers, retired army personnel, stockbrokers, accountants, doctors). Working-class widows and divorcees, particularly those who worked, also smoked, as did married working women. Young single women employed mainly in factory, shop and office work were also likely to be smokers, indeed few did not smoke. In contrast to these relatively affluent groups, working-class housewives, particularly the wives of labourers, were not usually smokers. Some of these home-based women declared that they would have smoked if they could afford to.[174] This point was reiterated by some of the full-time housewives in Zweig's study who, when asked about smoking, commented, 'I have given up smoking because it's too expensive, I can't afford it'.[175] As one woman explained, 'When I was in the factory I had more money to spare'; similarly a 47-year-old woman with three children reported that 'she can't even smoke as she used to when she was a girl, as she has no money now'.[176]

Money was usually no obstacle to smoking for most young and single working women, including the 103 working-class women aged between 14 and 20 years studied in 1945–46 by Pearl Jephcott. Jephcott discovered that virtually all her young women growing up near Piccadilly Circus in London, in Needham (a Northern industrial town) and Dowden Colliery (a pit village in County Durham) started smoking when they were 14, probably on leaving school and starting full-time work during the war. Typically, young women smoked only a few cigarettes initially, but smoking increased with age and they were usually heavy smokers by their late teens. Hilda Parker and her London friends typically smoked five cigarettes in an evening when they were 16, and twenty a day by the time they were 17. By the time Jephcott's young women were 17 or 18, they spent the major part of their pocket money on cigarettes. Dolly, a North Country girl, spent 2s 6d of her 5s pocket money on cigarettes when she was 17, and 5s of her 8s when she was 18½ .[177] A London machinist spent 5s of 23s pocket money when she was 16½, and 12s of her £3–£6 when she was 19.[178] It is worth noting that none of the 15–17-year-old women in Zweig's study mentioned smoking, and only a quarter of the 18-year-old women.[179] The high cost of cigarettes at the time of his survey may have been a disincentive to start smoking. In Rowntree and Lavers' study there were also occasional young workers from poor backgrounds who were unable to afford their own cigarettes because most of their low wages were contributed to the housekeeping.

Appearances were a key aspect of the smoking experience for Jephcott's young women. According to Jephcott, girls usually started smoking to look big or because everyone at work who is older smokes; in other words, smoking was a visual signifier of age and feminine sophistication. One woman aged 19 and married, recalled that she first started to smoke when she was 14 'to show my grandmother who was master'.[180] Jephcott noted of Hilda Parker and her friends that they followed the smoking habits of their set as closely as they monitored each other's 'make-up, reading matter and views on morality'.[181] This suggests that smoking practices were read carefully as visual signifiers, although Jephcott does not say of what. There is no indication, however, that there were any rules about where a young woman could respectably smoke even though there were rules about other matters. Hilda Parker's set, for instance, had rules for getting on with boys which included, 'don't show off; don't dress flash; and don't sing in the street or swear'.[182]

Smoking for visual effect – to look sophisticated, fashionable or competent – was often mentioned by the women who grew up in Scotland in the 1940s when interviewed by Elliot.[183] Choice of cigarette brand was one element of this: Bell changed to Du Maurier to 'improve my image', while Morag smoked Senior Service because it looked more 'respectable' than her previous brand.[184] Elliot found no evidence of women starting to smoke in imitation of film or advertising images, although these did provide a visual framework in which some women imagined themselves at the time and/or recalled retrospectively how they saw themselves (it being difficult to separate these different perspectives). As May put it, 'you can still see the image of yourself with the cigarette and the drink or your cocktail and it looks good. It was Hollywood'; Janet similarly recalled her smoking experience as 'a wee bit like on the pictures, you know, when the man comes up and lights your cigarette'.[185]

Although appearances were important, the smoking careers that Jephcott details suggest that habit and need gradually became equally, or more, pressing motivations for some women. One young woman smoked about fifty a day at 19, including some before breakfast. As Jephcott observed, she 'seems to be genuinely nerve-racked if no cigarettes are available'.[186] The ease with which smoking escalated from an occasional practice to a habit was not exclusive to working-class youth. Concern about the development of smoking careers prompted *The Guider* (the official Guide magazine) to denounce smoking as a 'temptation' that could lead girls and young women astray.[187] Although the *Guider* focused on excessive consumption, the implication was that even occasional smoking could get out of hand, as it is difficult to notice bad habits taking hold.

Sociability and relaxation were the main motivations that Zweig identified for women smoking. Going out to work, he explained, was conducive to smoking because women were more in the company of others who smoked and because many smoked to be sociable. Smoking ten cigarettes a day, or even fewer, was common among the women: 'often I was given figures as low as ten or twenty a week'.[188] Some of these women 'smoked only occasionally, some only over the weekend ... after a meal ... over a book or while listening to the wireless, and some only in company'.[189] Zweig concluded that: 'Women smoke mostly for relaxation, not so much for excitement, therefore often after a meal or in the evening near the fire.'[190]

Zweig stated that, although he had 'heard many stories about working women wasting their money on drinking, smoking and gambling', these stories were 'not borne out by the fact of my inquiry'.[191] Rowntree and Lavers were, in contrast, alarmed by levels of 'heavy' smoking and 'widespread addiction'.[192] The 100 female case studies they present do not reveal that women usually smoked as much as men, but about 20 per cent of the women more than 20 years old were described as 'heavy' smokers, and 30 per cent of women aged 20 and under. Although Rowntree and Lavers claimed that smoking 'gives much pleasure ... which is probably innocuous if indulged in moderately',[193] they were concerned about the ill effects of heavy smoking and the implications of dependence. Three key dependence issues were identified: that 'a substantial amount of real wealth is literally going up in smoke each year' as a proportion of US Marshall Aid was being used to purchase Virginian tobacco; that the nation was so dependent on tobacco that 'industrial production would undoubtedly be lowered' if tobacco were unavailable; the financial cost to individuals and families of addiction to tobacco products. Rowntree and Lavers' concerns about the social and health costs of tobacco consumption were not new. However, the experience of war heightened public awareness of dependency and the possible implications of this.

Conclusion

In 1920 the proportion of women who smoked was tiny and concentrated in the upper echelons of society, but 41 per cent of women from across the social classes were smokers by 1949. The image of the smoker also changed dramatically. Whereas in 1920 the image of the smoker was principally a male one, by the 1930s images of women smokers were commonplace. The feminization of smoking resulted from changes in the experiences of women – high among these was the way in which interwar women were engulfed in cigarette culture and how, within this, it became increasingly easy for them to conceive or indeed to see themselves as smokers. War conditions provided further reason to smoke and granted legitimacy to the practice for women from all walks of life. The discourses that were central to the feminization of the image of smoking from 1880 through to 1950 are explored in detail in Chapters 4–6, while Chapter 7 examines how women engaged with these discourses in the context of photographic portraiture.

Notes

1. *Daily Express*, 20 April 1920, p. 6.
2. Ibid.
3. Thanks to Cheryl Warsh for this point.
4. *Daily Express*, 21 April 1920, p. 5.
5. Nicolson and Trautmann, *Question of Things Happening,* pp. 175, 181; Glendinning, *Vita*, p. 95 and correspondence with Nigel Nicolson; Cadogan, *Richmal Crompton*, p. 96; Brittain, *Testament*, p. 354; Stocks, *Eleanor Rathbone*, pp. 121–2.
6. Player's DDPL 7/19/2 *Yorkshire Post*, 21 April 1920.
7. Wald et al, *UK Smoking Statistics*, p. 13.
8. On class see McKibbin, *Classes and Cultures.* Contemporaries used annual income as the dividing line between the middle and working classes; the middle class began at £250 per annum. McKibbin argues, however, that members of the minor clerical and distributive trades who often earned less than £250 per annum should also be included in the middle class. Although this group were usually of immediate working-class origins, they were middle-class in terms of education, lifestyle, salary, dress, deportment, social aspiration. The middle class also included higher and lower professionals. Members of the upper classes included most peers, extended royal family and senior functionaries of the court, the old aristocracy, parts of the gentry and many of the very wealthy. 'Society' included the socially active members of the upper classes as well as successful middle-class figures from the arts, cinema, literature and sports.
9. Mannin, *Young in the Twenties*, p. 33. Webb-Johnson, 'Women's Clubs', p. 91.
10. *Daily Mail*, 5 April 1927, p. 9.
11. Mannin, *Young in the Twenties*, p. 72. The prevalence of women smoking in some social circles by the 1930s and the etiquette which surrounded it is conveyed also in *Mab's Weekly* (17 October 1931, p. 8) which offered tips on catering for smokers when hosting a bridge party. Lady Troubridge's etiquette manual also discussed smoking, cited in MOA FR 3192, p. 125.
12. *Daily Express*, 17 May 1924, p. 7.
13. *Daily Express,* 16 May 1924, p. 1.
14. *The Sketch,* 16 May 1924, p. 1.
15. Charlton, 'Galsworthy's Images', p. 633. In the 1920s women smokers, especially 'big-game-hunters', appeared in P. G. Wodehouse's humorous novels of upper-class life.
16. MOA TC 63 Box 1.
17. *Modern Woman,* March 1939, p. 55.
18. *Men Only,* April 1937, p. 98.
19. *Daily Express*, 14 May 1920, p. 5.
20. MOA TC 63: 1/D Warrack; 1/B Franklin.
21. Rodaway, *London Childhood*, p. 152.
22. MOA FR 3192, p. 71.
23. MOA TC 63 1/B Franklin.
24. Wills 38169/M/8(c) Management Committee, 6 April 1927.
25. Cited in Hilton, *Smoking*, p. 145.

26. MOA FR 3192, p. 148. See also Margot Jones's shock at seeing a maid working with a cigarette in her mouth in 1937 (MOA TC 63 1/E).

27. *Glamour*, 3 June 1939, p. 9.

28. Priestley, *English Journey*, p. 82.

29. Brandt, *London in the Thirties*; see images 'An East-End Girl', p. 20, and 'Charlie Brown's, Limehouse', p. 22.

30. Jephcott, *Girls Growing Up*, p. 63.

31. ERA, Mrs S7P.

32. Elliot, '"Everybody did it"', p. 14.

33. *Daily Express*, 14 April 1927, p. 5.

34. *Vogue*, Early July 1924, p. viii.

35. For example, *TTR*: 1 January 1920, p. 19; 1 January 1927, p. 11; 1 July 1924, p. 37.

36. *Woman*, 14 August 1937, p. 2.

37. Wills 38169/M/8(a) Committee Reports, 10 March 1926; 38169/M/8/(c) Management Committee, 27 April 1927; 38169/M/8(h) Branch Selling Committee, 17 February 1930.

38. Wills 38169/M/8/(c) Branch Selling, Advertising & Supply Sub-Committee, 24 June 1927.

39. Hilton, *Smoking*, p. 154.

40. *TTR*, 1 January 1924, p. 13; *Manchester Evening News,* 1 April 1920, p. 6.

41. Storey, *Our Joyce*, pp. 169–170.

42. MOA TC 63 1/B: Corbett; T. Bosanquet.

43. *Manchester Evening News*, 12 April 1920, p. 3.

44. *Punch*, 15 June 1921, p. 470, cited in Doan, *Fashioning Sapphism*, p. 106.

45. Hilton, *Smoking*, pp. 119–22.

46. Dunhill, *Our Family Business*, p. 67. See also Rolley, 'Cutting a Dash'.

47. *TTR*, 1 June 1927, p. 24.

48. Dunhill, *Our Family Business*, p. 67.

49. Souhami, *Gluck*, p. 42; Nicolson and Trautmann, *Change in Perspective,* pp. 381–2; Summerscale, *The Queen*. Other pipe smokers are recorded in MOA TC 63: 1/E Iggulden; 1/B Lyn Evans. In MOA TC 63 1/C: Miss Roland liked a cigar, 'but never in public and only with people I know well'; so too did Mrs Hall.

50. MOA FR 979, p. 19; see also p. 20.

51. Tinkler, *Constructing Girlhood*, pp. 27–35.

52. Zweig, *Women's Life and Labour,* pp. 147, 180.

53. MOA TC 63 1/B T.Bosanquet, 1/E Iggulden.

54. MOA TC 63 1/D Taylor. See also TC 63: 1/B Cobb; 1/D Weaver; 1/C Miller.

55. MOA TC 63 1/B Bridgen.

56. MOA TC 63 1/E Rowland.

57. MOA TC 63 1/D Worden.

58. Hilton, *Smoking*.

59. Wills 38169/M/8/(a) Committee Reports, 19 May 1926.

60. Brandt, *English at Home*, p. 35.

61. See photographs of retail establishments, GMCRO. Libraries mentioned in Stevenson, *British Society*, p. 399.

62. See committee minutes in Wills 38169/M/8 (l), (m), (p).

63. Wills 38169/M/10(g) Reports of Advertising Sub-Committee, 12 November 1935.

64. Wills 38169/M/8(p) Advertising Sub-Committee, 2 February 1934.

65. BFI 'Most Graceful Cigarette Smoker?' 1921.

66. Doug Rendell, communication.

67. Hilton, *Smoking*, p. 93.

68. Wills 38169/M/8(n) Advertising Sub-Committee, 8 December 1932.

69. Wills 38169/M/8(g) Branch Selling Committee, 6 June 1929.

70. Wills 38169/M/8(n) Advertising Sub-Committee, 9 February 1933.

71. Hilton, *Smoking*, p. 106. Coupon schemes were first introduced briefly around 1900. Coupons were included in some cigarette packets and could be collected and exchanged for a range of goods.

72. Alford, *Wills*, p. 351.

73. *Daily Express*, 16 November 1928, p. 2.

74. Wills 38169/M/8(n) Selling Committee Minutes, 16 January 1933.

75. MOA TC 63 1/B Grant.

76. MOA TC 63 1/B T.Bosanquet.

77. Storey, *Our Joyce*, p. 71. MOA TC 63 1/B Beken described how 'much knowledge is gained by studying them [cigarette cards]' which was why she 'suffered' them gladly around the house.

78. Wills 38169/M/8(f) Branch Selling Committee Minutes, 7 January 1929. MOA TC63 1/D Terry describes the Player's Sailor appearing on 'the pin boxes and button boxes of my nurse and mother, and also on my first box of chalks and watercolour tubes'.

79. Wills 38169/M/8/(p) Advertising Sub-Committee, 9 February 1934, also 30 January 1934.

80. Wills 38169/M/8/(g) Branch Selling Committee, 6 June 1929.

81. *The Sketch,* 29 July 1925.

82. *Modern Woman*, March 1939, p. 58. Dr Grinsing also offered advice on moderate consumption: 'don't inhale or blow out through the nose', 'don't smoke before the age of twenty one', 'don't smoke before meals', 'smoke five or less a day', 'smoke only after meals and in the evening', 'always use a clean cigarette holder'. In a remarkably prescient statement the doctor warned also about the effects of passive smoking in that one 'can get the ill effects of over-smoking by inhaling a smoke-ladened atmosphere'. See also 'Smoke and be Healthy', *Daily Express*, 31 May 1924, p. 3.

83. *Daily Express*, 7 November 1928, p. 16.

84. *Daily Express*, 14 January 1930, p. 13. This point was also made in the advertisement cited above.

85. For example, *Modern Woman*, March 1939, pp. 55, 58; *Men Only,* January 1936, pp. 59–62. Advertisement in the *Daily Mirror*, 22 July 1939, p. 17, declared: 'you will be a healthier person in every way, free from headaches, dizziness, heart and nerve troubles, defective vision ... due to excessive smoking'. *My Weekly* had numerous anti-smoking advertisements. 'Cigarette smoking – mothers! Save your son's and girl's ruination. Secretly if necessary' (18 January 1930, p. 91). See also 1 February 1930, p. 151; 5 January 1935, p. 31. Despite the common belief that smoking aided digestion, medical evidence reported

in *Daily Express*, 31 May 1924, p. 3, identified tobacco, tea, coffee and alcohol as the four 'poisons' which are strong factors in indigestion. Some Mass-Observation respondents refer to health problems of smoking – for example, TC 63 1/D Terry: 'I am sure it is bad to smoke all day, as it takes away the appetite and in time destroys sense of taste and smell. I have heard that heart, lungs, liver and eyesight are affected, but I do not know if this is true.'

86. MOA TC 63: 1/B M.E.Bosanquet; 1/E Iggulden advised to stop smoking.

87. Webb-Johnson, 'Women's Clubs', p. 91.

88. *Daily Express*, 3 April 1934, p. 9.

89. D*aily Express*, 26 July 1939, p. 2. A woman who smoked heavily while playing bridge is portrayed as nagged by her conscience, 'Aren't we rather over-calling the smoking?' She is, however, reassured: 'the wool-filter absorbs half the nicotine and oils. So you can play ... and smoke ... till it's time to go home. Remember ... You needn't cut down smoking if you smoke cooltipt'.

90. Cited in Graves and Hodge, *The Long Weekend*, p. 43.

91. *Daily Express*, 21 April 1920, p. 5.

92. Cited in Graves and Hodge, *The Long Weekend*, p. 43.

93. Player's DDPL 7/19/2 *Evening News*, 24 March 1920, n.p.

94. *Daily Express*, 16 March 1925, p. 4.

95. *Daily Express,* 16 May 1924, p. 1.

96. MOA FR 3192, p. 78.

97. For example, MOA TC 63 1/E Barraud.

98. *Daily Mail*, 4 March 1920, p. 10.

99. *Daily Express*, 17 May 1924, p. 7; 22 May 1924, p. 7.

100. By 1939 women smokers had to be either famous or engaged in unusual activities to achieve visual prominence in the national press. For example, the back page of the *Daily Express* 25 July 1939 featured photo news of a woman: 'She smokes and swims – in a race at Ramsgate, when competitors had the difficult job of keeping their cigarettes alight.'

101. Wills 38169/M/8(h) Branch Selling Committee, 11 November 1929 and 28 November 1929.

102. Shackell, *Modern Fashion Drawing*, p. 44.

103. Colour posters which reproduced De Reske advertisements were also free in exchange for a cigarette box lid and a 2d stamp.

104. For example, *Eve:* January 1920, p. xvi; 25 March 1920, p. x; 29 July, p. f. Advertisements for Foyer cork-tipped cigarettes, although not depicting a woman, were clearly aimed at them: 'a dainty box containing dainty cigarettes, made of dainty macedonian tobacco leaves'. *Eve*, 8 April 1920, p. viii.

105. For example, *The Sketch*, 19 May 1920, p. xx and back page.

106. *The Sketch*, 26 May 1920, p. 137.

107. *Eve*, 1 Sept 1926, p. f; 6 October, 1926, p. g.

108. *Daily Express*, 13 April 1920, p. 10.

109. *Daily Express*, 17 May 1924, p. 1; 3 May 1924, p. 1.

110. Player's DD PL 6/22/1 Advertising stock lists. One Player's advertisement (*Eve*, 1 Sept 1926, p. 457) targeted women in the text only: 'In Player's Navy Cut cigarettes there is a subtle charm which will appeal to Eve's fair daughters.'

111. *Daily Express*, 2 November 1928.

112. *Daily Express*: 12 November, p. 8; 13 November, p. 19; 14 November, p. 1; 15 November, p. 19; 27 November, p. 3; 28 November, p. 1; 29 November, p. 19.

113. *Daily Express*, 14 November 1928, p. 1. See also 28 November 1928, p. 1; 29 November 1928, p. 19.

114. Wills 38169/M/8(h) 3rd Report of the Press Committee, 21 December 1929 – Three Castles cigarettes advertised from 1930 in *Weldon's Ladies' Journal, Modern Woman, Britannia, Eve, Good Housekeeping* and *Woman's Journal*. 38169/M/8(l) Press and Poster Committee, 11 January 1932, adverts in*: Woman's Journal, Woman & Home, My Home, Woman & Beauty, Wife and Home, Modern Home, Good Housekeeping, Modern Woman*. In 1933 advertisements also appeared in *Home Notes* and *Home Chat* – 38169/M/8(n) Press, 22 March 1933.

115. *Miss Modern*, January 1931, p. 65.

116. Dale, *Motion Pictures*.

117. *Daily Mail*, 6 April 1927; *Daily Express*, 21 November, 1928, p. 1.

118. Featured on the inside front covers of *Vogue:* Early July 1919, Early June 1919, Early May 1919.

119. For example, *Woman*, 1 July 1939, p. 51.

120. Brandt, 'Recruiting Women Smokers', p. 64.

121. Warsh, 'Smoke and Mirrors', p. 189.

122. Goodman, *Tobacco*, pp. 106–7.

123. Chapman, *Great Expectorations*, p. 21.

124. Schudson, *Advertising*, pp. 207–8.

125. Ibid., p. 183.

126. *Manchester Guardian*, 2 October 1926, p. 8.

127. Jackson, *Middle Classes*, p. 271.

128. Alexander, 'Becoming a Woman'.

129. Jackson, *Middle Classes,* pp. 141–6.

130. Ibid., p. 271.

131. Although Hilton (p. 150) claims that 'many Mass-Observation panellists' admitted to being influenced by screen stars, he presents only one example in evidence. My research, also that of Elliot ('Destructive but Sweet'), has not revealed further evidence of Mass Observation's women respondents testifying to the influence of cinema, although some did opine that film was probably a factor shaping trends (MOA FR 979, p. 33).

132. For example, *Poppy's Paper*, 16 February 1924.

133. MOA TC 63 1/E Poole.

134. Klein, *Cigarettes are Sublime*, p. 9.

135. Summerscale, *The Queen*, p. 91.

136. MOA TC 63: 1/D Warrack; 1/C Kempe; 1/B Bridgens; 1/E Hickling. Men, too, frequently recalled how they started to smoke in order to 'show' people that they were grown up and, most importantly, to appear manly, see MOA TC 63 Box 2.

137. MOA TC 63 1/B Corradine.

138. Mannin, *Young in the Twenties*, p. 72.

139. MOA TC 63 1/D Worden.

140. MOA TC 63 1/E Poole.

141. MOA FR 3192, p. 148.

142. MOA TC 63: 1/B T.Bosanquet; 1/E Poole. On men, Ms Warrack (MOA TC 63 1/D) commented: 'they are lucky as must save a lot of money, but I think men who do not smoke are a bit queer'. See also MOA TC 63 1/B Grant and FR 979, pp. 44–5.

143. MOA TC 63 1/B Cobb/Noble.

144. Tinkler, 'Smoking and Sapphic Modernities'.

145. MOA TC 63 1/B Bridgens.

146. MOA TC 63 1/B M.E. Bosanquet.

147. MOA TC 63 1/B Corbett.

148. MOA TC 63 1/B Evans.

149. MOA FR 3192, p. 136. See also, MOA TC 63: 1/B Corradine; 1/E Poole.

150. MOA TC 63 Box 1.

151. MOA TC 63 1/D Taylor.

152. MOA FR 3192, p. 141.

153. Wald, *UK Smoking Statistics*, p. 13, Table 2.1.

154. Graham, *Life's a Drag*, p. 6.

155. Wald, *UK Smoking Statistics*, pp. 34–5, Tables 4.11 and 4.1.2.

156. Alford, *Wills*, p. 399.

157. *Daily Mirror,* 26–31 July 1943. Advertisement in 26 July, p. 2.

158. *Daily Express*, 26–31 July 1943. Advertisements in 26 July, p. 4 and 28 July, p. 3.

159. McDowell, *Forties Fashion,* p. 50.

160. It was estimated that in 1943 (if part-time and voluntary work were included) 80 per cent of married women and 90 per cent of single women were contributing to the war effort. See Braybon and Summerfield, *Out of the Cage*, p. 168.

161. Mary Shuttleworth, communication.

162. *The Times*, 13 April 1943, p. 8.

163. Alford, *Wills,* p. 400.

164. Parliamentary Questions, June 1941, cited in Elliot, 'Destructive but Sweet', p. 222.

165. Avery, *London Morning*, p. 11.

166. MOA FR 979, p. 3; see also FR 3192, p. 79.

167. MOA FR 979, p. 10.

168. MOA FR 3192, p. 136.

169. Concern voiced in: *The Times*, 11 June 1947, p. 2; *Daily Mail*, 21 June 1947, p. 3. Details of scheme: *The Times*, 22 September 1947, p. 3.

170. *The Chord* [produced by the Stoke Mandeville Spinal Unit, Aylesbury] 1(4), Summer 1948, p. 30. Thanks to Julie Anderson for this article.

171. Cooper, 'Snoek Piquante', p. 38.

172. *Woman*, 25 September 1948, p. 32.

173. Zweig, *Women's Life and Labour*, p. 144.

174. Rowntree and Lavers, *English Life and Leisure*, for example p. 14, case study 24. The cost of smoking was also prohibitive for some middle-class people in the late 1940s, according to Lewis and Maude, *English Middle Classes*.

175. Zweig, *Women's Life and Labour,* p. 147.
176. Ibid., p. 180.
177. Jephcott, *Rising Twenty*, p. 59.
178. Ibid., p. 139.
179. Zweig, *Women's Life and Labour*, p. 61.
180. Jephcott, *Rising Twenty*, p. 59.
181. Ibid., p. 58.
182. Ibid., p. 17.
183. Elliot, 'Destructive but Sweet', pp. 303, 311, 313–15.
184. Ibid., p. 326.
185. Ibid., p. 295.
186. Jephcott, *Rising Twenty,* p. 59.
187. *Guider*, June 1940, pp. 149–50.
188. Zweig, *Women's Life and Labour*, p. 144.
189. Ibid., p. 145.
190. Ibid.
191. Ibid., p. 144.
192. Rowntree and Lavers, *English Life and Leisure*, p. 199.
193. Ibid., p. 200.

4

Modern and Emancipated Women

Women's liberation was often equated with the right to smoke. This is not surprising, because of the dominant association of smoking with men and masculinities. Women's rights were a key theme in late Victorian and Edwardian representations of women smokers irrespective of whether the claim was condoned or applauded. What marked a distinctive shift in the image of the woman smoker was the characterization of her practice as a 'modern' one. Modernity conferred a kind of status on women's smoking, or at least on the smoking of some women. The concept did not, however, represent a blanket celebration of change; as Rieger and Daunton argue, the attractiveness of the term 'modern' lay partly in its ability to convey ambivalence.[1] Representations of the woman smoker frequently reveal the management of ambivalent attitudes toward her 'modern' ways; this ambivalence, and sometimes hostility, stemmed from concern about the implications for gender and gender relations of women smoking. Before proceeding to explore the interwar image of the modern smoker, this chapter introduces the earlier association of women's smoking with women's rights.

Women who Claim the Right to Smoke

Smoking was associated almost exclusively with men during the nineteenth century, and a masculine discourse on smoking dominated. Although there was an established but subsidiary discourse on women and smoking, this aligned it with the sexuality of unrespectable women (see Chapter 5). In the context of demands for women's rights in the late 1800s, new female smokers came into the limelight, most notably the upper-class 'Pleasure Seeker' and the 'New Woman'. Both figures were presented as embracing new ways and claiming new rights. While the New Woman staked a claim to equal rights with men in a range of spheres including the economic and political, the Pleasure Seeker claimed her right principally to the *pleasures* enjoyed by male members of her class.

Drawing on a discourse of upper-class privilege and right to pleasure, and justified by a modern emphasis on women's rights, the Pleasure Seeker pursued her pleasures with little regard for convention or what the rest of society thought of her. The attraction of tobacco was, in large part, the properties claimed for it, namely its capacity to both soothe and stimulate. The masculine and sexual associations of smoking also contributed to the draw. The 'giddy society lady', as *Punch* called her, was a woman who, from an early age, was 'whirled perpetually round in a vortex of pleasures and excitements'.[2] The 'giddy society lady' was characterized by her hyper-heterosexuality but, suggesting that this woman had little regard for conventional morality, *Punch* describes how she marries and has children but 'dines often without her husband at smart restaurants'. The 'giddy lady' regularly attends Ascot and other Society events, she shops in Paris and, during the shooting season, does the circuit of country houses: 'She has been seen sometimes with a gun in her hands, often with a lighted cigarette between her lips. Indeed she is too frequent a visitor at shooting-luncheons and in smoking rooms, where a woman, however much she may attempt to disguise her sex, is never cordially welcomed by men.' A younger version of *Punch*'s figure emerged in 1891 in Eliza Lynn Linton's essay on 'wild women' in which she described 'half-naked girls and young wives, smoking and drinking with the men'.[3] A 'wild woman', Linton explained, 'smokes after dinner with the men; in railway carriages; in public rooms' and in this way 'thinks she is … vindicating her independence and honouring her emancipated womanhood'.[4]

Smoking remained a feature of *Punch*'s portrayal of Society women but by 1900 these were often more humorous than critical, as in a cartoon depicting four young women in their feminine finery, gambling and smoking (Fig. 4.1). One of the women asks 'Is Florrie's engagement really off, then?' to which another replies, 'Oh, yes. Jack wanted her to give up gambling and smoking, and goodness knows what else.' 'How absurd!' declared her friends.[5] The place of smoking in the lifestyle of the feminine 'smart set' was well established in the pages of *Punch* by 1914, thereby consolidating the association of smoking with a wealthy, hedonistic, fashionable female figure.[6] In the context of war, a new version of this figure emerged: the 'wartime flapper' was younger than her predecessor but, even in the midst of war, portrayed as a fun-lover. A sardonic *Punch* cartoon portrays the young FANY driver as someone who did not take her work and the war seriously. Standing in front of her truck, leisurely blowing smoke rings, the FANY advised her colleague not to worry if her vehicle broke down, 'Just send a wire to H.Q. You see, you have the whole British Army behind you if anything goes wrong.'[7]

While smoking was presented as a sign of a woman's right to pleasure, it was associated primarily with the demands of the 'New Woman'. Shaped by the long-established discourse of smoking and masculinity, and the more recent discourse of women's rights, the cigarette was one of several markers of a new type of femininity, one characterized by the assertion of equal rights with men and a claim to previously denied privileges such as access to public space, education,

*Figure 4.1   Pleasure-seeking women. Punch, 25 January 1905, p. 69. Reproduced
          by courtesy of the University Librarian and Director, The John Rylands
          University Library, The University of Manchester.*

professional work, the franchise and independent living. 'New Women' smokers
were discussed in press reports, while numerous 'advanced' young women
– students of higher education, graduates and professional women – sported
cigarettes in *Punch* cartoons and satirical pieces.[8] 'Mrs Shriek Shriekson', author
of 'A Saddis Aster', and 'Ann U. Woman', debated 'the advanced woman' who,
according to Mrs Shriekson, has 'her mind full of sex-problems she has not brains
enough to understand, and her breath stained with the traces of cigarettes she does
not care to conceal'.[9] By 1890 the New Woman brandishing her cigarette became
a recognizable motif in mainstream advertising. Dressed in bloomers and with
a cigarette in her hand, a woman explained that, 'Since taking Beecham's Pills
I have been a New Woman.'[10] An unusual advertisement for Ogden's Guinea
Gold tobacco in 1897 'sported an imperious woman astride a bicycle coolly
inhaling a cigarette'.[11] Although Ogdens, like most tobacco companies, usually
portrayed British women as non-smokers, it seems that a New Woman dressed
in bloomers and on her bike provided a 'legitimate' opportunity to titillate male
smokers with a glimpse of a shapely female leg. The association of smoking with

79

women's assertion of equal rights was reinforced in *Punch*'s representations of women's clubs.[12] In a feature on 'Novelties in Clubs' it described 'The Ladies' "Conservative"' which offered members 'special attractions' such as 'an extensive cigarette-room, a fencing saloon, and a ping-pong gallery'.[13] Ladies smoking featured in the background of a cartoon set in a woman's club at which an anti-man meeting is about to take place. Significantly, in *Punch*'s 'Coronation Procession' in 1911, only the 'contingent from the ladies clubs' were portrayed as smokers. Novels reiterated the association of smoking with women's emancipation, giving fictional gloss to an association presented in the print media.

There were a range of responses to the woman smoker, but among critics the problems were twofold. First, and this applied to Society smokers as much as to the New Woman, women were perceived to use smoking as a means to intrude into male space. This objection was, however, less serious than the second, which concerned the New Woman. Her smoking produced anxieties about a reversal of gender roles and the undermining of the heterosexual order. In one *Punch* cartoon, two New Women, who appeared rather masculine in dress, were abandoned by a young man because, as he explained, 'I can't get on without Female Society'.[14] A mock letter from a young man, 'one of the weaker sex', describes how, 'When Papa is not about' his sister 'lets me whiff one with her'.[15] While anxieties were managed with humour in *Punch*, in the pages of the *Girl's Reader*, a magazine aimed at young lower-middle-class women workers, the embryonic New Woman was treated more harshly, as seen in this description of Caroline: 'Her hair was cut short, she wore stand-up linen collars, while the general cut of her garments helped out the masculine idea. In addition, she often carried a silver-mounted walking-stick, smoked cigarettes, and went the length of making herself look even more ridiculous than Nature had intended, by wearing a monocle in her left eye!'[16] Unlike her peers, Caroline believed in equality of the sexes; 'some of them sneer when I say that a girl can do anything a boy does'. Caroline is described as unfriendly and unpopular with her female peers and a bully to younger girls. Predictably Caroline ends up in danger and in need of rescue by a feminine and popular schoolgirl. This proves a life-changing event and after this Caroline becomes a reformed character, a non-smoker, extremely feminine, quiet and quite forgettable.

Whereas prior to 1914 the 'semantics of modernity' were used 'to make sense of changes' in society,[17] women that smoked were not automatically described as 'modern'. More commonly the smoker was a 'New' or 'Advanced' woman. Perhaps this was an exercise in containment. In denying the smoker a 'modern' status, she was treated as a minority and, moreover, denied historical significance. After the war this changed abruptly and the woman smoker, as long as she was a member of the middle or upper classes, was loudly proclaimed as 'modern'. Indeed smoking became a recognized signifier of feminine modernity.

Women's Smoking and Interwar Modernity

In the 1920s women smokers became increasingly visible in the media, and this was invariably linked to the modernity of their smoking. The term 'modern' had a particularly high profile and status in the 1920s. Press reliance on the new and modern contributed to this: 'Newspapers are essentially records of modernity, and they inevitably focus attention disproportionately on the new and the unusual.'[18] The status of the 'modern' was also due to disenchantment with prewar life and a perceived discontinuity with Victorian and Edwardian values and manners. 'Modern' was clearly contrasted to the traditions associated with the late Victorian and Edwardian period. This distance, as Bingham shows, was repeatedly commented on in newspapers and visually represented in cartoons, and was also commonly articulated by comparing prewar and postwar women: 'The activities of women were an obvious and striking means by which this discontinuity could be measured and symbolized.'[19] For women, 'modern' meant engagement with the modern world and its changes and, most importantly, greater equality with men and emancipation from constraining Victorian models of femininity and gender roles. More specifically, modernity represented a rejection of the passive, subordinate and domesticated Victorian 'angel in the house' and the embrace of characteristics previously assigned exclusively to men, such as careers and professional ambition, intellectuality, an active sexuality, physical prowess and freedom of bodily movement, the franchise and access to public space and a public role. Smoking became part of feminine modernity. The cigarette, as a *Punch* cartoon illustrates, signified the difference between a modern young woman and her 'prewar' counterpart (Fig. 4.2).

With its emphasis on distance from everything prewar, interwar discourse on modernity neatly accommodated pre-established but marginal ideas about women's smoking. Interwar modernity was able to embrace the notion of a woman's right to smoke, and also draw on elements from the previously stigmatized discourse of smoking and female sexuality. In film, advertisements and interwar print, a range of modern women smokers emerged, including fashionable members of the higher social classes (successors of the 'giddy Society ladies' and the 'smart' set); publicly successful women in male domains, such as professional, literary, artistic or sports people (descendants of the New Woman); actresses and commercial glamour models (the respectable Western face of the sexualized smoker); and, most importantly, the 'modern girl' or 'flapper'. While some interwar modern smokers were new versions of prewar feminine smokers (for instance, the New Woman becoming a modern professional woman), the modern girl was a new figure. Although the modern girl was in evidence in *Punch* and some cigarette advertisements toward the end of the war,[20] it wasn't until a few years later that she became a staple ingredient in the popular press. The modern girl was clearly

Figure 4.2   The 'pre-war' girl. Punch, 22 August 1917, p.145. Reproduced by courtesy of the University Librarian and Director, The John Rylands University Library, The University of Manchester.

related to both the Pleasure Seeker and the New Woman, but she was also different because she was the product of a postwar generation. The modern girl was young, more concerned about her emancipation than the Pleasure Seeker, more frivolous than the New Woman, and her emancipation embraced the sexual sphere.

The association of smoking with the modern girl or flapper was of particular importance to the ascendancy of a discourse on women smokers as modern and emancipated. The 'modern girl' was the most pervasive image of a woman smoker interwar and, probably, the most talked about woman of the 1920s. Melman goes so far as to claim that 'the young woman ... came to embody the spirit of "modernity"'.[21] She certainly, as Bingham argues, represented the discontinuity of pre- and postwar life. This was achieved partly through her behaviour and appearance, but was also a product of her age. The modern girl was 'portrayed in *generational* rather than *sectional* terms';[22] her smoking was not, therefore, the practice of a minority group but a habit associated with a postwar generation of women, a cohort that by its very location in historical time was defined as 'modern'.

Modernity was, however, linked to specific types of smoking practice and, most importantly, to the smoking of cigarettes. The cigarette was, from the turn of the century, regarded as the modern form of smoking. Cigarettes were a relatively new product in 1900 and not weighed down by tradition. They were mass-produced and available in a standardized form. The mode of consumption was also compatible with the demands of modern, urban lifestyles in that it was 'convenient': 'The cigarette is the standardized, reliable, quick and easy smoke. It is the McDonald's of the tobacco trade, the fast food of smoking ... the preferred smoke for people aiming for a streamlined, cultural modernity, involved in the fast pace of city life'.[23] For women and men the cigarette, like the motor car, signalled an engagement with the spirit of the times. Significantly, cars and cigarettes were often twinned in advertisements, and interwar motor cars were often fitted with electric cigarette lighters and ash trays.[24]

The ease with which cigarette smoking became linked with aspects of feminine modernity, especially women's emancipation and greater equality with men, stemmed from the long-established association of smoking with men and masculinities and, to a lesser degree, from the alignment of smoking with female sexuality. Partly for these reasons, smoking had associations deemed by many to be problematic. Most notably, women smokers ran the risk of becoming too like men, of undermining gender differences that were the linchpin of heterosexual relations, and of usurping men's privileges and thereby destabilizing the gender order. Additionally, drawing on long-established sexual associations, women's smoking could also suggest promiscuity and sexual immorality, a point explored further in Chapter 6. Problems, tensions and feared consequences therefore characterized many of the media images of the modern practice of women smoking. This is not surprising, since modernity did not afford women smokers immunity from criticism. As Rieger and Daunton argue, the term 'modern' enabled contemporaries to express their 'ambivalence' about the positive and negative changes associated with historical change, and was more helpful than the positively loaded words of 'progress' or 'improvement': 'While concepts of the "modern" and of "progress" conceived the historical process as a succession of fundamental changes, they differed with respect to their assessment of the effects of transformations.'[25] 'Modern' practices could, therefore, be problematic. Arising from this, representations of women's smoking were frequently characterized by strategies which managed the potential consequences and contradictions of women's modernity. Advertisers, for instance, were, as Marchand describes them, 'missionaries of modernity' in that they both emphasize that which is new and changing and, at the same time, acknowledge, manage and alleviate signs of discontent with modernity.[26] Cigarette advertisements of the interwar years offer examples of this. On the one hand smoking is presented as the modern thing for women to do, but on the other, advertisements suggest a containment of the implications of modernity through a restatement, often quite subtle, of conventional gender relations.[27] Young women's magazines similarly engaged in an explicit exercise to manage representations of the *practice* of female smoking and to curtail how their readers interpreted its significance in ways which ensured the 'heterosexual career'[28] was not disrupted. These exercises in managing the implications of modernity could sometimes result in what Alison Light terms 'conservative modernity', representations that 'could simultaneously look backwards and forwards' and 'accommodate the past in the new forms of the present'.[29] In the following, I explore more closely representations of the modernity of the woman smoker, signalled primarily by her looks and her relationships with men.

Modern Looks

Smoking was central to the visual display of youthful feminine modernity and it was heralded in the media as one of the defining characteristics of modern young women.[30] Alongside a full-page photograph of two 17-year-old women (Fig. 4.3) perched on the arms of one chair with cigarettes joined at the tip, presumably lighting one cigarette from the other, *The Sketch*, explained that:

> The modern girl has been presented on the stage, and by artists and novelists, and at times their fancy portraits of Miss 1925, with her cigarettes, her short skirts, and her 'Eton' crop, have been condemned as exaggerations. The camera, however, cannot lie, and this page presents a genuine photograph of two examples of the Modern Miss, complete with 'fags,' cropped hairs, and neat ankles and dainty knees.[31]

(The apparent faith in the evidential force of this image was indicative of the contemporary status of photography.) Magazines targeting young working women similarly presented smoking as a visible sign of youthful modernity.[32] Illustrations for articles and fiction often depicted young modern women, perhaps an idealized reader, holding or smoking a cigarette. A particularly graphic representation of the alignment of smoking and youthful feminine modernity was where the trail of smoke from the modern girl's cigarette spelled out the story's title which was, appropriately, 'A Modern Girl'.[33]

As if to reinforce the association between women's smoking and modernity, old-fashioned women were not usually depicted as smokers. While there is a commercial logic for this in most advertising, it is notable that even magazine fiction suggests the incongruity of an old-fashioned woman smoking. Ruth, for example, was a young woman who, after a period of high living in London, had retreated to a quiet life in the Sussex Downs.[34] The reason for this was never made clear. In her London life, Ruth had dressed in sumptuous clothes, danced the nights

Figure 4.3 '*Knee and Crop and "Gasper": The Modern Miss!' The Sketch, 22 July 1925, p. 111. Reproduced by permission of The British Library (shelf mark LD52).*

away, wined, dined and smoked: she had been a 'modern girl'. In Sussex she assumed the guise of a spinster dressed in a sensible skirt, blouse and cardigan. Ruth's friends and neighbours just assumed she was a non-smoker because she was old-fashioned. However, though Ruth had rejected many aspects of her modern lifestyle, she continued to smoke a cigarette in private before retiring to bed. Indeed the cigarette served as a link between Ruth's past and present lives and as an indicator that Ruth was still modern at heart. When her friend discovered that Ruth even kept cigarettes in the house she was quite shocked. Eventually, however,

Ruth was compelled to re-emerge as a modern and sophisticated woman. Tellingly, the illustration portrays her, cigarette in hand, enjoying the company of a successful man whom she later marries. As *Punch* suggested in 1917, old-fashioned women were prewar in attitudes and style and usually opposed to women smoking while their modern sisters, in contrast, embraced smoking as a symbol of their modernity (see Fig. 4.2). Not surprisingly, some magazines suggested that young women smoked for 'fear of being thought old-fashioned'.[35]

Fashion was an important indicator of feminine modernity partly because it signalled that the wearer was up-to-date and, by definition, dissociated from prewar style. Women smokers, whether youthful modern girls or more mature modern women, were invariably dressed in the latest styles – the cocktail dress, masculine-style suit and sportswear. The place of women smokers in the vanguard of fashion was consolidated by their appearance in fashion spreads and advertising in elite magazines. One of the earliest examples was a half-page illustrated advertisement for gowns which appeared in *Vogue* in 1918.[36] By the mid-1920s, the cigarette routinely signalled the modernity of different styles of dress. For example, an advertisement by a leading London department store to promote the latest style in hats depicted a young woman in fashionable dress, cigarette in hand, having her cloche fitted.[37] The cigarette's role as a statement of modern style was confirmed in the mid-1920s as stylish cigarette holders of various colours and lengths became fashion items in their own right.[38] Although pipes were also promoted as fashion accessories, and some delicate and decorated examples were seen occasionally in public and in fashion features, these did not achieve the status of the cigarette and its holder.

Even more so than fashion, youthfulness was defined as modern because it located a woman in the postwar, rather than prewar, era. Additionally, it contrasted with the prewar emphasis on a more mature and matronly feminine ideal.[39] Youthful looks became fashionable and desirable for all women, and even when the boyish/youthful styles went out of vogue in the 1930s, a youthful face and figure remained the feminine ideal. In advertising and fashion promotions women smokers were always portrayed as young or as possessing youthful good looks. Interestingly, when youthful styles were all the rage, the cigarette served as a reminder of adult sophistication. As Steele observes, Iris Storm, the fictional counterpart of Society girl Nancy Cunard, was described as possessing 'an odd combination of childishness, with her dress printed with elephants, and sophistication, with her diamond-studded powder box and jade cigarette case'.[40]

The alignment of smoking with youthful feminine modernity was made particularly visible when women smokers appeared in their swimwear. In the mid-1920s, the sight of women in public with bare limbs was considered a sign of their emancipation.[41] Like smoking, parading in swimwear was seen as modern and, by some, as quite shocking.[42] Photographs of young women in their bathing suits and

Thómas Hardy, Arnold Bennett, who, in common with the "bourgeois" John Galsworthy, Anatole France, sisters of their trade, adopt a fanciful and H. G. Wells, Joseph Conrad,

FIRE-AND-WATER NYMPHS.

TANNING OPERATIONS AT CHISWICK OPEN-AIR BATHS.
Tasting the delights of sun bathing at Chiswick, where hundreds of girls are making the most of the heat wave.

Figure 4.4   *'Fire-and-Water Nymphs: Tanning Operations at Chiswick Open-Air Baths'. Daily Express, 22 May 1924, p. 7. Reproduced by permission of The British Library (shelf mark MLD 3).*

with cigarettes alight appeared in newspapers of the mid-1920s (Fig. 4.4); although ostensibly because of the novelty of the women's activities, the publication of these photographs also owed much to their titillation value. The pleasure for heterosexual men of looking at pictures of women with bare limbs was probably one reason why advertisements for Capstan cigarettes exploited the image of a woman in swimwear.[43] It seems, however, that the possibility of shocking the public by portraying semi-naked women actually smoking, discouraged cigarette advertisers from deploying this particular representation of the woman smoker until the late 1930s.

A fit, athletic, lively body was a hallmark of the woman smoker, and she was frequently portrayed engaged in a range of mainly middle-class leisure and sports pursuits. In press debates of the 1920s flappers were frequently described as avid dancers.[44] Golfers, swimmers and tennis players were presented smoking in fashion features and advertisements for non-tobacco products in magazines of the 1930s.[45] Active women were particularly prominent in cigarette advertisements which proliferated from the late 1920s. While in 1920 Evadne steered a punt with a De Reszke cigarette wedged firmly between her teeth, smokers of the 1930s swam, and played tennis and golf.[46] The active lifestyle and emancipation of the woman smoker is neatly conveyed in an advertisement for Bachelors cigarettes. The woman, attired in the latest sportswear, stands with her bag of golf clubs over her shoulder and a cigarette in her hand; in the background two men play golf. This woman smoker is not only active but, as implied by the backcloth, she can play the same course of golf as the men. What is more, she is sufficiently fit and independent to manage her own clubs. The text – 'Bachelors are different' – refers to both the cigarettes and the woman smoker.[47]

By the late 1920s, smoking was also implicated in the production of the modern figure. In the early 1920s, despite the preponderance of slender female models, advertisements suggest that being overly thin rather than over-weight was the more pressing concern for many women: 'How to become plump, popular and attractive' declared one advertisement in the *Daily Express*, 'How to get fat' declared another.[48] By the mid-1920s there was talk in the national press of a 'craze for slimness' and weight-reducing exercises were mentioned.[49] By the late 1920s advertisements for plumpness had disappeared, to be replaced by those for products, such as Ryvita crispbreads, which promised a slim look.[50] A series of cigarette advertisements in 1928 (modelled on the Lucky Strike campaign in the US) was particularly vocal in heralding the 'slim' female body. Tobacco had been mobilized as an appetite suppressant during the First World War (and repeated in the Second World War), but the explicit link between smoking and the attainment of the new feminine ideal was novel: 'I never *nibble* now, Jenkyn – I have a *Kensitas* and keep slim!'[51] This, and other advertisements in the series, identified and criticized the spread of a modern 'habit' – 'nibbling' – and offered the modern practice of smoking as the 'wholesome' answer for men and especially for women. But whereas fitness was the aim for men,[52] slimness was the aim for women: 'I've lost 5lbs. already this month. And I feel marvellous. All by substituting the wholesome habit of smoking Kensitas for the unwholesome habit of "nibbling".'[53] Two years later Kensitas resorted to a more dramatic appeal featuring photographs of 'charming', young and pretty women set against silhouettes of heavily overweight women (Fig. 4.5). Women were cautioned: 'How fascinating are the curves of the modern figure! Yet these alluring contours may be quickly lost by over-indulgence'; 'The comely, shapely curves of the modern figure are ever-appealing. Ugly fat, caused by over-indulgence ... soon ruins the charm of these soft outlines.'[54] Eating between meals was the main culprit, but the advertisements reassured readers that: 'Thousands of lovely women easily retain their modern figures without undergoing harsh dieting and drastic reducing methods condemned by the medical profession ... When tempted to over-indulge – to eat between meals, they say: "No thanks, I'll smoke a Kensitas instead".'[55]

*Figure 4.5   Kensitas cigarette advertisement. Daily Express, 16 January 1930, p. 3.
Reproduced by permission of The British Library (shelf mark MLD 3).*

Although the Kensitas campaign lasted only two years, it consolidated smoking as a slimming aid in the minds of at least some women. While there are direct references to this advertising in some women's recollections of the period,[56] there is also evidence that this approach permeated women's understandings of the relationship between smoking and body management. Miss Gandy noted that she smoked most 'when trying to eat less because I've been putting on weight', while Theodora Bosanquet explained that she smoked 'partly as a substitute for eating'.[57] Employing words and phrases that were remarkably similar to those used in the Kensitas advertisements, Miss Bridgens reflected that her smoking habit developed in part because 'it helped me not to eat sweets and chocolates or to nibble at odd bits of food in between meals'.[58] Medical advice reinforced this association. 'Smoking staves off the pangs of hunger', declared Dr Grinsing, and 'it may sometimes be a useful corrective to gluttony.' Echoing advertising copy, he advised that it was '[b]etter to smoke a few cigarettes a day than to be constantly nibbling at sweets and biscuits and moaning about being too fat!'[59] The 'location of smoking in a nexus of messages about slimness' was consolidated in women's magazines by the juxtaposition of advertisements for cigarettes and slimming aids and the feature of cigarettes in corset promotions.[60]

Smoking was associated with the fashionable, feminine, sporty look, and implicated in the production of the modern slender body; it also encouraged new ways of using the female body and, in the process, new ways of presenting the self and being seen. Victorian notions of feminine appearance, which emphasized modesty and constraint in posture and movement, were visibly challenged by the act of smoking. Descriptions of modern girls frequently referred to their unwomanly and expansive postures as they smoked while 'sprawled' or 'lolling' in armchairs.[61] Smoking also encouraged women to use the mouth in ways that infringed traditional conceptions of femininity. As Summers complained, 'All barriers of restraint and decency formerly hedging about womanhood are broken down, and we see women with cigarette holders a foot long sticking from their painted mouths'.[62] That smoking was initially perceived to disrupt feminine facial composure is not surprising: when smoking, the mouth was frequently open and/or pouting; an object was repeatedly put in and out of it, or kept there; and new ways of speaking were developed as a result of having a cigarette in the mouth. On the last point, even regular women smokers thought that this was not 'nice'.[63] The mechanics of the act of smoking also visually disrupted the division between the inside and outside of the body that was key to traditional constructions of femininity. The movement of the smoke during inhalation (out goes in) and exhalation (in comes out) visually transgressed these boundaries. It made the body's interior imaginable, and some parts, such as the inside of the mouth, visible. Smoking practice therefore disrupted norms about the way the female body should be presented, seen, known, imagined. Given all this, it is not surprising that late Victorian women smokers were often ambivalent about being *seen* smoking (see Chapter 2), but in the interwar years, smoking – like cosmetics and rapidly changing fashions – contributed to the production and display of modern womanhood. The media were quick to exploit the role of the cigarette in focusing attention on the mouth and other signifiers of female sexuality. Cigarettes, especially in holders, were used to accentuate graceful lines, or to draw attention to the made-up face, especially the mouth, and/or varnished nails. These devices were used regularly in cosmetics advertisements and in other commercial images of glamorous modern young women and the promotion of those – such as actresses – who traded on glamour.

Public acts of smoking, like the public application of make up,[64] were also a challenge to feminine norms because they drew attention to women in ways traditionally thought improper. In Victorian times only women of dubious morals had engaged in public display. The modern woman's exhibitionism was, however, quickly reproduced for a larger audience through newspapers, as Summers complained.

> Smoking cigarettes, they disported themselves, their short skirts and long legs from unauthorised seats on high walls along the towing path, and even *climbed trees*, like the ragged urchins of former generations! Thus they could effectively cheer and enjoy the subtle thrill of focussing public attention on their elegance. Their graceful deportment was duly photographed and published in the Press next morning, of course, the newspapers giving every encouragement to the 'advancement' of women, whose frivolities and vanities they carefully foster for the purpose of increased circulation.[65]

Summers was right about the media. The interwar press was keen to include images of pretty women for the interest of both their female readers and heterosexual men.[66] Photographs of the antics of some young women, whether genuine or contrived, were no doubt included more for titillation than for news. This may be one reason, alongside advertising revenue, why some newspapers were happy to feature on their front pages cigarette advertisements targeted at women.

Cigarette smoke also contributed to the visual presence of the woman smoker in the public domain, and it marked out her claim to spaces in which she was often a relative newcomer and, quite often, marginal to men. Additionally, women smokers often challenged the gender dimensions of space that smoking practices had historically served to construct and maintain. Traditionally, because of the strong smell produced by pipe and cigar tobacco, men retired from female company to specially demarcated rooms or places to enjoy a smoke. Tobacco consumption became, therefore, a means of demarcating male space. When men switched to cigarettes, the smoke was less offensive and men were no longer required to smoke in separate spaces which, if men desired, facilitated greater mingling of the sexes in leisure contexts. However, as women adopted the smoking habit they claimed their right to use designated smoking areas, such as smokers' railway carriages. This was often perceived by men as an invasion of their territory and was greeted with resistance in the late Victorian and Edwardian period,[67] although by the 1920s this had abated. *Where* women smoked was, therefore, contentious and as much about the gendered division of space as about shifting norms of respectable femininity. In the interwar years, newspapers eagerly displayed modern women smoking in public spaces; they depicted young women workers smoking cigarettes outdoors during their lunch break or while sunning themselves. Cigarette advertising was particularly keen to construct the cigarette as a passport to public spaces and, especially, modern ones. Women smokers appeared in hotel lobbies, art galleries, bars and airports and they were portrayed enjoying the freedom of movement offered by trains, cars and planes.[68] Importantly, these advertisements emphasized women's and men's mutual enjoyment of public and private spaces and, especially, the new and commercial. Only occasional cartoons gave visual expression to the continued fear of modern women invading male space.[69]

Acquisition of masculine looks and mannerisms were one of the consequences for women of the smoking habit, according to critics. In 'This Cigarette Business', a rare diatribe against women smokers published in a 1920s magazine for young working women, the author detailed the ways in which women who smoked lost their distinctiveness from men in terms of appearance, smell, behaviour and attitude.

[H]ow can he get the proper atmosphere when, on bending to extract the kiss that seals the bargain, he finds that her waving locks are perfumed with stale smoke instead of the sweet, subtle perfume that he has been given to expect, and that her answering kiss might be that of his best boy chum for fragrance?[70]

The author proceeded to describe the drastic consequences of women smoking for gender identity:

she might soon grow into a mannish, nicotine-stained and perfumed travesty of her former dear little self, lolling inelegantly on chair-arms, viewing the world through a cloud of smoke and cynical remarks. She might even – terrible thought – call me 'old thing!'

Even in articles where smoking was presented as acceptable, the spectre of 'mannish' women nevertheless lurked in the background, and readers were warned against emulating male smoking practices too closely. In 'Copy-Cattishness!' readers were explicitly cautioned against aping men. Careful not to be dismissed as old-fashioned, the author did not chastise readers who smoked but advised them to feminize the 'masculine' activity they adopted:

You may smoke, you may crop, you may be independent – only give it the girlish touch! He likes to see you have a cigarette ... if you manipulate it daintily, with a certain air of 'I'm not used to this, you know!' ... He doesn't like you to look professional, as it were. You lose all your charm then. That is *his* prerogative![71]

Explicit guidance on retaining 'the girlish touch' was unusual, but the spirit of this warning remained a feature of many representations of women smokers in the 1920s. Miss Bannerman who appeared smoking in *Eve* in 1926 was described as demonstrating how smoking, which could be thought 'masculine', could 'be adapted to feminine use'.[72] A 'girlish touch' was also key to the depiction of women smokers in many advertisements. It was also evident in newspaper reports about 'modern girls' such as the 'boyette', 'the latest type of young emancipated female', who 'dresses in every way as a boy' but who, according to the reporter, 'couldn't manage her cigarette' like one.[73] Ironically, women smokers were often criticized by men for their 'girlish touch', which was cited as evidence that women could not smoke 'properly' and, in periods of tobacco shortage, that they were less entitled than men to smoke.[74] Of course, these same men did not usually like to see women smoking 'properly': 'To see a girl smoking with all the nonchalance and air of use of the most hardened male smoker is, to me, horrible.'[75] Women were reminded that smoking should not undermine gender difference, as this would impair romantic opportunities. As we shall see, however, the cigarette did have a place in modern relations between the sexes.

Modern Relationships

Male companionship was a key feature of feminine modernity. This marked a radical departure from prewar custom when it was not generally considered respectable for young women to have male friends, or appear in company with young men without a chaperone: 'On the streets, the rules of etiquette required that a spinster under thirty submit herself to the "good-natured surveillance" of a chaperon. At home, the intricate rituals of cards and calls shielded her from the advances of unsanctioned male suitors.'[76] There was some relaxation of chaperonage from the 1880s for higher-class women, but it was not until the First World War that '[w]ar work and hospital visiting removed the vestiges of chaperonage, prompting Vera Brittain to declare it "quite thrilling to be an unprotected female"'.[77] In the 1920s, relaxed relationships with men were common for women across the social classes, as indicated in magazines for factory girls[78] and debutantes. As *Pam's Paper* explained to its teenaged readers: 'Gone are the days when girls had to be virtually engaged before they could enjoy a man's companionship.'[79] Although women smokers in the 1920s were occasionally depicted on their own in public, suggesting women's increased independence from men and family, this was unusual by the 1930s, and women smokers – whether portrayed on their own or in company – were invariably located explicitly or implicitly within a heterosexual framework. This heterosexual framework was, however, a modern one.

In interwar Britain, companionship became central to modern conceptions of heterosocial and heterosexual relations and, in particular, to the modern ideal of marriage. The 'keywords of companionship', as Marcus Collins explains, were 'equality' (of status not function) and 'intimacy': 'Intimacy was at once achieved and expressed through privacy, closeness, communication, sharing, understanding and friendship.'[80] Ian Tyrrell notes that in Australia tailor-made cigarettes were more suited than pipes or cigars to the needs of the modern heterosexual couple, in that they allowed men and women to remain together while men smoked and/or that they allowed couples to share cigarettes. Cigarettes, Tyrrell argues, opened up possibilities for 'companionate smoking'.[81] In Britain, smoking practices were portrayed as facilitating heterosocial and heterosexual associations (Fig. 4.6), they also embodied key aspects of the companionate ideal.

Figure 4.6   Player's Bachelors advertisement. Miss Modern, April 1931, p. 8. Reproduced by permission of The British Library (shelf mark 568).

Film, fiction, and advertisements offered graphic representations of women's smoking as a passport to modern relationships with men. They provided guidance on the role of cigarettes in managing new forms of heterosocial and heterosexual relationships. Cigarette advertisements were extremely vocal about the interpersonal significance of the cigarette, and they visually described a range of meanings attached to their use;[82] they provided an 'education in goods'.[83] Scenarios which presented cigarettes in implied or actual interaction contexts offered cues about how and when to use cigarettes and to what effect; in Goffman's terms they offered possibilities for making an impression and for influencing the definition of a situation.[84]

Smoking with men was portrayed as a key feature of life for modern women. It was presented as a sign of women's new equality with men and promoted as a fundamental component of the modern companionship ideal. In 1920 a series of advertisements for De Reszke cigarettes featured a number of modern girls smoking – Daphne, Sybil and Evadne. Although the series was entitled 'The Man's Year', in each advertisement it was the woman who occupied centre stage as she smoked in the company of men at various cultural and sporting events.[85] These advertisements presented women as equal to their male companions. Moreover, as suggested by the image of Evadne steering the punt she shared with her beau, these modern women were not simply passengers in heterosexual relationships but active drivers who could take their turn at the helm. The equality signified by shared smoking practices continued as a prominent theme into the 1930s. As Wills explained in an advertisement depicting a couple playing golf together: 'Romance to-day has none of the handicaps of past generations. Young men and women can share the same interests, play the same games, smoke the same cigarettes. The latter was inevitable once women learned to appreciate the man's cigarette'.[86] 'Daphne', who offered her male companion a cigarette in 1920, exemplifies another dimension of women's modern relationships with men.[87] Having cigarettes to offer, although not a typical scenario, suggested women's equality with men: modern women were able, and willing, to pay their own way. The implications of this were spelt out in an advertisement featured in *Woman*, which depicted a couple at the races.[88] The woman, dressed in a smart and sharply tailored skirt suit was shown leaning against a wall, cigarette in her mouth, binoculars held in one hand, programme and cigarette packet in the other. She was depicted looking openly at her male companion who was standing lower than she, lighting his cigarette. This advertisement portrayed a modern and independent woman who was not afraid to overtly appraise her male companion. Smoking, and more importantly having cigarettes to offer, was key to this particular representation of womanhood.

Women's right to smoke was a prominent theme in cigarette advertisements particularly in the 1930s. In one advertisement, the beautiful eyes of a woman stared out at readers from the front page of the *Daily Express*, with beneath them the demand – 'Give me a Gold Flake'.[89] The assertiveness of the modern woman was not restricted to cigarette advertisements, but was part of a broader attempt by advertisers to court women consumers. Advertisements suggested that recognition of women's wants was in fact recognition of their rights, and that women who used products previously associated with men, such as cigarettes or alcohol, were exercising their rights.[90] Modern relations between the sexes, according to many advertisements, depended on women being allowed to smoke. Men were advised to take note of this if they wished to be successful with women. Playing with words, adverts for Wills Gold Flake referred to women with 'wills of their own' and emphasized that 'there's no denying them'.

> It's a wise son who knows his own father-in-law – for here's the advice he gets: 'I know my daughter. She's not wilful – but she's one of the modern young women who like to have Wills of their own. So be sure to leave plenty of Wills's Gold Flake about the place'. Women certainly have taken to the flavour of the fine Virginia tobaccos of which Gold Flake are made. There's no denying that – and there's no denying them.[91]

Explicit references to women's 'modern' assertiveness was, on occasions, undercut by text which indicated that for married women this was restricted by dependence on a housekeeping allowance.

Equality between the sexes and intimacy were often visually represented by couples lighting their cigarettes from one another. A cover illustration for *War Budget* (Fig. 4.7), an illustrated wartime paper, provides an early but classic example and depicts a woman and her beau, clearly a heroic soldier (with a bandage round his head) on leave, lighting their cigarettes from one another over a tea table. Joining cigarettes end to end became a metaphor for modern heterosexual relations, and variations of this practice appeared in interwar newspaper photographs of modern couples.[92] The act could be romantic and resemble a kiss, but it could also suggest the union of marriage and, as we shall see in Chapter 5, hint at sexual relations.

The women smoker's status in heterosexual relationships was, however, often inconsistent – this was usually subtle but sometimes explicit. Although De Reszke was one of the first companies to promote assertive modern women smokers, it also on occasion portrayed a more passive figure. In 1926, for instance, a series of advertisements portrayed a woman, referred to as 'child', being introduced to the pleasures of smoking by an experienced older suitor.[93] The independence of the woman smoker was also undermined by the tendency to portray women as the recipients, rather than providers, of cigarettes; indeed, by the 1930s social etiquette usually required men to offer women cigarettes.[94] After 1930 the liberationist implications of women smoking were most visibly contained by a range of cues which signalled the differential status of the sexes and the superiority of men

Figure 4.7   Cover of War Budget, 3 February 1916. Reproduced by permission of The British Library (shelf mark 664).

relative to women. With few exceptions, the man stood or sat so that he was slightly taller than the woman, or he was depicted bending over her. Men usually had both legs firmly planted on the ground, signifying their solidity. In contrast, women either sat with legs crossed or curled up under them, in what Goffman describes as a characteristically child-like pose, or they stood with one leg bent, the 'bashful knee bend' which is again presented by Goffman as a hallmark of subordination.[95] In most advertisements which featured sports activities, women were not shown actively engaging in these activities even if their male companions were. In a series of Wills' advertisements, for example, two silhouettes were presented. The top one depicted a man engaged in sport, the lower one showed him sitting and having a cigarette with a woman who was attired in appropriately sporty clothes.[96] Even in advertisements such as the one of a couple at the races, where the woman is portrayed as independent and assertive, there was no suggestion that her male companion was her subordinate. His stance, with one leg firmly propped up in front of him, was masterful and stable.[97] Visible reminders of gender difference and gender order contained the liberationist implications of women's smoking.

Women were also more likely in some spheres than in others to be presented as equal with men.[98] The location of women's smoking within a heterosocial or heterosexual framework can be interpreted as a means of containing potentially disruptive implications of smoking for gender relations. Encouraging young women to smoke only to accompany men was one strategy that appeared in women's magazines of the 1920s. Keeping men, especially brothers, company was presented in one fictional forum as a particularly good reason why women should smoke.[99] As one character explained, 'when my brothers come home in the evening they like me to light up with them'. The heterosocial role of women smoking was forcefully restated by a male character: 'Smoke! I should jolly well think they should! … We like our sisters and girl friends to keep us company.' He went on, however, to specify that girls should only smoke at home: 'most of us men don't like to see girls of whom we think a great deal – our girl chums and our sisters – smoking in public places. I don't know how to explain it, but it seems to take the girlish freshness away from them. There should be moderation in all things.' (What this young man was unable to explain was that public smoking by women hinted at sexual impropriety, a point explored in Chapter 6.) Keeping men company was, in fact, a form of servicing. As such, women's smoking could be interpreted as an extension of traditional feminine behaviour and therefore embedded safely within conventional hierarchical gender relations. Early advertisements sometimes used this strategy to avoid provoking opposition to the representation of women as smokers.[100] Other ways in which women could service male smoking rituals were outlined by a man who condemned women's smoking: 'I should love her to provide me with lights, and blow out my matches, and, on those occasions when I favoured a pipe, fill it for me.'[101] Though no less containing, by the 1930s, and consistent with the companionate ideal, women's smoking was routinely portrayed as an aspect of a couple's mutual pleasure and shared intimacy. Feminine modernity was equated with the freedom to forge and enjoy heterosexual relationships.

The status and identity of the female smoker was usually linked to her relationships and leisure activities rather than to her paid work and public achievements. This is not surprising, given that advertising was a major contributor to smoking discourse, and that advertisements understandably stressed consumption and contexts in which smoking was easiest to pursue. Leisure and consumption nevertheless represented ways in which advertising contained the potentially threatening aspects of women's emancipation. Cigarette advertising only occasionally featured women in paid work. Even during the Second World War, only occasional illustrations depicted women smokers 'doing their bit'. In 1950 Gold Flake produced a series of advertisements which highlighted female skill in professional and sports activities. The ice-skating instructor smoked because, 'Keenness and vitality, essential at the rink, merit the solace of a quality cigarette. That is why many sportswomen relax with a Gold Flake'.[102] These women were, however, a rarity. The link between smoking and the modern woman's work and public achievement was more explicitly acknowledged in other media. Fictional modern girls in women's magazines were usually successful in paid work, although the specific details of their employment were stated rather than explored. Barbara, for example, was 'a modern girl' who featured in *Girls' Friend*. At nineteen she had already established herself as a well-respected and 'indispensable' private secretary to the head of an important firm.[103] Photographic and, occasionally, painted portraits of successful women smokers in the national press and elite magazines offered a more graphic consolidation of the link between women's smoking, work and feminine modernity (see Chapter 7). Nevertheless, the work-related aspects of the woman smoker's modernity were not dominant in visual culture.

Conclusion

From the 1880s, smoking became associated with women's rights and, in the 1920s, the right to smoke became a defining feature of feminine modernity. The alignment of smoking and interwar modernity ensured that the cigarette figured prominently in women's entry into the public eye and imagination and that it became a crucial element of what was the first media spectacle of (female) youth. The cigarette was not just symbolic of female liberation and modernity, but also contributed to it by producing the modern female body, assisting in the modern appropriation by women of public space and facilitating modern forms of companionable heterosocial and heterosexual relationships.

Women's smoking, though aligned with modernity, was often problematic. This was because women's smoking was aligned with the disruption of pre-1914 gender identities and gender relations: it resonated with overtones of masculinity and was associated with women challenging traditional gender hierarchies and usurping male privileges. However, in representations of modern women smokers the disruptive and possibly dangerous gender associations of smoking were often contained through heterosexual relations. Indeed, throughout the interwar period one of the increasingly significant ways in which women's smoking was deployed (and established as a feminine practice) was in the context of romantic relations with men.

Notes

1. Rieger and Daunton, 'Introduction'.
2. *Punch*, 15 March 1890, p. 124.
3. Linton, 'Wild Women', p. 604.
4. Ibid., p. 597.
5. *Punch*, 25 January 1904, p. 69.
6. For an early example, *Punch*, 28 December 1889, p. 304.
7. *Punch's Almanack*, 1918.
8. In *Punch*, New Women smokers included a journalist (15 June 1895, p. 281), art student (26 April 1899, p. 197) and a young woman with 'a classical education' (25 April 1900, p. 292).
9. *Punch*, 22 September 1894, p. 142.
10. Hindley and Hindley, *Advertising in Victorian England*.
11. Cited in Law, 'New Woman Novels', p. 23 (fig. 3).
12. *Punch*, 6 March 1907, p. 175; 7 June 1911, p. 441.
13. *Punch*, 21 May 1902, p. 368.
14. *Punch*, 15 June 1895, p. 282.
15. *Punch*, 22 January 1898, p. 25.
16. *Girls' Reader*, 22 January 1910, p. 798.
17. Rieger and Daunton, 'Introduction', p. 15.
18. Bingham, *Gender, Modernity and the Popular Press*, p. 50.
19. Ibid., p. 48.
20. For example, *Punch*: 1 August 1917, p. 76; 5 September 1917, p. 181; 13 February 1918, p. 104; 5 March 1919, p. 182.
21. Melman, *Women and the Popular Imagination*, p. 24.
22. Bingham, *Gender, Modernity and the Popular Press,* p. 82.
23. Schudson, *Advertising*, p. 199; see also Schivelbusch, *Tastes of Paradise*, chapter 6.
24. MOA TC 63 1/B T. Bosanquet.
25. Rieger and Daunton, 'Introduction', p. 7.
26. Marchand, *Advertising the America Dream*, p. xxi.
27. Hilton, 'Advertising', notes that a combination of the past and the future was characteristic of British cigarette advertising more generally.
28. Tinkler, *Constructing Girlhood*, p. 3; see also discussion of editorial management of other aspects of feminine modernity.

29. Light, *Forever England*, p. 10.

30. See photographs in: *Daily Mail*, 4 March 1920, p. 10; *Daily Express* 17 May 1924, p. 7 and 22 May 1924, p. 7. See also images in *Punch*. In film too, the cigarette contributed to the definition of the 'modern miss', see Haskell, *From Reverence to Rape,* and Rosen, *Popcorn Venus*.

31. *Sketch,* 22 July 1925, p. 111.

32. This also occurred in the Irish press, see Ryan, 'Negotiating Modernity'.

33. *Girls' Friend*, 30 May 1925, p. 12.

34. *Girls' Friend*, 5 September 1925.

35. *Girls' Favourite*, 18 March 1922, p. 164.

36. *Vogue,* Early April, 1918, p. viii.

37. *Vogue*, 7 March 1928, p. 14.

38. Mannin, *Young in the Twenties*, p. 72.

39. Steele, *Fashion and Eroticism*, chapter 11.

40. Ibid., p. 240.

41. Clyde, *Eve's Sour Apples*, p. 148.

42. Summers, *What's Wrong with England?*; Clyde, *Eve's Sour Apples*.

43. *Sketch*, 9 July 1930, p. 78. Richards, *Commodity Culture*, chapter 5, especially pp. 228–31, demonstrates that the sexual attractiveness of the female bather had been used in advertising from the 1870s.

44. For example, *Daily Express*, 12 November 1924, p. 1.

45. *Vogue,* 13 June 1934, pp. 23, 40. *Miss Modern,* August 1931, p. 45.

46. *Vogue*, Early July 1920, inside front cover. Examples of: tennis, *Miss Modern*, July 1931, p. 62; golf, *Sketch,* 9 July 1930, p. 99; swimming, *Woman*, 7 August 1937, p. 17.

47. *Sketch,* 9 July 1930, p. 99.

48. *Daily Express*, 11 May 1920, p. 7; 21 May 1920, p. 9.

49. Melman, *Women and the Popular Imagination*, pp. 22-3.

50. *Daily Mail*, 15 November 1928, p. 18.

51. *Daily Express*, 13 November 1928, p. 19.

52. *Daily Express*: 4 November 1928, p. 19; 28 January 1930, p. 2.

53. *Daily Express*, 13 November 1928, p. 19; 27 November 1928, p. 3.

54. *Daily Express*, 14 January 1930, p. 2; 16 January 1930, p. 3.

55. *Daily Express*, 14 January 1930, p. 2.

56. Mannin, *Young in the Twenties*, p. 72**;** Marjorie Hughes, communication.

57. MOA TC 63 1/B: Gandy; T. Bosanquet.

58. MOA TC 63 1/B Bridgens.

59. *Modern Woman*, March 1939, p. 58.

60. Warsh and Tinkler, 'In Vogue'; Tinkler and Warsh, 'Feminine Modernity'.

61. Summers, *What's Wrong with England*, p. 36; *Girls' Favourite*, 4 December 1926, p. 411; *Daily Express*, 10 June 1918, p. 2, cited in Doan, *Fashioning Sapphism*, p. 66.

62. Summers, *What's Wrong with England*, p. 82.

63. MOA, TC 63.

64. Touching up one's make-up in public had similar implications in North-American society according to Peiss, *Hope in a Jar.* Through this activity women 'claimed a public

space, stopping the action, in a sense, by making a spectacle of themselves' (p. 186; also p. 39). Make-up was promoted 'as a tool for women to explore and portray their individuality in the modern world' (p. 144).

65. Summers, *What's Wrong with England*, p. 36.

66. Bingham, *Gender, Modernity and the Popular Press*.

67. See *Punch*, 15 March 1890, p. 124; also Chapter 2 on women smokers on trains. There was also opposition to non-smoking women entering male smoking space, see *Punch*: 8 August 1885, p. 66; 5 May 1894, p. 208.

68. *Vogue*, 5 March 1930, p. 84; 5 February 1930, p. 79. Also advertisements in *Woman* 1937.

69. For example, *Men Only*, April 1937, p. 98. Space was also a contentious issue in Canada and the US: see Warsh, 'Smoke and Mirrors' and Tate, *Cigarette Wars*.

70. *Girls' Favourite*, 4 December 1926, p. 411.

71. *Girls' Favourite*, 23 October 1926, p. 271.

72. *Eve*, 9 June 1926, p. 511, cited in Doan, *Fashioning Sapphism*, p. 115.

73. *Daily Mail*, 19 April 1927, p. 7.

74. MOA FR 979, p. 31. More recently the drinking habits of 'ladettes' have received similar treatment: see for example Jackson and Tinkler, '"Ladettes" and "Modern Girls"'.

75. *Girls' Favourite*, 4 December 1926, p. 411. See also MOA FR 979, p. 32.

76. Collins, *Modern Love*, p. 20.

77. Ibid., p. 38.

78. Tinkler, *Constructing Girlhood*.

79. *Pam's Paper*, 1 March 1924.

80. Collins, *Modern Love*, p. 93.

81. Tyrrell, 'Limits of Persuasion', pp. 47–8.

82. Offering cigarettes was presented by advertisements as: an indication of friendship and goodwill; essential to social intercourse; a means of establishing social credentials; the sign of a good host. For examples see *Miss Modern*, April 1931, p. 8; *Daily Mirror*, 26 July 1939, p. 5; *Woman,* 1 July 1939 p. 51; *Woman*, 8 July 1939, p. 26.

83. Schudson, *Advertising*, p. 208.

84. Goffman, *Presentation of Self*.

85. *Vogue*, inside front cover, Early May 1920, Early June 1920, Early July 1920.

86. *Sunday Express*, 9 July 1939, p. 18.

87. *Vogue*, Early May, 1920, inside front cover.

88. *Woman,* 3 July 1937, p. 17.

89. *Daily Express,* 5 April 1934, p. 1.

90. Using similar phrases to those of Wills tobacco company, Barclays Lager was heralded as 'the one beer which the daughters of Eve have made their own', it is 'the drink for a ladylike thirst' (*Sketch*, 22 July 1925, p. xvi).

91. *Miss Modern*, February 1939, p. iii.

92. For example, *The People*, 27 March 1927, reproduced in Doan, *Fashioning Sapphism*, fig. 11. Earlier examples: *Sketch*, 30 June 1915, p. 4; *Daily Mail*, 31 July 1913, front page.

93. *Eve*, 15 September 1926, p. 573; also 29 September 1926, p. 705.

94. MOA TC 63.

95. Goffman, *Gender Advertisements*, pp. 40–1, 45.

96. For example, *Woman*, 17 July 1937, p. 31; 14 August 1937, p. 22. Similar motifs of heterosexual companionship, sports activity and differential status of the sexes are apparent in advertisements for other products such as ale, see *Sketch*, 7 August 1935, p. 285.

97. *Woman*, 3 July 1937, p. 17.

98. Similar themes and scenarios were employed to promote lagers and ales, previously the preserve of men, to women. In one advertisement a young man is portrayed losing his last drop of lager to his female companion. Although the advertisement suggests that this incident could raise doubts as to the woman's suitability as a wife, her good taste is a sign that she is marriageable. *Sketch*, 22 July 1925, p. xvi.

99. *Girls' Favourite*, 18 March 1922, p. 164.

100. *Sketch*, 26 May 1920, p. 137.

101. *Girls' Favourite*, 4 December 1926, p. 411.

102. *Vanity Fair*, October 1950, p. 59; also, June 1950, p. 4.

103. *Girls' Friend,* 21 March 1925, p. 1.

5

The Sexual Promise

Women's relationship to tobacco has, for over a century, been filled with sexual promise. This chapter traces the detail of this promise. It begins with the equation of tobacco products and smoking with men's enjoyment of women's bodies, an association that was common prior to 1915 and which continued in the interwar years. Following this, the chapter examines the image of the woman smoker that emerged pre-1914 and the strong association of smoking with women's sexuality. The third section explores the highly visible heterosexualization of women's smoking, which was facilitated by the growth of mass – and image-based – media and new ideas about heterosexual relations and female sexuality. Michael Koetzle argues that 'the notion of the cigar or cigarette in a woman's hand has become imbued with an extraordinary ambivalence'; 'nicotine becomes a metaphor, a symbol: as expressive of degradation as of emancipation'.[1] The sexual connotations of women's smoking are key to this ambivalence. As this chapter demonstrates, they underpinned the feminization of smoking, contributing to both its respectable and its unrespectable connotations.

The Equation of Tobacco with Women's Bodies

Smoking has a long-standing association with women and female sexuality in that tobacco has, since Elizabethan times, been personified as a woman: 'It became a cliché for a man to speak of his cigarette or cigar as his lover, a rival of his fiancée or wife'.[2] Rudyard Kipling's description of his favourite Cuban cigars as 'a harem of dusky beauties tied fifty in a string', indicates 'prevalent associations between the color of tobacco and that of an "exotic" woman's skin and between ways in which women and cigars were both held in "captivity" to await an owner's need'.[3] The association between tobacco consumption and the possession of the female body was frequently given material expression in smoking and tobacco paraphernalia. Mayhew, in his investigations into mid-nineteenth-century London life, noted the sale of cheap snuff boxes decorated with pictures of young women. In stylish shops in Oxford Street, according to one of Mayhew's informants, there were also 'pipe heads of a fine quality, and on them is painted, quite beautiful, naked figures of women, and there's snuff-boxes and cigar-cases of much the same sort'.[4] 'Indecent snuff-boxes', mainly of French manufacture, were also sold on the streets of London to wealthy young men.[5]

The association of female sexuality with men's tobacco consumption was reinforced in late Victorian and Edwardian tobacco packaging.[6] Cigar labels commonly used images of women. *El Secreto* cigar labels, for example, featured two Spanish women, one whispering to the other.[7] Turkish, Spanish, Native American and African women, 'all representing cultures and regions important in tobacco cultivation and manufacture', were also featured on tobacco products imported from the US.[8] The Middle-Eastern woman was the most passive type in US tobacco art. Dolores Mitchell argues that many parallels exist between such women and tobacco products. Harem women, like cigars, are commodities that need to be kept in a controlled environment where they could be 'kept ... in perfect condition to provide their masters with sensual fulfilment'.[9] Advertising also utilized woman as a symbol of the pleasures of tobacco use. Wild Woodbine cigarettes by Wills, for example, featured a woman standing at a rustic fence with hands clasped, smiling sweetly at the presumably male viewer.[10]

In 1920 it was still common to compare women with tobacco: women, like fine cigarettes or cigars, were objects of desire. Advertisements of the early 1920s frequently suggested parallels between the possession of a woman and consumption of tobacco. An advertisement for Bond of Union tobacco aligned the act of pipe smoking with that of taking a wife. In the illustration, the man had one arm around a woman whom he was kissing passionately, in the hand of the other arm he holds a lit pipe: 'I shall never tire of you or it.'[11] This alignment was also used in a series of advertisements for Kenilworth cigarettes targeted at men and women in 1920: 'Just you and I – and a box of these delightful Kenilworth Cigarettes. What more could any man want?'[12] An advertisement depicting a tobacconists in which a coy young shop girl lights a cigarette for an admiring male customer played on the theme of women's bodies being available to the male smoker.[13] The alignment of smoking with possession of a woman was also reinforced in comparisons made between women and tobacco: 'Her eyes are blue as summer seas, Or azure rings of cigarette'.[14] This possession of women through male smoking practices persisted in a range of forms. Perhaps indicative of the sexualization of tobacco and smoking, the sailor's head, which adorned packets of Player's Navy Cut cigarettes,[15] is rumoured to have revealed more than naval demeanour to some male smokers. From the right angle, and with the aid of a mirror, the sailor's mouth could be made to represent a vulva that could be opened and shut. Apparently this unintentional effect was later utilized by manufacturers in cigarette cards.[16] Even in 1939, advertisements such as those for Black Cat cigarettes continued to equate women's bodies with the pleasures of smoking. Four scantily clad beauties, each shown holding a large photograph of herself, were offered to the smoker: 'meet the girls from the Black Cat Pack. See and collect these magnificent studio portraits of famous film beauties found in every packet', although it quickly added that 'more important still is the fine, full flavour and quality of Black Cat Cigarettes'.[17] The heterosexual male smoker was, no doubt, the principal target but, given that so many women were captivated by movie stars,[18] this advertisement may well have appealed also to women smokers.

Under the Influence: Tobacco and the Sexualization of Women Smokers pre-1915

Although the (hetero)sexualization of tobacco products and male consumption practices has a long-established history, there were few images of women smokers prior to 1914. However, where women were portrayed smoking, the link between tobacco consumption and female sexuality was often consolidated. Most of these depictions were not widely accessible because they were out of the media – and therefore the public – eye, and because they circulated in contexts accessible primarily to the affluent, cultured and well-travelled. Images of women smokers could be seen in prestigious art galleries,[19] on the packaging of specialist tobacco products purchased in, or imported from, France and the US, at the theatre and, for the right price, in pornographic photographs purchased 'under the counter'. However, in the course of working in upper-middle-class and upper-class homes, domestic servants probably encountered some images of women smokers in, for example, their employers' magazines or in the packaging of cigars or tobacco. The working and lower middle classes may also have encountered women smokers in erotic and pornographic postcards. As Lisa Sigel demonstrates, by the early 1900s sexualized postcards, some of which featured women smoking, were available from corner stores, markets, newsagents, tobacconists and street traders and on display in shop windows.[20] So, long before smoking emerged in popular visual culture and everyday life as a feminine practice, the woman smoker occupied a place in the imagination of the British public. Representations of Oriental women and, more broadly, colonial subjects contributed prominently to this highly sexual visual discourse.

Paintings of Middle-Eastern and Asian women provide the most common examples of women smoking. A painting by Francesco Renaldi of a *Muslim Lady Reclining* (1789) is typical of early depictions of Middle-Eastern women which ostensibly described the appearance and lifestyle of Oriental women.[21] Renaldi portrays a young and very petite Indian woman sitting against a cushion boulder with one knee raised. She is dressed in beautiful cloth from head to toe with a veil over her head and ornate jewellery in her nose and ears, and on her wrists, fingers and ankles. Her embroidered slippers are discarded to reveal one bare foot, adorned with toe rings. With eyes cast down, and in a meditative pose, this woman seems unaware of the viewer as she firmly holds a hookah pipe in her hand. The light from a shuttered window illuminates her finery and her isolation. In this painting, the hookah appeared alongside other 'exotic symbols' such as jewellery, cushions, veils and dress as constituents in the construction of 'the Other'.[22] As Malek Alloula comments, 'There is no Orient without the hookah.'[23] The hookah contributes to the eroticization of Oriental women, not least because Western women were not usually represented as smokers at this time. More specifically, the hookah contributes a sexualized significance to these paintings partly because of the snake-like pipe from which the woman inhales tobacco smoke but also, importantly, from the properties attributed to tobacco.

The narcotic effects of tobacco were well established by the nineteenth century. The explicit link between nicotine and sexuality is summed up in a poem depicting the Shah's visit in 1872 to the London house of a famous madam:

> With deftness roll the fragrant cigarette.
> The weeds they light we Nicotina call,
> And dreamy ecstacy comes down on all;
> And what happs next, not ours it is to deal,
> For clouds of smoke ascend and all conceal.[24]

However, whereas men's tobacco consumption could stimulate the mind as well as sexual desire, and promote contemplation as well as physical relaxation, for women tobacco consumption was expressly related to their sexuality. Women, it seems, were engulfed by the influence of nicotine and, in this state, they became sexually uninhibited, possibly vulnerable, invariably available.

The effect of tobacco on women was articulated explicitly in late Victorian paintings. Harem women, in particular, were frequently depicted as under the influence both of their 'master' and of nicotine: the odalisque was quite literally enslaved. Jules-Jean-Antoine Lecomte du Nouy's *The White Slave-Girl* (1888) depicts a naked white woman in profile, one leg crossed under the other, with fabrics draped over part of her body, exhaling the smoke from her cigarette through pouting lips. The woman looks in front of her and upward, perhaps toward her 'master'. There are plates of uneaten food beside her; the peeled fruit, broken into segments, and as yet uneaten, is symbolic of her virginity. This passive and subdued white woman represents just one version of a male fantasy of woman's sexual enslavement under the effects of tobacco. Another version highlights the role of tobacco in loosening a woman's inhibitions, arousing her desire and heightening her powers of seduction. Edouard Richter's *Dreams*, for instance, depicts a young, heavily made-up woman propped against cushions in an oriental setting (Fig. 5.1). One leg is crossed underneath the other, her shoe is half off her foot, she leans back

*Figure 5.1   Dreams, Richter, Edouard Frederic Wilhelm (1844–1913). Galerie Nataf,
Paris, France. Bridgeman Art Library.*

with one arm behind her head and stares coquettishly at the viewer. The pipe from
the hookah coils around her and snakes around her wrist, and purple smoke trails
from the hookah. Suggestively, a partially eaten orange is cast on the floor.

The sexual associations of women's smoking were reinforced and publicised
more widely from 1900 by the craze for photographic postcards which included
images of Middle-Eastern and other colonial women smoking. With their
'ethnographic alibi', these postcards 'popularized anthropological beliefs about
nonwhite sexuality', 'played up the exoticism of foreign sexuality' and 'naturalised

ideas of sexual availability'.[25] Whereas it was illegal to openly send postcards of white women with their nipples, genitalia or pubic hair exposed, the same restrictions did not apply to the nudity of colonial subjects.[26] The exposure of the colonial woman's body made visually explicit the link between women's use of tobacco and sexual availability. The hookah was a particularly graphic symbol in these postcards: 'The simple evocation of the hookah, associated with hashish, suffices to give life to a world of dreamy feminine presences, in various states of self-abandonment and lasciviousness, welcoming and without reserve.'[27] While the hookah was the most usual symbol of the sexual responsiveness of the Oriental woman, from around 1900 the cigarette also played a role in her sexualization.[28] Unlike the hookah, the cigarette is a symbol that articulates and plays with the connections between Europe and its colonies. It is illustrative of the 'dialogic' relationship between western-European nations and their empires.[29] On one level, the photographer uses the European-style cigarette to signal that colonial women were touched by Western mores, and to suggest that colonial women were receptive to further associations with white Europeans, including sexual ones. On another level the meanings attached to the colonial woman smoker and to the cigarette in these postcards testifies to the flow of significations between the colonized and colonizers. When the colonial woman, particularly in a state of nudity or semi-nudity, smoked a cigarette, the sexual nature of her practice had implications for the meanings attached to the cigarette. The flow of sexual connotations was, however, two-way. The cigarette's utility for the colonial photographer was evident because the cigarette was already associated with prostitution[30] and was established as an erotic prop in artistic and pornographic representations of white European women (to be discussed shortly). The interconnection between the Western woman and the colonial subject were also apparent in another way, as evident in a postcard of a semi-naked African woman with a cigarette, entitled *The Cigarette Girl*. As Sigel comments: 'the title wryly contrasted her [the African woman] with white cigarette girls, who – though a bit racey – certainly did not appear naked in public. By accentuating the contrast between types of cigarette girls, the photographer heightened the awareness of the African woman's nudity within British society.'[31] While the comparison served to heighten the African woman's otherness, the portrayal of the colonial woman as a cigarette smoker served also as a commentary on smoking by white women. The juxtaposition of cigarettes and the sexual promise of 'the Other' woman hinted to British viewers of the sexual possibilities inherent in the white woman's gesture of modernity.

The eroticism of smoking was not entirely displaced on to images of Eastern or African women. Dreamy women smokers were also apparent by the 1880s in paintings of European women. Francisco Masriera (1842–1902), whose paintings were on exhibition and winning awards in Madrid and Paris in the 1870s and 1880s, utilized the theme of tobacco's soothing effects in his painting *Young Girl*

Resting. Replicating characteristics of harem painting, Masriera portrayed a young Spanish woman in delicate laces reclining on a sofa amid opulent furnishings. With a fan in one hand and a lit cigarette in the other, the woman has closed her eyes as she dreamily exhales the cigarette smoke. French commercial art of the 1880s and 1890s developed further the theme of nicotine-induced stupor. Alphonse Mucha's art-nouveau posters, which gained international acclaim in Europe and the US and were used in advertisements for cigarillos and JOB cigarette papers,[32] characteristically depicted women smokers as either naked or draped in soft flowing robes that revealed the shoulders, neck, parts of the breast and often the ankles. Intermingled with curling locks of hair, smoke swirls from their cigarettes in ribbons that appear almost as an extension of their clothing and, like their hair, something that enfolds them. Embraced by cigarette smoke, the women gaze dreamily into the distance or close their eyes. At least one of these women, according to Mitchell, 'swoons in a cigarette-induced orgasm'.[33] Sexual pleasures are also evident in other images of women smokers. Masturbation, for example, is suggested in caricatures of women smoking alone in their bedrooms, often supine and in a state of disarray.[34] An occasional image found its way into the British press. The front page of *The Sketch* in 1920 featured a painting by Suzanne Meunier, *La Dame Qui Fume* (Fig. 5.2). Propped on cushions, a woman smokes a cigarette apparently unconcerned that her robe has slipped to reveal her naked shoulders and breast. An open book is discarded on the floor, reinforcing the impression that some form of sexual abandon has just taken place either in company or in isolation. Such a sexually suggestive, and high-profile, representation of a white woman's enjoyment of smoking was rare in Britain.

While most women smokers appeared subdued by nicotine, some were portrayed as possessing an active, independent sexuality that was manifest in flirtatious, seductive and/or promiscuous behaviour. *Carmen*, written in 1845 by Prosper Mérimée and recreated on the London stage in 1890, no doubt contributed to this impression. Mérimée 'transposed harem imagery' to Spain: 'His cigarette factory, like a harem, is a place where "no man can go without a permit," because the women strip to undergarments to lessen the heat.' However, the heroine, Gypsy, who works in the factory, is no passive harem woman but a 'sorceress who smokes, is "very fond of the smell of tobacco," and enslaves her lovers much as tobacco does.'[35] The heroine's Romany heritage is proffered as part explanation for her behaviour and allure. Sexually lively young women were also featured in French tobacco packaging available from select British tobacconists. Figures, such as the cigarette girl portrayed by Jules Chéret (1895), seem to 'flirt with the viewer, appearing to offer their bodies as well as their cigarettes'.[36] In this instance the woman casts a coquettish glance over her bare shoulder with her hand supporting a cigarette in her mouth. Flirtatious women smokers also appeared in tobacco trade advertisements promoting products for female British consumers. In

*Figure 5.2   La Dame Qui Fume by Suzanne Meunier. The Sketch, 26 May 1920, front
page. Reproduced by permission of The British Library (shelf mark LD 52).*

1898 the pleasures of 'Sweet Cherry-tipped cigarettes' were promoted by a feisty
young woman in a short, low-cut dress smoking a cigarette in a holder.[37] Frossard's
Cavour cigars which were 'mild and fragrant' were targeted at the British 'New
Woman'.[38] But the woman who appeared in this advertisement, created by French
artist Henri Meunier, wore a short skirt and frothy pink petticoats, a tight band at
her waist, a low bodice decorated with flowers and a flamboyant hat. Smiling as

she raised a cigarette to her mouth, this 'New Woman' was more intent on flaunting her underskirts than on staking her claim to equality with men. This is a classic example of the 'New Woman' as a 'highly sexual being'[39] and, more particularly, as heterosexual. This image was far removed from the usual portraits of British New Women. Indeed, typical of commercial representations, the woman smoker is portrayed as always 'Other', in this case as continental European.

While white British women did not appear as smokers in commercial tobacco art, nationality was often ambiguous in erotic and pornographic postcards of seductive white women smokers (Fig. 5.3). In photography, according to Michael Koetzle, the erotic possibilities of the cigarette were recognized by 1900. Like

Figure 5.3   Erotic postcard. Own collection.

stockings, high heels, veils and boudoir or moorish furniture, the cigarette and its holder became an erotic prop with the 'projected aim of sexual arousal'.[40] Koetzle argues that what distinguished the erotic photograph from the 'artistic' nude was that, whereas 'the nude photograph engages in a kind of "interior monologue", the erotic portrayal seeks dialogue with the camera, or with the anonymous consumer. The erotic photograph therefore has the enticing gaze into the lens, the come-hither gesture, the sweet smile, the illusion of intimate togetherness.'[41] In photographs, unlike in paintings, the erotic possibilities of women smoking were heightened by the illusion of a reality captured by the camera (i.e. this is a real woman who has actually been posturing like this with a cigarette). The photograph, more readily than the painting, conveyed to the viewer the illusion of voyeurism. In erotic photographs the sexual elements were also frequently heightened by the deliberately provocative use of the cigarette. The cigarette dangled between the teeth drawing attention to the woman's parted lips and inviting look, and suggesting various oral pleasures. Cigarettes, especially in holders, were also inserted into the mouth or studied intently while the model assumed a sexually inviting position in order to insinuate sexual possibilities, often some form of intercourse. These explicit images of white women remained illegal and could not be purchased openly or sent through the post.

A visual link between tobacco consumption and the sexuality of women was well established in art, theatre, tobacco packaging, advertising and erotic and pornographic photographs by the outbreak of the First World War. Although this was not the dominant discourse on smoking, as tobacco use was firmly associated with men and masculinities, it was nevertheless an important one. This sexual discourse provided the foundations for the highly visible feminization of smoking that occurred after 1914.

The Heterosexualization of Smoking, 1915–1950

The feminization of the image of smoking was inextricably tied to its hetero-sexualization and equation with middle-class style, a process beginning tentatively during the First World War and gathering momentum during the interwar years. In the context of rapidly expanding – and increasingly image-based – mass media, the sexual implications of women's smoking became more visible, with an explicit link made between cigarette consumption and heterosexual attractiveness, heterosexual encounters and sexual intimacy.

Attractive Women

Cigarette advertisers were particularly keen to exploit and promote the hetero-sexual possibilities of smoking in advertisements targeted at women, because this made smoking compatible with the assumed ambition of many women to secure a male partner and/or to remain heterosexually attractive, and because the heterosexual framework contained potential threats of smoking as a sign of women's modernity (see Chapter 4). An advertisement for De Reszke cigarettes (which came in three sizes, the smallest of which were 'soprano' for ladies) which appeared on the rear cover of *Sketch* in 1915 was entitled a 'Naval Engagement'.[42] This advertisement portrayed a young couple leaning toward each other over a dining table, their cigarettes meeting end to end, presumably to light one from the other. Framed by a large heart, the act of lighting the cigarettes appears like a kiss. Five years later, a Kenilworth advertisement portrayed a man and woman dancing – they have already moved away from the main crowd of dancers as he persuades her to join him for a cigarette. Perhaps because this is an early advertisement, and advertisers were wary of being too bold, the woman seems prepared to smoke only to keep her beau company. Harping back to the familiar equation of tobacco and women, and alluding to fears about the sexual promiscuity of women in wartime, the advertisement presented both the woman and the cigarette as 'untouched' by the war: 'Like all the best things in life the War has left Kenilworths untouched.'[43]

Although during the 1920s cigarette advertisements featured independent women, or women in female company, the explicit or implied heterosexual context increasingly became a staple feature of cigarette advertising to women, and by the 1930s it was the principal one.[44] Attractive women were depicted enjoying a smoke with men at the races, while alighting from a plane, sitting in a cafe or at a bar table, while motoring or cycling in the countryside, after a game of tennis or following a swim.[45] The heterosexual significance of smoking was also conveyed through social gatherings in which beautiful women and well-dressed men engaged in relaxed discussion.[46] Handsome men competing to light a woman's cigarette became a classic sign of a woman's heterosexual success, and was reiterated in advertising for other products such as women's beauty preparations.[47] Heterosexual success was also conveyed implicitly by hinting at a male admirer or companion. In a Craven 'A' advertisement, for example, a woman was shown holding a cigarette near her mouth.[48] Although there was no visible trace of a man, nor any reference to one in the text, the model's facial expression – lips slightly parted, eyes cast to the left and outside the frame of the advertisement, one eyebrow raised – suggested that she was engaging with someone outside the advertisement in a relaxed, intimate and slightly sexual manner. By the mid-1930s, photographs of glamorous women, which drew on Hollywood ideals of feminine beauty and dramatic lighting techniques, facilitated the heterosexualization of the image of the woman smoker.[49] The romantic – and often sexual – resonance of Hollywood dramas was imported into the advertising frame, contributing to the sexual promise of the cigarette.

By the 1940s, as Lorraine Greaves points out, smoking was established as 'a way of increasing one's attractiveness to men'.[50] Heterosexual attractiveness and romantic encounters were a crucial feature of cigarette advertising directed at women. Fashion also played an important role in aligning the cigarette, and occasionally a dainty pipe, with attractive and stylish femininities. Graphic examples of the place of cigarettes in heterosexual encounters were provided by magazine fiction from the mid-1920s and, most notably, by film. However, where respectability was important, there was often a tension between the promotion of a sexual framework and the control of unruly sexual elements. Issues of respectability were particularly important for cigarette manufacturers who, in the pursuit of an expanded female market, were anxious to cast smoking as a respectable feminine practice; but respectability was also a preoccupation in other mainstream media either by choice or by compulsion. The long-standing association of smoking with female sexual laxity often threatened to disrupt the respectability that was essential to mainstream representations of attractive women smokers. Perhaps in an effort to distance cigarettes from these associations, women smokers were usually presented in cigarette advertisements, and in mainstream British media more generally, as middle- or upper-class; signifiers of social class were presented as guarantors of respectability and unimpeachable (hetero)sexual standards (see Chapter 6).

From 1928 the sexual tension which threatened to disrupt the respectability of female smoking practices was not exclusively heterosexual. Prior to the highly publicized trial of Radclyffe Hall's novel of lesbian love, *The Well of Loneliness*, in 1927, 'No manner of smoking (the cigarette in its holder, a pipe or cigar) signalled sexual preference'.[51] This is not to say that there had been no conjecture about smoking practices and sexuality before this. Havelock Ellis had, in 1897, written that lesbians 'frequently' had 'a pronounced taste for smoking cigarettes' and 'a decided taste and toleration for cigars'.[52] Smoking practices had also been used to suggest sapphism in early erotic and pornographic imagery, including Oriental postcards produced to satisfy the fantasies of heterosexual men.[53] The sapphic associations of smoking had not, however, achieved mainstream recognition; the trial of *The Well* changed this. Images of Hall, which were popularized in the national press, presented her with 'short hair, bow tie, cigarette protruding from her mouth or even clenched between her teeth, and hand tucked nonchallantly into a jacket pocket'.[54] These features, as Laura Doan demonstrates, became 'distinctive marks of a lesbian subculture'.[55] In the decades following the trial, the dominant media image of Hall's smoking style resurfaced in other representations of lesbians and, occasionally, of misguided heterosexuals. Daisy Brentley, for example, a career woman who came to regret her initial disdain for marriage, smoked with 'her shingled head flung back, her hands in her velvet jacket pocket, laying down the law'.[56] Dr Bellows, head of a women's college and predatory lesbian, 'looked like a handsome, energetic man' when she was not wearing her hat, she 'dug her hands into the front pockets of her skirt and stood rocking on her toes and heels' and 'laughed boyishly'.[57] Indicative of her predatory style and the influence of Hollywood film noir, Dr Bellows also used lipstick, plucked her eyebrows and lounged around with 'a cigarette drooping from her scarlet lips'. The popular face of sapphism, even in the 1950s, remained that of Radclyffe Hall, though the details of her dress and smoking style were often recalled inaccurately.[58] With the increased public awareness of lesbianism after 1927, the media could hint at sapphic versions of the desirable woman smoker. Nevertheless, the mainstream image of the desirable woman smoker remained pointedly heterosexual. Defined by sexuality and social class, the line between respectable and unrespectable smoking was a fine one for women. While respectability was a constraint on representations of the sexualized woman smoker, the suggestion of sapphic and unruly heterosexualities still surfaced in some mainstream media.

Hetero-sexual Encounters

The cigarette was graphically embedded in the modern ideal of companionship between the sexes. Smoking practices were portrayed as facilitating communication, contact and physical closeness which were precursors to romance and essential elements in the maintenance of intimacy. A frequently repeated scenario in advertisements depicted a man offering a woman a cigarette from a packet from which he had already extracted a cigarette for himself.[59] The act of offering a cigarette meant that the man and woman had to be in close contact. The point at which the woman extended her hand to accept a cigarette brought their bodies, more precisely their skin, into near contact. Eyes were particularly important at this point: invariably the woman's eyes were cast down as she selected a cigarette in a submissive and coy manner and, usually, her lips were parted slightly. The man was portrayed either as being focused on the packet and the meeting of their hands or with his attention concentrated on the woman's face in admiration of her demeanour and her taste in cigarettes. Smoking practices were also promoted as facilitating shared leisure and interests. This was the respectable role of smoking in (hetero-)sexual encounters, and the one most visible in the media as was shown in Chapter 4.

Smoking practices were also implicated in predatory heterosexual encounters and could even serve as a feminine device for ensnaring men. This was made explicit in 'A symphony in smoke', an advertisement for De Reszke cigarettes which featured on the back cover of *Sketch* in 1915: 'She almost goes to sleep, and yet, though lulled by booming honey-bees, She keeps alight her cigarette. A winsome, clever, cool coquette'.[60] The illustration depicted a young woman, reclining on a hammock, with eyes closed and one leg hanging gracefully over the edge and across that of a young man lying in the crook of a tree. Although apparently asleep, the woman still managed to keep her cigarette alight; she was, as the poem explained, flirting. Reminiscent of themes in earlier representations, the advertisement suggests that tobacco has a narcotic, 'dreamy' effect, one that enhances the sensuality of the woman smoker and which can be used, surreptitiously, in the seduction of men.[61] Seduction was also a theme in advertisements for 'ladies'' cigarettes of the early 1920s which frequently used Orientalism as a context for depicting the smoker as a heterosexually desiring woman. Fabian's Eram Khayyam amber-perfumed cigarettes were 'remindful of the mysterious charms, visions, and alluring sweetness of the Romantic East'.[62] Set against a backdrop of stars and minarets, a young woman with a veil over her hair sits smoking as a young man comes up behind her, lured by the fragrance of her cigarette. Occasional advertisements were more explicitly sexual in a manner reminiscent of Edwardian erotic postcards (Fig. 5.4). 'Alluring and seductive', declared an advert for Kiamil cigarettes, referring both to the cigarettes that satisfied 'connoisseurs' and to the young woman who is portrayed sitting at her dressing table in only her petticoat with the strap fallen from her shoulder and her bare thigh revealed above her stocking. Peering back and over her shoulder, with head tilted down but eyes looking straight at the viewer, the woman holds a burning cigarette in one hand as she reaches for her powder puff with the other.[63]

Eastern contexts of feminine allure and seduction had disappeared in cigarette advertisements by 1930. Once the large tobacco companies decided to target women they needed to foster women's smoking as respectable. Overtly seductive images were inappropriate and suggested that smoking was only fit for the boudoir. The importance of introducing cigarettes into all areas of life was recognized by American Tobacco president George Washington Hill. With the help of public-relations expert Edward Bernays, Hill sought to make smoking in the streets acceptable for American women so as to maximize the times when they could smoke.[64] It seems likely that similar processes were at work in Britain. The theme of the flirt's feigned innocence also disappeared by 1930. This, and the demise of the Oriental theme, may have followed also from the expectation that modern women could more openly associate with – and fall in love with – men.

Consistent with this, by 1930 advertisers indicated that heterosexual love and the pleasures of smoking were as interconnected for women as they had traditionally been for men. For example, a De Reszke advertisement depicts a couple smoking, but the text suggests that the term 'love' refers both to the relationship between the man and woman and, also, to the relationship between the woman and her cigarette. Reminiscent of love talk, the advertisement refers to 'little murmurs' of thanks to De Reszke from 'soft lips all over the world'.[65] Paying lip service to the idea of women's new heterosexual freedoms and suggesting that cigarettes and men were comparable pleasures, an advertisement for Player's 'Medium' Navy Cut Cigarettes cheekily proclaimed that while 'Men may come and men may go', 'Player's are

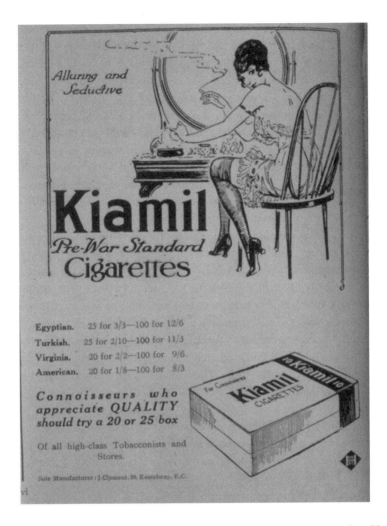

Figure 5.4   Kiamil cigarette advertisement. Eve, January 1920, p. xvi. Reproduced by permission of The British Library (shelf mark 335).

constant ever'.[66] Occasional advertisements still presented the woman smoker as flirtatious. 'Stainless Stephanie', a 'modern girl' with 'cherry ripe lips', appeared in a series of advertisements for cigarettes with red tips. Stephanie used cosmetics to heighten her attractiveness to men, she is 'a work of art' 'got up to kill': 'Lucky cigarette, to be caressed by those cherry-ripe lips!'[67] In 1930s advertisements, the modern woman's heterosexual desire was not camouflaged as in depictions of her late Edwardian predecessors, nor displaced on to an Oriental Other, but openly acknowledged. The construction of the sophisticated and sexual modern woman owed much to the popularization of the ideas of Freud and other psychoanalysts, sexologists and sex reformers. But although by the 1920s a woman was recognized as a sexual being, and by the 1930s she was expected to be a willing partner in an active sex life with her husband, she was still expected to be the passive sexual partner and to engage in sex only within marriage.[68] The predatory implications of Stephanie's smoking practices were, therefore, made less threatening by her use of cherry, rather than scarlet, lipstick. (Implications of this are discussed shortly.) The dilution of Stephanie's seductiveness was a necessary ploy given that cigarette advertisements were restricted to portraying only respectable women with whom viewers could identify, or attempt to emulate. Other media had more scope to portray less respectable women smokers or women smokers in sexually explicit contexts, though there were still constraints.

Whereas in erotic and pornographic images the cigarette was visibly associated with sex and sexual arousal, in mainstream media, even in images designed for titillation, this could only be hinted at. By December 1935 when the magazine *Men Only* was launched in Britain, the cigarette had secured a place in the bedroom, but there were still limits to how women's smoking could be legitimately portrayed. From its launch, *Men Only* attempted, in a frequently misogynist fashion, to create a specifically 'modern' male space for middle-aged middle-class men, 'we won't have women readers', and this magazine will not be like the 'castrated nonsense' found at railway bookstalls.[69] *Men Only* featured articles on 'Style for men', hobbies, sports, the male body – 'Forty – and Fat', as well as general interest features such as 'Office wives', 'Telepathy' and 'Betting may be good for you'. 'Saucy' cartoons were a common feature and frequently depicted women smoking. In these contexts women's smoking was usually associated with premarital sex, although for the men this could be extramarital; presumably the infidelity of married women was deemed too risqué, and/or unsettling, for *Men Only*'s married male readers. During the Second World War the smoker was likely to be a naive young woman hopeful that marriage would follow from sex; before 1939 she was typically a young single woman who slept with her elderly employer, suggesting the exchange of sex for perks.[70] These cartoons commented on sexual mores but, more specifically, on the morality of modern young women. Propped up in bed, an elderly man in pyjamas leans toward a young woman dressed in a skimpy nightdress. He offers her a cigarette which she declines disdainfully: 'Thank you, Mr Westinghouse, I don't approve of smoking.'[71] These cartoons suggest that the genre of comedy was necessary for the explicit portrayal of smoking in sexual contexts. Comedy did have its limits, and while nudity could be suggested, the woman's body was always covered. Nude women, whether photographed or sketched, were never portrayed smoking or toying with cigarettes or cigars; this remained the territory of pornography. Images of nude women were a special feature of *Men Only*, initially one coy voyeuristic colour sketch per issue aptly titled 'Studio Peeps' and, from August 1937, several black and white photos. Photographs portrayed the naked woman as youthful, innocent, beautiful, graceful and in tune with nature, associations that were often reinforced by titles such as 'Youth', 'On the Dunes' and 'Reverie'. Even the 'Studio Peeps' portrayed the nude woman as demure. Smoking threatened to disrupt the carefully constructed vision of feminine innocence that was key to the 'tasteful' depiction of female nudity.[72] Side by side, nude portraiture and cheeky cartoons rearticulated the classic 'Madonna and whore' distinction. Disrobed, and with a cigarette in her hand, a woman invariably had only a tenuous grasp on feminine respectability.

Hollywood film prior to 1934 was less constrained in its depiction of women smokers than cigarette advertising or, more generally, mainstream British film and fiction.[73] Smoking was exploited in Hollywood film as a sexual sign and, in this way, the sexual connotations of women's smoking achieved pre-eminence alongside that of modernity in the 1920s. In films of the 1920s, smoking was associated with sexually sophisticated and often experienced ultra-modern or 'deviant' young women, though not all 'bad girls' smoked. There were rebellious flappers (Clara Bow in *Dancing Mothers*, 1926), 'worldly' women and mistresses (Edna Purvience in *A Woman of Paris*, 1923; Louise Brookes in *Pandora's Box*, 1928), lower-class women (*Carmen*, 1916; Betty Compson in *The Docks of New York*, 1928), criminals (Kay Francis in *The Cocoanuts*, 1929) and 'tough girls'. In the 1930s, numerous stars contributed to the high-profile association of smoking with female sexuality, including Marlene Dietrich in *Morocco* (1930) and *Blue Angel* (1930) and Loretta Young in *Platinum Blonde* (1931). This sexuality was often an unruly version of heterosexuality and sometimes laced with homoerotic elements. Though cabaret singer Amy Jolly (*Morocco*) had her eye on legionnaire Gary Cooper, she exuded homoeroticism when she sat smoking, dressed in a tuxedo and with legs parted; this was even before she teased the on-looking legionnaire by approaching a female nightclub patron and kissing her full on the lips. By the 1930s, however, smoking was as much a feature of respectable womanhood as of feminine deviance. In *Ladies in Love* (1930), for instance, both the 'nice' girl and the two-timing bad girl, smoked. According to Dale's study of Hollywood films in 1935, heroines were more likely to smoke than female villains, but Dale's numerical indicators of good and bad types of woman smoker do not reveal the extent of smoking or the influence of the smoker or smoking scenes;[74] it is likely that some smokers and smoking scenes had an influence far in excess of their numerical preponderance. An explicit link in Hollywood film between smoking and unruly female sexuality disappeared under the Hays Production Code which was formally introduced in 1934.[75] Depictions, or even suggestions, of indecency, immorality and violence were strictly controlled, thereby curtailing on-screen as well as off-screen space. Smoking still retained strong associations with sexual desire and pleasures. Under the Hays regulation, as Parr notes, 'screen lovers kept one foot on the floor and cigarettes to hand at all times ... all the sex to be had was sublimated: good girls kept their lips unparted, while wicked women sent smoke signals of sensuality and sophistication, unmistakable invitations to a seduction'.[76]

Sexual Intimacy: The Language of Sex and the Cigarette

Although smoking had associations with sexual signalling that pre-dated 1914, the language of sex and the cigarette was given widespread publicity through fiction illustrations in popular magazines and, albeit cautiously, some cigarette advertising. Film enabled a particularly graphic rendering of the sexual possibilities afforded by smoking practices. It was not just that new – and mass – media enabled the widespread visibility of a link between women's smoking and sexual possibilities, the interwar period also witnessed changes in the perception of female sexuality. It is not mere speculation that Freudian meanings underpinned some representations of women smoking, although this reveals nothing about the significance for viewers of these images. In the US, the psychiatrist Brill advised Bernays on advertisements for American Tobacco: 'Two people should appear, one man and one woman. That is life ... The cigarette is a phallic symbol, to be offered by a man to a woman. Every natural man or woman can identify with such a message.'[77] By the 1940s, particular styles of lighting up, inhaling and exhaling smoke, and holding cigarettes were well-aired signs of sexual experience, desire and activity.

Film and popular fiction often spelt out the shifting levels of intimacy that smoking practices revealed. In 'Strangers To-day', a story featured in *Woman* in 1937, the growing feeling between Belling and Audrey was indicated by shifts in their smoking practices.[78] At the outset, Audrey was depicted smoking alone in the hotel lounge. When Belling first approached Audrey he offered her a cigarette and then, when she accepted, he leant forward to light it for her. She then offered him a cigarette and he lit both their cigarettes. Within twenty-four hours, and in the final scene in which Belling confessed that he had fallen in love with Audrey, he lit a cigarette for Audrey and passed it to her before he lit one for himself. Lighting cigarettes, as this example illustrates, was full of sexual nuance.

Lighting rituals were key to the sexual significance of smoking, and they often sizzled with sexual tension. A classic lighting ritual, first exploited in erotica and subsequently used in illustrations, cigarette advertising, and film, involved two people lighting their cigarettes end to end. The significance of the connection spoke for itself, although depictions in mainstream print media were often coy compared to film's more graphic exploitation of the sexual connotations. More usually men lighted cigarettes for their female companions. The sensual dimensions of this act were graphically conveyed in 'That Dreadful Miss Cardew', a story from *Girls' Friend* in 1925.

He rose and handed her his case. She took a cigarette and slipped it between her lips, waiting for him to give her a light. For a moment he hesitated, for there was something in the way her soft, red lips closed round the cigarette that covered him with confusion … He lighted a match and held it to her cigarette, and again he noticed how red and curved were her lips.[79]

The cigarette highlighted the sensuality of the woman's lips, and this was further illuminated by the light from the match. The act of smoking was also erotic; Daisy 'slipped' the cigarette into her mouth and her lips 'closed round' it. As befits a 1920s magazine heroine, however, Daisy was unaware of the sexual signalling of her smoking practice. An advertisement for Wills' Gold Flake also illustrates clearly the sensuality of this lighting ritual (see Fig 5.5).[80] In this full-page colour advertisement, a man in evening dress with a lighted cigarette in his mouth stood behind a beautiful woman attired in a sumptuous gown. The picture captured the moment that he leaned over her to light the cigarette that she had between her teeth. In this posture, the woman's neck was extended and the bareness of both her neck and collar bone, recognized erogenous zones, were accentuated. The woman's eyes were wide open, suggesting her sexual availability and submissiveness, as she looked deeply into those of her male companion. This posturing was erotic and clearly conveyed shared intimacy. Even when a woman did not have a cigarette in her mouth she was often depicted in advertisements in a sexual manner with her lips moist and parted slightly (the other common pose being the smile). To avoid suggesting that the woman was attempting to seduce the viewer – an obviously promiscuous prospect for cigarette advertisements – the woman was usually depicted with her eyes cast down or looking intently into those of her companion. The role of cigarettes as a prelude, or adjunct, to sex was often conveyed graphically by variations on this lighting ritual, as when a man lit a cigarette which he then inserted into the mouth of his female companion as in *Johnny O'Clock* (1947). In reverse, this gesture could be an explicit sign of female desire, as demonstrated by actresses Ruby Keeler and Joan Blondell in Hollywood's *Gold Diggers* (1933). In tone or phrasing, a woman's demand for a light was also frequently laced with sexual innuendo. In *Morocco* (1930), for instance, Marlene Dietrich demands of her escort, 'cigarette me, big boy'.[81]

The flame used in lighting a cigarette was also a valuable narrative and visual device in its own right. It facilitated action by providing illumination of the face, thereby highlighting attractiveness and rendering emotion visible. Although the lighting of a cigarette was used in scenes between women, it was in the context of heterosexual romance that it was most popularly employed. Daisy Cardew's lips were illuminated by the light from a match and, in the Wills' advertisement, the flame from the lighter highlights the lovers' mutual attraction. Revealingly, the illustration for 'Strangers To-day' also portrayed the moment of illumination.

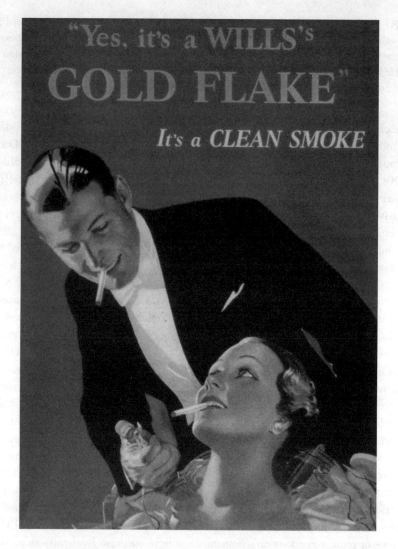

Figure 5.5   Wills' Gold Flake advertisement. Woman, 19 June 1937, p. 5. Thanks to
Imperial Tobacco. Reproduced by permission of The British Library (shelf
mark 419).

Indeed, in this story Belling was described as deliberately offering a lone woman a cigarette in order to sneak a glimpse of her face which was otherwise hidden by the shadows in the dimly lit hotel lounge. Belling was, however, 'unprepared for the loveliness the flame revealed'.[82]

Flames also served as symbols of love and sexual attraction: in the following exchange a flickering flame symbolized the awakening of passion.

The window behind them was wide open, and the breeze from the sea made the match-flare flicker between them, and Simone put her hand over Thurston's to make a shield for it. She could feel his eyes upon her, and presently she looked up with slow deliberation, but the smile died from her lips as she saw the expression of his face, for it was as if he said 'I love You'.[83]

In this extract from *Mabs Weekly*, it was significant that Simone placed her hands over those of Thurston in order to protect the flame that was their newly sparked love.

All types of women smoked in film and fiction, but the significant difference between women who were sexually innocent and those who were sexually experienced, promiscuous and/or dangerous lay in the extent to which they smoked and their style. Sexually experienced women smoked most often and most graphically.[84] Women with the capacity to seduce men – and sometimes women – and lure them to their downfall invariably wore scarlet lipstick as they smoked. Sadie Bracken, the multiple murderer, 'paced silently up and down the bedroom, a cigarette between her scarlet lips',[85] while Dr Bellows, the lesbian scholar and sexual predator, is described with 'a cigarette drooping from her scarlet lips'.[86] Meta Carter, a wealthy and promiscuous widow, had a cigarette constantly 'between her scarlet lips' and, consolidating her status as an immoral woman, she 'flicked her ash on to the floor with a scarlet, pointed nail' and 'dropped the end of her cigarette onto the cement floor and set her high white heel on it'.[87]

Inhalation of cigarette smoke was often associated with female sexual sophistication. In *Woman* magazine, Meta Carter was a stylish and proficient smoker who inhaled deeply. Thirteen years later in 1950, this style of inhalation was not restricted to promiscuous women in the pages of *Woman,* but was also typical of sophisticated and sexually experienced married women, such as Connie, who 'lighted a cigarette and drew on it dramatically … She inhaled deeply … and the smoke curled about the black cavern of her mouth.'[88] This depiction reflected the eroticization of married women,[89] a process that had begun in the 1930s, and it clearly differentiated Connie from younger women, such as Margy, whose sexual innocence is confirmed by the way she smokes, 'the cigarette tremble[d] in Margy's lip and she spiked the flame'.[90]

Sexual experience was also suggested when a glamorous woman dangled her cigarette, especially in male company. An unsupported cigarette either jutting or dangling from a woman's mouth was most often presented as a utilitarian gesture. Typically the woman's hands were portrayed as temporarily too busy to allow her to hold her cigarette.[91] In most cases where a woman had an unsupported cigarette in her mouth, it jutted straight out at a right angle to her face and signified her equality with men.[92] The non-utilitarian dangling cigarette was, in contrast, a sign of sexual sophistication and seduction. Film made much of the sexual possibilities of the dangling cigarette. Though cigarette advertisers were always keen to exploit possibilities, and the dangling cigarette was used in some advertisements, they invariably qualified the gesture. In the mid-1930s an advertisement for Bachelor's cigarettes, which appeared in *Miss Modern* and *Vogue* magazines, presented a photograph of a woman with blonde hair swept back tightly from her face and a cigarette dangling from one corner of her painted mouth (Fig. 5.6). The girl's

Sweet & twenty

'BACHELOR' GIRL ... *Her frocks ..her hair... her eyes proclaim a charming serenity ... her cigarette a worldly wisdom*

Figure 5.6   Bachelor's cigarette advertisement. Vogue, 9 January 1935, p. 67.
Reproduced by permission of The British Library (shelf mark LD 89).

cigarette, the advert declared, proclaimed 'worldly wisdom'.[93] Precisely what this meant is deliberately ambiguous. The text and the image did, however, work to contain the sexual significance of this descriptor. 'Her frocks ... her hair ... her eyes' proclaimed 'a charming serenity' and clearly marked her as feminine. The sexual suggestiveness of the term 'worldly wise' was further tempered by the emphasis, in the photograph, on the model's large eyes which dominated her face and which, in their openness and slightly averted gaze, conveyed a childlike innocence. If this woman had looked the viewer straight in the eyes she would have appeared brazen. That this advertisement had to work to contain the connotations it unleashed testifies to the prominence of the sexual interpretation of the glamorous dangle.

Alongside the dangling cigarette, the exhalation of cigarette smoke was also revealing of sexual experience and intent. Cigarette smoke directed into a man's face was a particularly graphic sexual invitation employed in Hollywood film. Jean Harlow in *Platinum Blonde* (1931) expelled twin streams of thick smoke from her nostrils just inches from a man's face; Bette Davis in *It's Love I'm After* (1937) blew smoke into her fiance's face; Marlene Dietrich, as a saloon singer in *Seven Sinners* (1940), exhaled straight into a man's face; and Joan Crawford, in *Strange Cargo* (1940), exhaled thick streams of smoke from her nose and mouth into the leading man's face before kissing him on the mouth.[94] Blowing smoke into someone's face could also be an insult. In *Bulldog Drummond* (1929), a British '"talkie" thriller', the merciless and glamorous crook played by Lilyan Tashman blows smoke into the face of her female captive, played by Joan Bennet.[95] When done by a woman to a man, however, the insult was invariably laced with sexual connotations, a tease or a sign of sexual contempt.

Conclusion

In late Victorian and Edwardian Britain, women's relationship to tobacco was portrayed principally as serving men's pleasures. This representation was, however, for a restricted audience. After 1920, the sexualization of women's relationship to tobacco continued, but it became visible to a wider audience due to the expansion of the print press and the establishment of cinema as a mainstay of British leisure. In the context of new understandings of female sexuality and new ideals of heterosexual relationships, the sexualized interwar woman smoker looked very different to her prewar counterpart. Smoking was inextricably tied to the modern woman's attractiveness and her ability to negotiate the demands of modern relations with men. This high-profile heterosexualization of smoking was key to the feminization of the process. However, smoking continued to have associations with unruly heterosexualities and even sapphism. These unruly elements were played out in film, sometimes in fiction, and cautiously toyed with in advertising. By 1940, smoking was firmly associated with sexual allure and sexual signalling.

Notes

1. Koetzle, *Seductive Smoke*, p. 7.
2. Mitchell, 'Images of Exotic Women', p. 329.
3. Ibid.
4. Mayhew, *London Labour*, pp. 441.
5. Ibid., p. 440. In both French and Dutch, the verb 'to pipe' has 'lewd connotations', thereby contributing 'to this perception of the masculine, carnal implications of smoking'. If in seventeenth-century England a middle-class married woman was seen with a tobacco pipe, the implication was that she was cuckolding her husband. Dry Drunk Exhibition website.
6. Also demonstrated by the display in shop windows of young women rolling cigarettes or cigars by hand (Souhami, *Gluck*, p. 25). This practice is referred to in Arnold Bennett's novel, *Lion's Share*, cited in MOA FR 3192, p. 67.
7. Alford, *Wills*, colour plates 3.
8. Mitchell, 'Images of Exotic Women', p. 329.
9. Ibid., p. 331.
10. See examples in Alford, *Wills*.
11. *Sketch*, 19 May 1920, p. *n*.
12. *Sketch*, 23 June 1920, p. 283. See also *Sketch*, 26 May 1920, p. 137.
13. *Manchester Guardian*, 26 March 1920, p. 7.
14. *Sketch*, 2 June 1915, p. 4.
15. Hilton, *Smoking*, pp. 102–3, recounts the history of this icon.
16. Thanks to Lisa Sigel for this information from Dingwall's catalogue of the Milford Haven Collection, p. 8, Victoria and Albert Museum. This 'lewd picture' is also mentioned by MOA TC 63 1/D Terry. This effect can be produced with advertisements from the Second World War, see *Vogue*, October 1940, p. 93.
17. *News of the World*, 9 July 1939, p. 19.
18. Stacey, *Star Gazing*.
19. In 1870, William Powell Frith exhibited *At Homburg* at the R.A. This painting of a woman smoking in public was 'mercilessly attacked' because public smoking suggested that the woman was a prostitute and this was not deemed a fitting subject of art (Wood, *Victorian Panorama*, fig. 1). Paintings of women using hookahs were not so controversial in Britain, and may have been on display or in private collections, since Orientalist paintings were very popular in the nineteenth century, especially with the new-moneyed northern

industrial manufacturers. (Thanks to Rosemary Betterton for this point). Women smokers, especially harem women using hookahs, were also on display in the Louvre (Kalmar, 'The *Houkah*') and other prominent French and Spanish galleries.

20. Sigel, *Governing Pleasures*, pp. 121–2. By 1909, 800 million postcards were sent in England each year (p. 122).

21. Bridgeman, 152740.

22. For other examples of the use of exotic symbols see Koetzle, *Seductive Smoke*; Sigel, *Governing Pleasures*, pp. 128–9; Alloula, *Colonial Harem*.

23. Alloula, *Colonial Harem*, p. 74.

24. Cited in Laver, *Age of Optimism*, p. 99.

25. Alloula, *Colonial Harem*, p. 52; Sigel, *Governing Pleasures*, pp. 124, 125, 130.

26. Sigel, *Governing Pleasures*, p. 123.

27. Alloula, *Colonial Harem*, p. 74.

28. Although Alloula comments only on the hookah's significance in the postcard of the 'algérienne', several of the postcards he reproduces feature women smoking cigarettes: see pp. 29, 53, 69, 79, 104.

29. Haggis, 'Gendering Colonialism or Colonising Gender?'

30. Public reaction to an unusual painting by Frith of a European woman smoking in public is revealing of this assumption (note 19), see also the poem (note 24) and discussion of working-class young women smokers (Chapter 2). See also Kalmar, 'The Houkah', p. 224.

31. Sigel, *Governing Pleasures*, p. 128.

32. Hoole and Sato, *Alphonse Mucha*, p. 7.

33. Mitchell, 'The "New Woman" as Prometheus', p. 4.

34. Ibid., pp. 4, 6.

35. Mitchell, 'Images of Exotic Women', p. 333.

36. Mitchell, 'The "New Woman" as Prometheus', p. 4.

37. *TTR*, 1 February 1898, p. 6.

38. Bridgeman, 130224.

39. Cited in Mitchell, 'The "New Woman" as Prometheus', p. 5.

40. Koetzle, *Seductive Smoke*, p. 14.

41. Ibid.

42. *Sketch*, 30 June 1915, p. 4.

43. *Sketch*, 26 May 1920, p. 137.

44. An advertisement for Spinet cigarettes in 1920 was unusual in portraying two women smoking together over tea (*Vogue*, late June 1920, p. 104). Although the 'female friends' scenarios was marginal in cigarette advertising it was a staple of fashion imagery.

45. Examples in *Woman*, 1937.

46. For example, *Miss Modern*, April 1931, p. 8.

47. *Sketch*, 26 April 1950, p. iv (back page); also beauty product advertisement, *Miss Modern*, February 1939, p. 63.

48. *Miss Modern*, February 1939, p. 46.

49. For example, *Woman and Home*, January 1935, p. 36; *Modern Woman*, April 1939, p. 12; *Woman*, 18 February 1950, p. 28.

50. Greaves, *Smoke Screen*, p. 21.

51. Doan, *Fashioning Sapphism*, p. 107.

52. Jeffreys, *Spinster and her Enemies*, p. 106.

53. Alloula, *Colonial Harem*, Chapter 9.

54. Doan, *Fashioning Sapphism*, p. 99.

55. Ibid., p. 122.

56. *Girls' Friend*, 15 March 1930, p. 3.

57. *Glamour*, 8 July 1939, p. 18.

58. Gardiner, *From the Closet*, pp. 34, 90.

59. See also fiction. In 'White Flowers' a woman is persuaded to have a cup of tea with a complete stranger in return for a light for her cigarette. *Woman*, 30 January 1943, pp. 12–13.

60. *Sketch*, 2 June 1915, back page.

61. See also advertisement for Abdullah cigarettes: 'each Abdullah spells a radiant Dream' (*Eve*, 27 May 1925, p. 448). The dreamy, vulnerable and sensual woman smoker appears also in an illustration of the devil watching a woman, her eyes closed while smoking beside a river (*Sketch*, 16 July 1930, p. 121).

62. *Vogue*, late June 1919, p. lviii. See also, advertisements for Ambar cigarettes (*Sketch*, 23 June 1920, p. *k*); Abdullah cigarettes (*Eve*, 27 May 1925, p. 448); Morris's cigarettes (*Daily Express,* 13 April 1920, p. 10); Muratti 'Ariston' cigarettes (*Sketch*, 19 May 1920, p. xx).

63. *Eve*, January 1920, p. xvi.

64. Brandt, 'Recruiting Women Smokers', p. 65.

65. *Daily Express*, 22 January 1930, p. 16. See also *Sketch*, 23 July 1930, p. 191. Similar sentiments were expressed in the Player's caption, 'The Bachelor way to a woman's heart' *Sketch*, 10 July 1935, p. 111.

66. *Woman and Home*, April 1927, p. 44.

67. *Woman*: 1 September 1937, p. 2; 14 August 1937, p. 2. It was not just women who became more alluring when they smoked, an Erinmore advertisement depicted a middle-aged man smoking his pipe while two young and attractive women fawned over him: 'What's he got that other men haven't got?' (*People*, 14 February 1943, p. 5).

68. Hall, *Sex, Gender and Social Change*.

69. *Men Only*, December 1935, pp. 13–14.

70. *Men Only*, August 1937, p. 37; see also January 1941, p. 68.

71. *Men Only*, October 1937, p. 39.

72. Lisa Sigel explained to me that: '"tastefulness" was based on unspoken restrictions coming from the government. Newsagents and vendors wanted a list of censored works or censorable attributes, but the Home Office kept insisting there wasn't one (whereas there was). To keep from getting their entire stock confiscated, they kept the bar at "tasteful" continuing the de facto Victorian codes of legality', especially around body hair and genitals.

73. All films mentioned were released in Britain. I used the 'Female Celebrity Smoking' website to trace films with women smokers.

74. Dale, *Motion Pictures*. British films also aligned smoking with respectability, for example, in *Night Must Fall* (1937) a very ordinary young woman smokes while playing cards with her mother.

75. A version of the Code is reproduced in Docherty, *Pre-Code Hollywood*. By the 1950s the Code was often ignored by film producers but it was not replaced by a film ratings system until 1968.

76. Parr, 'S for Smoking', p. 31.

77. Brandt, 'Recruiting Women Smokers', p. 65.

78. *Woman,* 25 September 1937, pp. 8–10, 40.

79. *Girls' Friend*, 16 May 1925, p. 8.

80. *Woman*, 19 June 1937, p. 5.

81. Katherine Hepburn, *Bringing Up Baby* (1938), demands that her boyfriend 'cigarette me'.

82. *Woman*, 25 September 1937, p. 8.

83. *Mabs Weekly*, 17 October 1931, p. 7.

84. Sexually experienced women who smoked featured in *Anna Christie* (1930), *Blonde Venus* (1932), *Baby Face* (1933). Dancers, performers and criminals, all with a reputation for sexual promiscuity, were usually smokers – for example Lola in *Blue Angel* (1930) and Amy Jolly in *Morocco* (1930). Wealthy socialites and flappers were also smokers – for instance Joan Prescott in *Montana Moon* (1930).

85. *Lucky Star*, 14 September, 1935, p. 4.

86. *Glamour*, 8 July 1939, p. 18.

87. *Woman*, 17 July 1937, p. 21. Smoking was also used in fiction to denote tension, anticipation and anxiety, the latter by virtue of making more visible the subject's shaking hands, 'Hating, brooding, smoking a chain of cigarettes, drinking endless cups of tea, she walked up and down the room, hour after hour ... Sadie sank into an arm-chair and watched the cigarette trembling in her fingers' (*Lucky Star*, 19 October 1935, p. 5).

88. *Woman*, 1 April 1950, p. 7.

89. Hall, *Sex, Gender and Social Change*.

90. *Woman*, 1 April 1950, p. 7.

91. *Woman*, 3 July 1937, p. 17.

92. *Vogue*, Early July 1920, inside front cover; *Daily Express*, 9 January 1930, p. 14, 30 January 1930, p. 6; *Woman*, 25 November 1939, p. 44.

93. *Vogue,* 9 January 1935, p. 67.

94. See 'Female Celebrity Smoking' website.

95. Promoted in *School-Days*, 24 August 1929, p. 2.

6

Respectable Smoking: A Class Act

Women smokers were invariably portrayed in the mainstream print media of the period 1920–1950 as respectable, but respectable smoking was always a class act. It is no coincidence that women smokers were usually middle or upper class in appearance – the visibly working class were not seen smoking. Respectability can be broadly defined as having good social standing and as having socially or conventionally acceptable morals and standards. Although respectability is a slippery and subjective category,[1] 'dominant notions of respectability'[2] tend to represent the values of dominant social groups. Respectability, or more accurately dominant notions of respectability, have 'always been a marker and a burden of class'.[3] They have also been gendered, most notably in the ways in which respectability has been aligned with specific models of feminine sexual conduct.[4] Another key aspect of respectability for women is refinement. Refinement required attention to the finer details of appearance and depended on careful maintenance and control/containment of the female body. Janice Winship, in her discussion of the 'neat and tidy' interwar woman, and Beverly Skeggs in her study of young women in the 1990s, both identify care of the female body as an important aspect of feminine respectability.[5] A version of refinement that includes care and containment of the home and locality also had a long-established relationship with respectability. As Judy Giles demonstrates, the practice of 'keeping yourself to yourself', which was the linchpin of suburban respectability throughout the period 1900–1950, was principally concerned with containment.[6] Aside from appearance, refinement also required a certain posture (elegant and contained) and behaviour (polite, not coarse). Given the importance of refinement for feminine respectability, it is no surprise that it was key to the visual representation of respectable smoking.

This chapter explores the parameters of respectable smoking for women by examining dominant images of female smokers in print media – modern girls, glamorous ladies, smart middle-class women and women at war. It shows how working-class women were excluded from the category of respectable smoker until the late 1930s and how, even in the context of the Second World War, the respectability of the working-class woman smoker remained fragile. The final section considers the effort involved for women smokers in keeping up the appearance of respectability, and the efforts of some women to visibly rebel against this.

Modern Girls

Modernity had a complex relationship with respectability, and this had implications for the status of the modern woman smoker. Change often involves the disruption of dominant and traditional notions of respectability and/or the emergence of new forms of behaviour that, at least initially, are not coded as respectable. This was the case with women's smoking. As demonstrated in Chapter 4, smoking contributed to the production of modern femininity, one that transgressed Victorian notions of refined femininity. It also, as discussed in Chapter 5, challenged the long-standing association of women's smoking with sexual laxity. Only those in secure social positions (upper and upper-middle classes) were in a position to embrace smoking publicly, but then social elites were the arbiters of fashion and in a position to code the new as consistent with an updated/modern version of feminine refinement and respectability. The public adoption of smoking by social elites was one way in which this 'modern' feminine practice was redefined as respectable. Media representation also played a role and, in the interwar years with the growth of the mass media, it was the forum in which the alignment of smoking with feminine respectability was given widespread publicity and visibility. This was assisted by the willingness of the press to devote 'endless copy' to the antics of Society's 'Bright Young Things'.[7] It also stemmed in part from the media interest in aesthetically pleasing and novel images. In this context, women smokers were featured and, moreover, portrayed as attractive and respectable.

The 'modern' and respectable woman smoker was invariably depicted in the press and advertising as upper-middle or upper class, and often as a member of 'Society'. For example a series of advertisements for De Reszke cigarettes in 1920 featured Society belles at Henley, Lords and the Royal Albert. While in 1920 these advertising images were exclusive to the elite press, by the late 1920s they were commonplace in daily newspapers. De Reszke's 'gallery of girls', which appeared in the *Daily Express* in 1928, included 'Joan. A girl with a soul – to say nothing of her outward graces. Easy to get on with, so long as she's not asked to tolerate anything second-best ... Joan says breeding will show – in cigarettes as well as in human beings.'[8] Other markers of class included affluent settings and servants. Fashion features in elite periodicals further aligned the act of smoking with the constellation of attributes that constituted affluent youthful modernity, in particular sophistication (social and sexual), independence (social, sexual, economic) and style (Fig. 6.1). Advertisements for non-tobacco products also employed these associations, indicating that advertisers perceived the attractive, and socially exclusive, meanings of smoking as widely recognized by their intended audiences.[9] The association of smoking with social elites was also made visible in magazine fiction for young women of the lower-middle and upper-working classes. Modern girls who smoked were invariably depicted as middle class, or as women who

*Figure 6.1   Fashion promotion. Vogue, 11 January 1928, p. 25. Reproduced by
permission of The British Library (shelf mark LD 89).*

had risen to fame, fortune and the ranks of Society through acting.[10] Hollywood
flappers reinforced the mainly middle-class (lower or upper) credentials of the
flapper.[11] Working-class girls were not presented as smokers unless they aspired to
join the ranks of the affluent and/or the 'modern' set who were invariably middle
and upper class.[12]

The association of smoking with visibly middle- or upper-class women and
lifestyles, particularly in cigarette advertisements, needs to be interpreted as a
marketing device; aspirational images were a common feature of all sorts of

advertising. However, the absence of obviously working-class women smoking in the interwar period is revealing of how respectability could be visually represented at this time. Obvious indicators of being a working-class woman in the 1920s included occupation (mill and factory work, domestic service); poor housing (signified by a small cramped home, although domestic servants could be portrayed working in affluent households); dress (more specifically a lack of modern and stylish clothes, or the uniform of domestic service). However, the working class was widely perceived to be divided into two key social groups, the 'respectable' working class or 'deserving poor', and the 'undeserving' poor or 'rough' working class.[13] Images of respectable poor women had to be constructed carefully so as not to cross the fine visual line between respectability and unrespectability.

The lack of images of obviously working-class girls smoking suggests that if a domestic maid or a factory girl had been depicted with a cigarette, this would have undermined any attempt to portray her as refined and respectable. In a work context, smoking signified a woman's half-hearted approach to her task and, alongside markers of being working class, suggested that this woman was slovenly and unrespectable. The threat that smoking posed to the respectability of working-class women was heightened by the association of working-class women's smoking with sexual immorality. Psychologist Cyril Burt included in his study, *The Young Delinquent*, photographs of two young women smoking, to 'give the visualising reader some concrete picture of the cases [of sexually delinquent girlhood] that illuminate the text'.[14] Oral history also reveals that, for 'ordinary women', smoking still had connotations of sexual impropriety in the interwar years. As May, born in 1926, recalled in her interview with Rosemary Elliot: 'It was sort of looked down upon', 'It was only a certain type of woman who smoked, cheap, cheap, cheap class of woman.'[15] Jess, born in 1916, recalled that working-class women may have smoked in secret but 'it was just frowned upon, it wasn't thought to be very respectable if you smoked, and yet … all those jazzy kids … had their long cigarette holder and their cigarettes'.[16] As Jess's recollections suggest, unlike their working-class peers, middle- and upper-class women could smoke without endangering their reputations. The refinement and respectability of the visibly middle-class woman was not precarious in the way that it was for her visibly working-class sister. Moreover, smoking was consistent with modernity and this very visual identity was associated primarily with the *look* of the middle and upper classes. Although the upper- and middle-class girl's smoking could symbolize modernity and increased sexual sophistication, the working-class girls' smoking could too easily symbolize prostitution.

The difficulty of representing working-class women as smokers gradually disappeared in interwar magazines, as visible features of the lives of these young women changed. Whereas in the 1920s working-class young women were represented chiefly in domestic service, mill and factory work, by the 1930s these characters were more likely to work in offices and shops (this being consistent with changes in the employment of young women at this time[17]). Given that office and retail work attracted young women from both working-class and middle-class backgrounds, it became more difficult to discern a woman's social class simply from the representation of her paid work. These new types of women's employment were predefined as 'modern' and, because widely perceived as 'clean' forms of work,[18] they were consistent with the representation of refinement and respectability. Although, judging by the text, some of these young workers may have been working class, it was difficult to tell this from the visual images of these characters; the office or shop girl who smoked always *looked* like a modern young woman from the respectable middle classes.

The availability of fashionable styles for the masses was another factor that facilitated the dissolution of visible working-class indicators. If women could not afford to buy couture, there were ready-made alternatives and, increasingly, patterns to enable women to make their own versions of fashionable dress.[19] The simplicity of fashionable dress further blurred visible class difference: 'A version of the little black dress, perhaps with a white Peter Pan collar, could be worn by duchess and shop girl alike, as could the grey or navy suit, or the simple wrap-over or edge-to-edge coat in black or beige.'[20] It was, as one contemporary noted, 'much harder ... to tell what class someone belonged to by looking at [her] clothes'.[21]

However, class differences in the clothes and bodies of young women did remain.[22] Moreover, while the latest fashions were more accessible to young and single working-class women in paid employment, the standard of living experienced by many working-class mothers would not have facilitated fashionable dress.[23] Consistent with this, images of older working-class mothers usually portrayed them as old-fashioned and as poorly, but neatly, dressed as they went about their work in the home. Whereas employment and leisure venues provided contexts in which class was often difficult to read, the home remained a visibly classed environment. With class so blatantly signalled in the home environment, the working-class mother, unlike her social 'superiors', was not portrayed as a smoker.[24]

Sophisticated and Glamorous 'Ladies'

In the early 1930s, a more mature and demure image of the woman smoker came to the fore, although the themes of affluence and modernity were still evident. This smoker had been visible in the early 1920s but only in elite magazines; by the 1930s the lady smoker appeared in newspapers and magazines catering for all social-class groups. Whereas smoking was a marker of the 'modern girl's' identity, in these images smoking was principally a leisure and lifestyle motif. Fashion features in *Vogue* regularly featured well-dressed, sophisticated young women smoking in a range of settings. The style of some of these images was reproduced in cigarette advertising where symbols of exclusivity remained a popular feature,[25] it also appeared in advertisements for non-tobacco products. An advertisement for Dolcis summer sandals, priced beyond the reach of working-class women at 12*s* 9*d* to 14*s* 9*d*, appeared in the middle-class magazine *Miss Modern* (Fig. 6.2). This advertisement featured two stylish and affluent women sitting at a restaurant table on a summer's day with the sea and cliffs visible in the background, with a waiter, dressed in bow tie and tails, in attendance. There were long, presumably cold, drinks on the table and one woman smoked.[26] This image could have been taken from a *Vogue* fashion plate and it became a cliché for affluent feminine leisure well into the 1960s. A similar scenario, also with a woman smoking, but this time while sharing a pot of tea or coffee with a friend, was used to emphasize the superiority of Menex sanitary towels – 'For ladies of discrimination'.[27] The terms 'ladies' and 'discrimination' were mutually reinforcing, and emphasized that these women noticed, and cared about, fine details and differences: these women were refined and sexually respectable.

Visual images of 'lady' smokers often portrayed them as glamorous. Glamour denotes a beautiful, stylish, but showy, appearance achieved largely through artifice (most obviously expensive clothes, accessories and cosmetics); it also includes the confidence and self-assurance to carry off this look.[28] Owing to the emphasis on a specifically adult feminine display, glamour is also, quite often, highly sexualized. From the outset, smoking was associated with glamorous British femininities, particularly the affluent femininity of leisured Society women which, by the late 1930s, was often Americanized. Women smokers were often portrayed in contexts in which being 'noticed' was of paramount importance, for example in fashion features and some advertising. Glamorous women smokers were also evident in fiction illustrations of women dressed for special evening events, for example Dixie who had 'everything – beauty, wit, charm and money' and Cecile, a glamorous top model, 'One Hundred Per Cent Town Girl'.[29] Once again, the visible woman smoker was of high social-class status, either by birth or by virtue of a successful career in modelling or film. The glamorous smoker was also, necessarily, portrayed as refined.

Lynn Pearce argues that 'glamour is always read as "degrading" unless "protected" and defended by other marks of middle-class respectability (such as education or wealth)'.[30] The importance of markers of respectability, especially refinement, for the portrayal of the glamorous smoker stemmed from the long-established association of overt sexual display with working-class prostitution and, relatedly, the widespread distrust of working-class women who loved finery and display. Valverde notes that during the nineteenth century there was a widespread assumption that the pursuit of finery by a working-class woman inevitably led to prostitution.[31] Mayhew's descriptions of Victorian prostitutes referred repeatedly

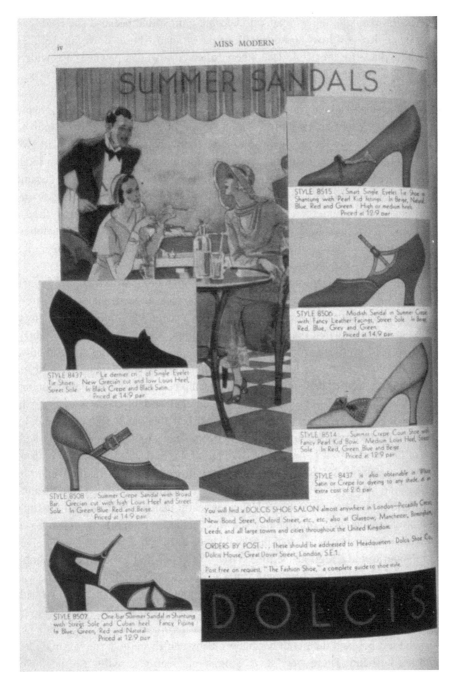

Figure 6.2   Dolcis Shoes advertisement. Miss Modern, July 1931, p. iv. Reproduced by permission of The British Library (shelf mark 568).

to this: for example, the woman who became a prostitute because she could not satisfy her 'love of dress and display', or the woman whose 'downfall' resulted from a fondness for dress.[32] Indeed, finery (often borrowed or pawned) was widely perceived as a trademark of the prostitute in the early stages of her career.[33] These associations remained in the interwar years[34] and were heightened by Hollywood representations of glamorous but 'immoral' lower-class women on the lookout for easy money and an easy life.[35] The adoption of glamorous attire, combined with smoking, was therefore problematic for working-class women in two reinforcing ways. Finery signalled sexual immorality, and smoking had a long-standing association with sexual promiscuity. Even as women's smoking became increasingly normalized, the actual practice of smoking retained strong sexual overtones. The campaigner, Vera Brittain, herself a smoker at the time, fired a maid in 1918 because she wore make up and smoked expensive Turkish cigarettes. Together these practices indicated to Vera that the maid was a prostitute rather than a glamorous 'modern woman'.[36]

The potentially deviant sexual associations of glamorous working-class women smoking were evident in some women's magazines. Indeed, magazines rarely portrayed working-class women as glamorous except when modelling a gown for a customer or when masquerading as an upper-class woman; importantly, when dressed up these women did not smoke. A rare magazine story about a married woman who 'sold love for money' illustrates the dangers of glamour for working-class women and signals the relationship between smoking, glamour and respectability. The 21-year-old Jean struggled against debt and was unhappy in her marriage to Davey: her husband often worked away and, when at home, he quarrelled with Jean about their mounting debts. Jean's lot contrasted starkly with that of her working-class neighbour, Iris: 'Iris Langford was surrounded with so many of the things I couldn't help longing to possess. Clothes ... the wealth of dresses and hats and furs and undies that were crammed into boxes and trunks and wardrobes in her bedroom.'[37] Jean soon learnt that prostitution paid for Iris's glamorous appearance, and one day she was persuaded by Iris to borrow a gown ('a white satin gown with stockings and shoes to match and a sea-green velvet wrap') and to have a go at 'selling kisses'.[38] On her first expedition to a hotel notorious for prostitution, Jean met Evan who recognized straightaway that she was 'not the Park Hotel-lounge type of girl'. Jean thought she had fallen in love with Evan and, after having sex with him once, she conceived a baby. Jean, however, quickly realized the error of her ways and, after a tortuous time during which her husband left her, and then both her unborn baby and Evan died, she was reunited with her husband. There were several signs that Jean was really a respectable, if misguided, young woman; the fact that she did not smoke was one of these signs. In contrast Iris, an obviously 'Park Hotel-lounge type' who regularly and unashamedly sold sex, did smoke heavily. For working-class women the spectre of being labelled sexually promiscuous always loomed large. In this context, the combination of smoking (which was already associated with independence and sexual sophistication) and glamour easily disrupted the display of sexual modesty and innocence that was crucial to the working-class woman's respectability. For the sexually unrespectable and showy working-class woman, who was usually described as 'cold' and 'self-assured', smoking merely served to enhance her display of sexual sophistication and confirm her sexual deviance. The display of finery and the practice of smoking were both problematic for the respectability of working-class women; the glamorous woman smoker had to be visibly refined and clearly not of the working classes.

Ironically, given the obvious influence of cinema depictions of glamorous women smokers and the use of female stars to promote cigarette brands, Hollywood Studios prohibited the release of photographs of their actresses smoking except when in character. A photograph of Lana Turner, for instance, was retouched to remove her cigarette before it was considered acceptable for public release in the early 1940s.[39] This rule testifies to the potency of the cigarette as sexual signifier. It was no doubt introduced to safeguard the fragile sexual reputations of women performers. There was, it seems, an important distinction between what female characters could do on screen and what actresses could do in real life. With reference to glamour portraits of women smokers in the 1930s and 1940s, Koetzle claims there was 'only a thin line between "fashionable/elegant" and "lascivious"', as indicated by the ambivalence in many of these images.[40] The reasons for this lie in the long tradition of sexual associations discussed in Chapter 5.

Smart and Serviceable or 'Respectable Ordinariness'

By the late 1930s smoking was visibly consistent with a less affluent but *smart*, middle-class femininity. The smart woman smoker was presented as stylish, attractive and discerning; she was concerned with quality and value for money. For example, an advertisement for 'three knots British hosiery' depicted a well-dressed woman posed with a cigarette in a holder: 'Fashionable, comfortable, hard wearing, this sums up the smart woman's demands when buying hosiery'.[41] The smart and attractive middle-class woman smoker became a staple of cigarette advertising targeted at women. Middle-class British actors and personalities such as Florence Desmond, Peggy Wood and Gracie Fields extolled the virtues of cigarettes, Fields even offering a 'ten minute smoke for intelligent folk'.[42]

The 'respectable ordinariness'[43] of this middle-class woman smoker was often reinforced by reference to her paid or unpaid employment; for these women, smoking represented a brief reprieve from the demands of work. In some cases, particularly in advertising for domestic products, the smart and serviceable woman smoker was portrayed as a housewife engaged in the care of the home. In spite of her work, this smoker was always portrayed as refined. Even in an advertisement for floor cleaner, the smoker was depicted dressed in a neat apron and high-heeled shoes as she perched gracefully on a pouf smoking a cigarette while waiting for her floor to dry.[44] Although this woman's outfit seems ill-suited to domestic work, young middle-class wives were frequently advised to dress smartly for housework: 'Like most of our film actresses Elizabeth Allan likes to have jumpers and slacks for "off-duty" times – New Year Brides might adopt the idea for housework'.[45] This advice to readers was motivated partly by the belief that a woman should remain visibly feminine and attractive at all times in order to please her husband and other male family members.[46] It was also about the presentation of respectable middle-class domestic womanhood. In the context of paid work in the interwar years, Winship posits a hierarchical distinction between work in which bodies were required to *act on* materials and work in which bodies were engaged in *acting-with* people. Winship argues that 'those symbolically placed on the side of the latter strive fiercely to protect this class marker and status' by carefully managing their appearance.[47] Although Winship does not address unpaid domestic work, it seems likely that personal appearance was also critical to the status of women who worked in the home at this time. A woman's appearance conveyed whether she engaged in dirty housework – that is, housework dependent principally on the woman's own labour power, carried out in conditions of poverty – or whether she engaged in clean housework in a modern, middle-class home with the latest domestic appliances. The emphasis on refinement in images of the domestic woman smoker clearly conveyed that this woman worked in her own modern and well-equipped home and that she was therefore of the respectable middle classes.

The importance of refinement for representations of the smart domesticated woman smoker is revealed clearly in an advertisement for washing flakes in which two women are depicted having tea together and smoking cigarettes (Fig. 6.3).[48] The advertisement made two main points. First, it stressed that Sylvan washing flakes were the best that money could buy. Secondly, the advertisement focused on the 'dishpan hands' of one of the smokers: 'Harsh soaps and powders quickly ruin lovely hands.' 'Dish pan hands' illustrated the threat which domestic work could pose to the presentation of respectability. Although a daily help was affordable by most moderately well-off families with an income over £400 per year, many middle-class families, whose income fell below this level, could not have afforded this expense.[49] In the context of sensitivity to markers of social class, 'dishpan hands' loudly proclaimed that a woman did her own washing and, as Giles explains, the 'routines, drudgeries and daily tasks involved in maintaining a home were considered unbecoming for middle-class women'.[50] 'Dishpan hands'

Figure 6.3   Sylvan Flakes advertisement (edited). Woman, 28 October 1939, p. 44.
Thanks to Proctor & Gamble. Reproduced by permission of The British
Library (shelf mark 448).

also indicated that a woman did not take sufficient care of her appearance. This lack of refinement threatened to undermine the display of respectability although, in the Sylvan example, the woman's respectability was confirmed by other signs of refinement and by the woman's obvious embarrassment at her lapse in personal care ('What must she think of my hands ...'). As Winship argues, being 'neat and tidy' was, for the lower-middle-class woman in the interwar years, fundamental to the presentation of a respectable middle-class body. This 'nice and neat' body was the product of new self-disciplines for women as they attempted to 'define their bodies and lifestyles as superior ... and as, metaphorically and literally, the embodiment of class'.[51]

Working-class women were rarely depicted as smokers even in the late 1930s. As argued earlier, visibly working-class women smokers were not featured in advertisements, magazine fiction and articles. Given the taboos on smoking in streets, especially for working-class women, working-class women smokers were also absent from press photography. On 22 July 1939, however, a photograph of a working-class 'housewife' accepting a light for a cigarette appeared in most of the national newspapers (Fig. 6.4). The image, and the response to it, is illuminating.

*Figure 6.4   A modern housewife. Daily Express, 22 July 1939, p. 5. Thanks to Daily
Express. Reproduced by permission of The British Library (shelf mark LD52).*

Mrs Theis is photographed in her living room accepting a light from Mr Walter
Elliott, Minister of Health. Mrs Theis was a resident of the recently completed
White City Estate in Hammersmith, London, built to house working-class families.
Her photograph, like that of her neighbour Mrs Carter who posed on a balcony,
were clearly staged as publicity and they deliberately employed visible signifiers
of upward mobility. Mrs Theis is portrayed as a 'modern' housewife who lives in
'modern housing' with a tiled bathroom, labour-saving kitchen and sun balcony.
Speeches in the opening ceremony referred to 'the new life being born for
housewives – the modern tools and equipment that were there for the profession
of housekeeping'.[52] Mrs Theis is also dressed in modest but fashionable clothes;
the full-length photograph of Mrs Carter (not smoking) provides an even clearer
example of the modern and stylish clothes worn for the occasion. Mrs Theis and
Mr Walter Elliott sit around a table, at which a place is set with shiny cutlery for
at least three courses, and on which stands a jug of water and glasses. A vase
of flowers stands on a sideboard in the background. Emphasizing the spacious
modernity of her new environment, Mrs Theis says, 'I had only two rooms in my
old place and like the extra space'. The smart fashionableness of her dress, her
status as a 'modern' housewife, and her 'modern' home filled with symbols of
middle-class domesticity, make it acceptable for Mrs Theis to be seen smoking:

she does not appear working class in appearance or setting. Smoking, in this context, contributes to her modernity and it is plausible that the episode was staged to convey this and, possibly, to represent the government's 'gift' to working-class women and their families. Public reactions to this photograph are revealing. The respectability of the smoker was not a primary concern, although not all approved of the women smoker. The main issues were the irony of the Minister of Health encouraging smoking and, in relation to a working-class woman, condoning a financially wasteful practice.[53]

Women at War

Representations of Service women and other war workers joined the ranks of respectable women smokers with the outbreak of war. This was justified by women's legitimate need for tobacco (see Chapter 3); this need was both personal and social.

The notion that tobacco helped people to cope with stress was used to justify women's smoking in wartime. The link between smoking and stress first achieved public prominence during the First World War, and by the late 1930s this was widely accepted as a rationale for smoking. Dr Grinsing, writing in *Modern Woman* in 1939, observed that most women smoked for pleasures that stemmed from the way 'smoking soothes their nerves and encourages tranquillity'. Moderate smoking, he argued, had 'good effects: a cigarette will often turn a harassed, jaded person, ready to "fly out" at anyone, into a calm human being who is nice to know.' Those who smoked too much, the doctor noted, did so because they were finding life 'difficult', an observation repeated by researchers 40 years later (see Chapter 8). Heavy smokers may 'be lonely, bored, worried or unhappy in their personal relationships. They may be living in conditions which are a constant irritation and strain. They may be overworking – running a home and an exacting office job, with dependants thick about them – a dual enterprise that would make most men sag at the knees after a week of it.' Irritated by some people's disapproval of smokers, the doctor continued:

> Among the heavy smokers I know is a professional woman who has a full-time job and also runs her home, with inadequate help. Her husband died after a long illness, their capital has gone, and she has two school children and an old father to keep ... Yes, she smokes too much. Is it surprising? Hers is not an isolated case. There are hundreds of such women.[54]

Dr Grinsing was not the only medic to extol the comforts of smoking. Mrs Clayton described how: 'I have several times even tried to acquire the habit. On one occasion this was at my doctor's suggestion. He said, "Don't worry about things ... but sit down quietly and have a cigarette."'[55] Fiction also reinforced the link between smoking and emotional control – heavy smoking was a comfort to both the good and the bad. In *Love Betrayed*, a 'nice' young woman is described 'smoking cigarette after cigarette, for what seemed like hours' when in a state of considerable anxiety after being framed for theft by her fiancé.[56] After being cornered into a confession of murder, the 'daughter of Satan', Sadie Bracken, smoked a chain of cigarettes as 'she walked up and down the room, hour after hour'.[57]

Because of its soothing effects, smoking was also lauded as a promoter of social harmony. Ms Corbett, for instance, argued that the 'only good thing about smoking is that it soothes the nerves of most people, thus making for peace and quiet in circumstances where without tobacco there might be unrest'.[58] Smoking was also heralded as a facilitator of social interactions. This was a prominent theme in advertising: 'Breaking the ice' declared one cigarette advertisement featuring a woman and two men smoking together.[59] By 1939 many of the women smokers who responded to a Mass-Observation survey on smoking extolled the personal and social benefits – indeed the necessity – of cigarettes: the consensus was that, as one woman expressed it, 'it is more sensible to smoke a little'.[60]

Smoking was presented as an appropriate response by women to the strains and new social situations they experienced in wartime. With the outbreak of hostilities women smokers appeared in advertisements for a range of products, for example the uniformed 'butterfly' at the wheel of an ambulance in a cosmetics advertisement and a WAAF (Women's Auxiliary Air Force) in a government information poster promoting Post Office Savings.[61] Illustrations of women smoking while 'doing their bit' also featured in occasional cigarette advertisements (occasional primarily because advertising was restricted during the war and increasingly male-oriented: see Chapter 3[62]). In 1939 an advertisement for Wills' Gold Flake featured a woman from the Auxiliary Fire Service with a cigarette in her mouth: 'A specialised job for trained personnel. Driving staff cars and light lorries, and important work in the watchroom and at the switchboard'.[63] A decade later, Player's portrayed a land girl atop her tractor leaning down to take a light for her cigarette from a passing young man.[64]

Recognition that tobacco was a legitimate need for women as well as men, rather than merely a luxury, was articulated in a series of advertisements for sweets. One targeted at workers in 'looms, lathes, launderies', where 'it's no smoking by order', portrayed a serious-looking woman worker.

When smoking's not allowed work can be a misery. But pop a Rowntree Fruit Gum or Pastille into your mouth – at once that craving goes – that 'want something in my mouth' feeling goes. Life's brighter – work's easier. There's more than the taste of fruit in Rowntree's Gums or Pastilles – they *soothe* and *protect* the mouth and throat in a way no other sweets can. Lasting relief![65]

A language of dependence is used without censure in this advertisement. 'Craving' and 'misery' are experienced by smokers denied a cigarette but, when they are satisfied by a substitute, life becomes 'brighter' and easier' once again. Cigarette advertisements during the war often emphasized this theme. At the outbreak of war, Player's advised magazine and newspaper readers to 'Keep that happy expression'.[66] As the advertisements explained: 'When the problems of the day seem beyond you, light up a "Player". In the enjoyment of its fragrant aroma difficulties become less formidable and composure is restored.'[67]

The woman smoker's respectability was not, however, automatically safe-guarded by the prevalent discourse of need. Public displays of smoking by women were often frowned upon. Taboos still existed against women smoking in the streets, as evident in letters to *The Times* in 1944.[68] Even women smokers were often opposed to this practice: 'This sounds very silly coming from me, but I just can't bear to see a woman smoking in the street, not even in these days.'[69] The respectability of woman in uniform, especially those in the Auxiliary Territorial Service (ATS), was particularly fragile, as conveyed in a cartoon in *The Sketch*.[70] An ATS girl in full uniform, heavily made up and with a cigarette in her mouth, goes into a cosmetics shop and explains to the assistant: 'I want toning down a little – I'm going home on leave'. ATS director Leslie Whateley, received 'various complaints and criticisms ... as to the bad impression created by auxiliaries smoking while walking in the street, sitting in a bus or standing on a station platform'. Whateley 'agreed with these criticisms, for to my way of thinking such habits looked unattractive and unfeminine in civilian clothes, and in uniform worse.'[71] In response to these concerns, Whateley issued an instruction in March 1944 whereby auxiliaries were not allowed to smoke in public. The instruction was, however, too vague and, following many queries, a set of rules were issued. As *The Times* explained,

Smoking is not permitted now when on duty, except where normally permitted by local rule; in streets or built-up areas; on railway stations or in station approaches, except in station buffets; in railway station, cinema or theatre queues; in buses, trams, tubes, or underground trains, or in shops, except in the tea rooms or restaurants. Members of the A.T.S. may smoke on long railway journeys, in smoking compartments, or in the corridors, and at sports meetings and similar events in the open air. When smoking is permitted the officer or auxiliary need not remove her cap unless she wishes to.[72]

In the House of Commons it was argued that preventing members of the ATS from smoking in public would 'ensure that the appearance of the auxiliaries did credit to their Service'.[73]

Objections to women – and in particular those in the ATS – smoking in the streets reveal the continued significance for women smokers of the relationship between social class, sexuality and respectability. For reasons similar to those on the precariousness of glamour for working-class women smokers, a uniformed woman who smoked in the street was seen to parade herself, to make a spectacle of herself and to thereby imply sexual laxity. The reason for which the smokers of the ATS, rather than other Services, was picked on was that the ATS was the 'Cinderella service' with a reputation for sexual immorality, a reputation no doubt enhanced by its principally working-class composition compared to that of other women's Services.[74] The ATS woman was, however, in a double bind. If she smoked and emphasized her femininity and heterosexuality she was criticized for being brazen and unrespectable. If she smoked, but played down signs of her femininity, she risked appearing too masculine and this smacked of aping men and/or expressing a lesbian identity, neither of which were respectably feminine.

A Matter of Appearances

Respectable smoking was a matter largely of appearances, and refinement was key to this. Refinement was, however, not always easy for smokers to achieve. Lipstick marks on a cigarette were an 'unforgivable sin', according to one cosmetics advertisement.[75] Red-tipped cigarettes were specially designed to remedy this and ensure that lipstick did not leave the 'shameless smear that has taken the edge off so many promising affairs':[76]

> The modern girl is a work of art. She knows how to make the most of her looks. But she is also careful not to offend. Observe those cherry-ripe lips. Then observe the end of the cigarette they have been caressing. Her escort's eyes are upon it. Are they affronted by an ugly smear of lipstick …?[77]

Smoking also posed other threats to refinement, as some cigarette advertisements made explicit: '[I]t is the little refinements of a woman's appearance that men notice – whiteness of hands, softness of lips. You who smoke have to be particularly careful about these details.'[78] The importance of managing the finer details of appearance was also emphasized in promotions for products to counteract the visible effects of smoking. As an advertisement for Eucryl explained with reference to the 'modern girl', 'Modern in ideas and ways she smokes quite a lot, and never questions whether anything will stain her teeth or not. But she does not neglect them.'[79] This and other advertisements for dental preparations portrayed the female smoker as attractive and young. Heavy smoking was not deemed a problem as long as the visible threats to beauty were counteracted and refinement was protected.

Most women wanted to be perceived as respectable when they smoked, and the increased respectability of smoking in the years 1920–1950 therefore facilitated women's adoption of the cigarette habit. However, respectable smoking could be elusive for working-class women, particularly prior to 1939. Although dominant conceptions of feminine respectability were changing, they did so more slowly for working-class women than for their sisters higher up the social scale. As the cases of the glamorous working-class woman and the ATS woman reveal, the sexual respectability of the working-class woman smoker was fragile even in the context of the acceptance of smoking as a legitimate individual and social need. However, as Andrew Davies notes, subjective definitions of respectability are remarkably fluid and most people want to class themselves as respectable.[80] It seems likely, then, that – irrespective of what others thought – most working-class women smokers were not intent on appearing 'fast'. Indeed they frequently mentioned that they wanted to look 'posh' or 'smart' when they smoked. As the choice of words suggests, these women envisaged themselves acting-up in class terms: the cigarette facilitated the performance of 'class'. Indeed, the cigarette was often part of a carefully crafted appearance, and women took considerable care with their grooming. 'Bell', who started smoking in Glasgow in the 1950s, was advised to 'make sure you brush your teeth, use a fresh hair spray'.[81] Concerns about respectability did, however, inhibit some – mainly working-class – women from smoking in public until after the Second World War. Whether working-class women smoked in private or in public, and whether this was condoned or not, they could still be part of an 'imagined community' of respectable, modern and glamorous smokers, a community produced in visual culture through advertising, fashion and film.

Not all women smokers were concerned to be thoroughly respectable. Challenging dominant and/or traditional notions of respectability was the attraction of smoking for some, usually upper-middle and upper-class women. The challenge that smoking posed to feminine respectability was two-fold. First, the shocking attractions of smoking were its symbolic association with 'fast' women. Second, the challenge related to definitions of refinement and whether the practice of smoking infringed these. Prior to 1914, women's smoking challenged *dominant* conceptions of feminine respectability. The social standing of elite women allowed them some leeway to play with notions of feminine respectability, partly because their sexual reputations were not as fragile as those of their working-class sisters. Moreover, when they challenged dominant conceptions of respectability they retained some protection from social censure by virtue of their class status, although not all middle- and upper-class women smokers were safe from criticism or even harassment (see Chapter 2).

By the interwar period, because conceptions of respectability were changing, especially among the upper and middle classes, smoking could more effectively be used to challenge *traditional* conceptions of respectability. Because of this, smoking could be employed as a sign of modernity and rebellion against one's elders. In this instance the shock value of smoking stemmed from age-related differences in perspective. Generation became of increased importance in the twentieth century, particularly after 1919. In the 1920s, as Mannin noted, the generation gap was not just among the 'bohemians' but also among the 'respectable middle classes'.[82] While smoking increasingly achieved respectability for younger members of the middle and upper classes, older members of these class communities often operated with different, and more traditional, notions of respectability. Smoking served for some young women, therefore, as a means of shocking the older generation and of asserting their independence and difference from them. By the mid-1920s, especially in London, the shock value was much reduced. Two women 'bought "Amber" scented cigarettes at five for a shilling, and smoked in public at a teashop'. Though they thought this 'very fast', they were, according to Mass Observation, 'disappointed when there was no apparent sensation'.[83] A generational shock was more easily produced outside the large cities. Margaret Rowntree remembered that 'it was "fashionable" to have a surreptitious smoke occasionally – not usually "done" in this provincial town [Fleetwood, Lancashire]'.[84]

Conclusion

Sexual reputation and refinement were both key to respectable smoking for women, but bodily refinement was pivotal to the *display* of respectability. Refinement was a visual marker and, therefore, important in a world that relied heavily, and increasingly, on visual cues.[85] The emphasis on appearance, and especially the body, was not incidental, it is a visible surface and has long been used to represent respectability;[86] moreover, as Bourdieu argues, the body is the 'most ubiquitous signifier of class'.[87] The absence of unrefined images of women smokers indicates the visual parameters of respectability and the implicit class nature of this. As Skeggs notes, the 'display of respectability' was 'a signifier of *not* being working class'.[87] In the period 1920–1950, feminine respectability was visually compatible with being working-class, but only if a working-class woman did not compromise her refinement, and thereby her respectability, by being seen to smoke. The absence of images of working-class women smokers between 1920 and 1950 suggests that smoking was visibly inconsistent with refined and respectable working-class femininity.

The prevalence in visual culture of refined middle- and upper-class women smokers was not solely due to the promotion of a particular conception of respectable smoking. It was also the outcome of aesthetic considerations. Although advertisements obviously used images of attractive and refined women smokers, this also applied to other visual media. Visual images of women's bodies, or parts of them, were regularly, and increasingly, used to attract attention, to sell goods and services, and to give pleasure. There was little demand for unattractive images of women, let alone unrefined women smokers.

Notes

1. Davies, *Leisure, Gender and Poverty*, pp. 67, 172. See also Giles, *Women, Identity and Private Life*, especially Chapter 3.

2. Nead, *Myths of Sexuality*, p. 190.

3. Skeggs, *Formations*, p. 3.

4. Nead, *Myths of Sexuality*; Skeggs, *Formations*; Giles, 'Playing Hard to Get'.

5. Winship, 'New disciplines'; Skeggs, *Formations*, p. 84.

6. Giles, *Women, Identity and Private Life*, Chapter 3. Victorian representations of the respectable poor were also characterized by containment: see Nead, *Myths of Sexuality*, p. 37.

7. McKibbin, *Classes and Cultures*, p. 28.

8. *Daily Express*, 15 November 1928, p. 19.

9. *Vogue*, 8 February 1928, p. 10.

10. For example Daisy Cardew, *Girls' Friend*, 16 May 1925, pp. 7–8, discussed in Chapter 5.

11. Haskell, *From Reverence to Rape*, p. 79.

12. *Girls' Friend*, 23 May 1925, p. 6. For further discussion see Tinkler, 'Refinement and Respectable Consumption', p. 347.

13. Giles, 'Playing Hard to Get', pp. 242–3; McKibbin, *Classes and Cultures*, pp. 198–201; Nead, *Myths of Sexuality*, pp. 37, 179.

14. Burt, *Young Delinquent*, Preface, pp. ix–x (figs 9 and 20).

15. Elliot, 'Destructive but Sweet', pp. 300–1.

16. Ibid., p. 301.

17. Tinkler, *Constructing Girlhood*, pp. 27–35.

18. Winship, 'New disciplines'.

19. Breward, *Culture of Fashion*, pp. 183, 187; Wilson and Taylor, *Through the Looking Glass*, Chapter 3; Alexander, 'Becoming a Woman', Buckley and Fawcett, *Fashioning the Feminine*, Chapter 4.

20. Wilson and Taylor, *Through the Looking Glass*, p. 88.

21. Cited in Steele, *Fashion and Eroticism*, p. 237.

22. Wilson and Taylor, *Through the Looking Glass*, pp. 88–9; Horwood, *Keeping Up Appearances*.

23. See for example Rice, *Working-Class Wives*.

24. For example *Woman*, 14 August 1937, pp. 18–19, featured a story about a women's lodging house that was home to extremely poor women who were, with the exception of one middle-class woman who had fallen on hard times, of working-class background. There was no reference to smoking in the illustration or the text.

25. For example, an advertisement depicted a woman in a French couture evening dress (*Miss Modern*, January 1931, p. 66).

26. *Miss Modern*, July 1931, p. iv.

27. *Woman*, 24 June 1950, p. 33.

28. Stacey, *Star Gazing*, p. 154.

29. *Glamour:* 9 September 1939, p. 15; 4 November 1939, p. 11.

30. Cited in Skeggs, *Formations*, p. 110.

31. Valverde, 'The Love of Finery', pp. 169–88.

32. Mayhew, *London Labour*, p. 257, also pp. 216, 220.

33. Nead, *Myths of Sexuality*.

34. 'Dire poverty is less often a reason for such behaviour [sexual promiscuity] than is the desire of girls earning a moderate wage to have a good time and to dress in the prevailing fashion.' Cited in Durant, *Problem of Leisure*, p. 94.

35. Jacobs, *Wages of Sin*; Rosen, *Popcorn Venus*; Haskell, *From Reverence to Rape*.

36. Brittain, *Testament*, p. 429.

37. *Glamour*, 9 September 1939, p. 19. The series ran to November 1939.

38. Ibid., p. 34.

39. Kobal, *Hollywood Portrait Photographers*, p. 51.

40. Koetzle, *Seductive Smoke*, p. 11.

41. *Miss Modern*, March 1931, p. 8.

42. *Woman*: 15 July 1939, p. 33; 5 August 1939, p. 40; 1 July 1939, p. 51.

43. Walkerdine, 'Dreams from an Ordinary Childhood', p. 162.

44. *Woman*, 2 January 1943, p. 16.

45. *Miss Modern*, January 1939, p. 39.

46. Tinkler, *Constructing Girlhood*, pp. 153–61.

47. Winship, 'New disciplines', p. 32.

48. *Woman*, 28 October 1939, p. 44.

49. McKibbin, *Classes and Cultures*, pp. 61–2.

50. Giles, *Women, Identity and Private Life*, p. 151; see Samuel, 'Suburbs under Siege', p. 28. Alexander, 'Becoming a Woman', p. 250 refers to hands ingrained with dirt being 'the mark of poverty and domestic labour' and as therefore incompatible with feminine respectability.

51. Chris Shilling cited in Winship, 'New Disciplines', p. 31.

52. *Daily Express*, 22 July 1939, p. 5. See also *Daily Mirror*, 22 July 1939, p. 24.

53. National Archive, MH 58/649.

54. *Modern Woman*, March 1939, pp. 55, 58.

55. MOA TC 63 1/B Clayton; also, MOA FR 979, p. 28.

56. *Glamour*, 24 June 1939, p. 32.

57. *Lucky Star*, 19 October, 1935, p. 5.

58. MOA TC 63 1/B Corbett.

59. *Daily Mirror*, 26 July 1939, p. 5.

60. MOA FR 979, p. 44.

61. *Miss Modern*, February 1940, p. 27. McDowell, *Forties Fashions*, p. 50.

62. In North America the woman smoker remained commonplace in wartime advertising (Warsh and Tinkler, 'In Vogue').

63. *Woman,* 25 November 1939, p. 44.

64. *Sketch*, 4 January 1950, p. 1. Also see use of WREN's head on showcards, countercards and tins for Player's Medium. Player's DDPL 6/22/1 Advertiser's Stock Lists.

65. *News of the World*, 2 July 1939, p. 4.

66. *Sunday Express*, 30 July 1939, p. 3.

67. *Vogue*, October 1940, p. 93; see also August 1940, p. 60.

68. *The Times*, 1 November 1944, p. 5; also 4 November 1944, p. 5.

69. MOA, FR 3192, p. 71. This taboo was also noted by Barraud, MOA TC 63 1/B.

70. *Sketch*, 10 March 1943, p. 114.

71. Hartley, *Hearts Undefeated*, p. 113.

72. *The Times*, 29 March 1944, p. 2.

73. Comment from Sir John Grigg. Hansard 4 April 1944.

74. Braybon and Summerfield, *Out of the Cage*, pp. 163–5.

75. *Woman*, 13 February 1943, p. 2.

76. *Woman*, 11 September 1937, p. 2.

77. *Woman*, 14 August 1937, p. 2.

78. *Woman*, 28 October 1939, p. 43; see also 8 July 1939, p. 2.

79. *Woman and Home*, February 1935, p. 75.

80. Davies, *Leisure, Gender and Poverty*.

81. Thanks to Rosemary Elliot for this quotation from her interview transcript with 'Bell', p. 6.

82. Mannin, *Young in the Twenties*, p. 51.

83. MOA FR 3192, p. 72.

84. MOA TC 63 1/C Rowntree.

85. See Chapter 1 and, in relation to magazines specifically, Stein, 'The Graphic Ordering of Desire', p. 146.

86. Nineteenth-century art represented a distinction between respectability and non-respectability in terms of physical deviancy (Nead, *Myths of Sexuality*, p. 172).

87. Skeggs, *Formations*, p. 82.

88. Ibid., p. 47.

7

Look at Me Smoking: Revealing Portraits?

Propped against the wooden post of a porch or terrace, an Edwardian woman stares at the viewer, a lit cigarette in her hand, the ash building up (see Fig. 7.1). The woman, Lallie Charles, stands out because she appears to be smoking in a period when this was a minority practice among women and, moreover, rarely depicted in a photographic portrait. Patricia Holland advises that although photographs 'may tempt the reader to engage in the detective project and to deconstruct stories

Figure 7.1 Lallie Charles by Compton Collier (NPG x68996). © reserved; collection National Portrait Gallery, London.

155

from these tentative clues, the empirical historian would do well to treat them with extreme caution'.[1] However this portrait of Lallie Charles remains enticing. Is it revealing of women's relationship to smoking and, if so, in what ways?

Roland Barthes asserts that a distinctive feature of a photograph is its 'evidential force'.[2] The photograph provides evidence that what is in the frame was actually in front of the camera at some point in time. Barthes does 'not take the photograph for a "copy" of reality' – for him, the photograph's significance is that it is 'literally an emanation of the referent. From a real body, which was there, proceed radiations which ultimately touch me'.[3] The emphasis, as Marianne Hirsch explains, is not on the content of the photograph but the presence it records; but this is a 'controversial reading of photographic reference'.[4] For critics of Barthes, the importance of photographs does not lie in a reality that 'lies "behind" the paper or "behind" the image'.[5] There are two main reasons for this. First, '*every* photograph is the result of specific and, in every sense, significant distortions which render its relation to any prior reality deeply problematic and raise the question of the determining level of the material apparatus and of the social practices within which photography takes place.'[6] Second, as photographs are only ever made sense of by social beings, what lies 'behind' the paper/image for the viewer is necessarily only 'reference': that is, 'a subtle web of discourse through which realism is enmeshed in a complex fabric of notions, representations, images, attitudes, gestures and modes of action which function as everyday know-how, "practical ideology", norms within and through which people live their relation to the world.'[7] John Tagg insists that the question we should ask of a photograph is, therefore, 'how does it animate meaning rather than discover it; where must we be positioned to accept it as real or true; and what are the consequences of doing so?'[8] 'Evidential force' is, Tagg argues, 'a complex historical outcome and is exercised by photographs only within certain institutional practices and within particular historical relations'.[9] How people see colour is a case in point. In the 'photographic world' of the early twentieth century, as photographer Madame Yevonde lamented, 'you would stroll in the gardens and gaze on black geraniums, and sit on a white lawn under black trees' because this world was 'entirely without colour'. Photographers thought colour was 'unnecessary and *unnatural* (my emphasis)' and the general public had 'become so used to photographs in black and white that a colour photograph seems to them to be an error in taste'.[10]

Rather than asking abstract questions about whether a photograph can be trusted as evidence, Howard Becker suggests, we need to think about the question(s) a photograph *could* answer.[11] My concern in this chapter is not to ask whether a photograph of a woman holding a cigarette is evidence that women smoked.[12] Rather, I am interested in discovering why women were willing to appear in photographs as smokers and what they hoped to convey about themselves. Addressing these questions directs attention to the photographic image and also to the 'materiality of the photograph' illuminating it 'as an object which was posed, taken, made, acquired, circulated, used, collected'.[13] As Susan Sontag notes, 'one never understands anything from a photograph' because understanding is based on discovering how something 'functions': 'And functioning takes place in time … Only that which narrates can make us understand.'[14] To understand the meaning of photographs involves locating them within two interconnected narratives – the production of the image and the uses made of the photograph-as-object.

Contextualization is key to this project. The context of the photographic occasion is constituted by the interpersonal dynamics between photographer and subject(s), the motivations and skills of the photographer and the aims of the subject(s). It also involves the possibilities afforded by photographic technologies, photographic conventions, and visual discourses. Photographs can also be contextualized in relation to how they have been used and the meanings invested in them by the owner(s). Unravelling the meaning of a photograph is problematic because as with all sources the historian must distinguish between the meaning for the users/owners as opposed to the readers/audience.[15] Discovering the subject's/user's meanings is complicated further by the context in which the photographs are encountered. If we are lucky the original frame is still intact and some of the owner's meanings can be teased out – for example, if the photo appears in the original photograph album or in the form of a postcard that has been used by the subject(s).[16] More often, though, the photograph is dislodged from its original frame and context. Sometimes a thread of connection anchors the image in general terms, as when a photograph surfaces among possessions inherited by a grandchild, but often, 'with the passage of time its moorings come unstuck. It drifts away into a soft abstract pastness, open to any kind of reading'.[17] The loss of original context need not be a product of history. Photographs can be reframed deliberately and recontextualized for the purposes of contemporary media. As demonstrated by Laura Doan's charting of photographs of the author Radclyffe Hall that were initially released to the press in 1926 and subsequently reused by newspapers to fit changing perceptions of Hall, this process produces new meanings and ones not necessarily intended by the subject.[18]

Photographs of women smoking are not just about women's relationship to tobacco, but about women's relationship to tobacco within the photographic frame. In the context of personal and/or commissioned photographs, the meanings attached to smoking are inextricably bound up with the meanings attached to being visually recorded. This chapter explores the shifting photographic opportunities for women to appear smoking and how some women used these opportunities to make statements about themselves. It begins with the late Victorian and Edwardian period when images of women smokers began to appear in private photo collections, both 'joke' photographs and also 'serious' photographs intended as 'identity statements'. The chapter then proceeds to the interwar period and the emergence of professional photographic portraits of women smokers, which frequently circulated widely and publicly.

Late Victorian and Edwardian Photographs

Photographs of women smoking are scarce prior to 1920. While this is indicative of smoking as a minority practice among women, it is revealing, more importantly, of photographic conventions and the status both of women and of smoking. Being photographed smoking was inconsistent with the conventions of late Victorian and Edwardian portrait photography. Inherited from the tradition of portrait painting, professional photographic portraits were 'one of the symbolic acts by which individuals from the rising social classes made their ascent visible to themselves and others and classed themselves among those who enjoyed social status.'[19] Portraits were commissioned to celebrate achievements in the public sphere, to commemorate marriages and the building of a family, and to chart the development and even the death of children.[20] Smoking was not commonly regarded as consistent with femininity – even if women did smoke it was unseemly to be seen doing so and inappropriate to be recorded for posterity with a cigarette in hand.[21] Frivolous use of professional services was a possibility for the affluent, but these experiments were for private purposes and, for the most part, unconventional photographs have escaped the historical record. Photographers were unlikely to admit publicly to producing pictures that could jeopardize standards of propriety and threaten their social and professional standing. Being for the most part members of the 'petite bourgeoisie', photographers had much invested in protecting their respectability.[22] When Richard Speaight was asked to photograph a 'lady of title' in her 'knickers and camisole, smoking a cigarette' and sitting with her 'legs crossed', he insisted the photographs were unsigned while his client insisted that the plates be destroyed.[23] For the less affluent, itinerant photographers offered an affordable service, but there was still a tendency to adhere to the conventions of professional photographic studios; propriety was still a concern for this group.[24] Aside from this, as Holland observes: 'The poorer the community, the less directly are their daily activities reflected in the pictures they keep. Those who lived in the inner city tenements remained anxious to record the formality and dignity of their life'.[25]

Around 1900, photographic practices began to change. Itinerant photographers, especially those working at the seaside, began to digress from portrait conventions to produce less formal and more intimate photographs of people at leisure.[26] Amateur photographs, facilitated by the launch of the Kodak camera in the 1880s and then the box Brownie in 1900, also expanded opportunities for women to appear in new ways. In the context of shifts in photographic opportunities and conventions, women were occasionally featured smoking. Although some professional photographs of women smoking can be found, most photographs of women smoking prior to the 1920s are amateur productions. The low visual profile of women smokers in professional photography mirrored that in the print media and, indeed, in public (see Chapter 2). Early photographs of women smoking, whether professional or amateur, were for personal use. While amateur photos could sometimes catch women smoking unawares, in most posed photographs it was rarely incidental for women to appear smoking.

In late Victorian and Edwardian Britain smoking remained primarily associated with men and masculinities. Although women's smoking was increasingly aligned with modern womanhood, it nevertheless retained its older associations with feminine licentiousness. The masculine and sexual associations did not, however, prevent women from playing with the significations of smoking in front of the camera.

'Joke' Photographs

With a cigarette in the corner of her mouth and wearing a soldier's uniform, Bessie Clinton playfully posed for the camera as a man; only her dainty shoes belied her gender.[27] Within the photographic frame other women toyed with the sexual connotations of smoking. In Bolton, around 1915, three women posed for a photograph (Fig. 7.2). Two of the women, each holding a cigarette, sit either side of a table on which there are glasses of dark fluid; a soda siphon gives the impression that this is liqueur. A third woman leans on the back of her friend's chair with one hand on her hip and the other holding a cigarette. The aim was to suggest that the women were 'fast'. The women's poses were particularly revealing (the seated have their legs crossed and the standing woman has her hand on her hips), and in clear disregard of photographic conventions. The following advice from 1861 represented standard photographic practice well into the 1900s: 'The pose of a lady should not have that boldness of action which you would give a man, but be modest and retiring, the arms describing gentle curves, and the feet never far apart.'[28] As Linkman explains, men, in contrast, 'were allowed greater assurance and assertiveness. This was achieved by means of crossed legs, elbows out at angles, with canes and umbrellas projecting into the space around them.'[29] The posture of the standing woman reminds us that the physical act of smoking was in itself a radical departure from feminine standards of appearance and gesticulation. The bar/lounge setting, the alcohol and cigarettes, were essential props that worked in conjunction with the poses of the women to suggest sexual licence. This photograph was a 'joke', and clearly so.

For the joke to work, the idea the photograph conveyed – that the women were 'fast' – had to be far-removed from reality. In this instance, the sexual propriety of the women had to be so clearly established for their intended viewers that the

*Figure 7.2   A 'joke' photograph (DPA 608/31). Reproduced by permission of the DPA,
Greater Manchester County Record Office.*

sexual meaning of the image could not be mistaken as real. To safeguard against
misreading the photograph, its construction was also made visible. The photo was
clearly contrived and no effort had been made to hide signs of this. The domestic
or lounge-bar setting was achieved by the use of a backcloth that ended abruptly
within the photographic frame, the flagstones of the yard were also visible on one
side of the photo, and there was a discarded chair in the photo which suggests that
some experimenting took place before the right effect was achieved. Whether this
contrivance was revealed to friends and family was a matter of choice. How this
picture was shown to viewers, and in particular how it was framed, could hide or
reveal evidence of the production of the image.

   This photo was most likely orchestrated by the women who posed for it, for what
purpose is unknown. That this particular copy of the photo belonged to their friend,
Mrs Florence Robinson, suggests that the 'joke' was shared with at least one friend
and perhaps others. The photograph reveals a modern fascination with image and
image making. But the representation of smoking reveals a more complex relation
to modernity. The photograph testifies to the dominant and long-established idea
of women's smoking as a practice engaged in principally by the disreputable. It

also hints at the new and complex relationship for women between smoking and modernity. Although in some social circles smoking was being redefined as a signifier of women's modernity and emancipation, these interpretations did not apply, or they did so only shakily, to smoking by women from the lower-middle and working classes: only the most socially secure could play with the modernity of smoking without damaging their social standing. Although the women came from fairly prosperous upper-working-class backgrounds,[30] these women could not openly smoke without endangering their social status (see Chapter 6).

Seventy years later, when this photograph was archived, the playful nature of its content was stressed. Reflecting an awareness of the instability of meaning, Mrs Robinson's daughter thought it appropriate to fix this through explanation. This was probably because the reputations of the women and their friend, Mrs Robinson, hinged on the 'correct' interpretation of the photo – the donor pointed out that the cigarettes and drink were not real, the women were just 'pretending to be fast'.[31] Whether Mrs Robinson's friends actually smoked cannot be ascertained from this image. What is more important is that for these women, posing for the camera as smokers was probably only possible, or desirable, in the context of play-acting or joking. At this particular time, the modernity of smoking was beyond the reach of these women even if the respectability afforded by their upper-working-class status facilitated the making of jokes about smoking. It is unlikely to be a coincidence that the archives reveal upper-working-class and middle-class women making 'joke' photographs of themselves smoking, but there is no evidence of a similar practice among women lower down the social scale. Social class was an important factor shaping whether women felt able to smoke in a photograph and how. Not all women who were photographed smoking did so as a 'joke'. For some women, usually those from the upper echelons of society, smoking could be used to make identity statements.

Identity Statements

The constructions of femininity achieved by women who were photographed smoking were very different to those typical of most professional portraiture, whether photographic or painted. The portrait is traditionally, as Tagg explains, 'a sign whose purpose is both the description of an individual and the inscription of social identity'.[32] Tagg does not elucidate the relationship between these elements but, as Audrey Linkman shows, social identity provided the lens through which description could occur. Victorian photographers worked with fixed notions of how to represent women, men and children from different social classes.[33] Character was a pivotal concern of portrait photography, but for the majority this was interpreted through stereotypes. Women's character was invariably defined through the dominant feminine roles of daughter, wife and mother. Eminent people required attention to the individuality of character,[34] but public distinction, with few exceptions (Queen Victoria), was a masculine domain. Professional portraiture, whether painted or photographic, denied women individuality. For instance, the portraiture produced by professional photographer Lallie Charles, 'was not about the representation of individual character, nor the portrayal of ideas, but of the personification of the late Edwardian type, the softly-proportioned and languid beauty.'[35] In the realm of professional photography this did not change until the 1920s, and even then individuality remained the prerogative of specific social groups.[36] Entitled 'The New Feminine photography', a *Punch* cartoon in 1926 depicted an elderly male photographer attempting to photograph a bold and boyish modern woman who insisted, 'I don't want one of those sloppy pictures. Just get the character and let it go at that.' This, as Doan points out, is a 'complicated task' for the photographer, given the 'the apparent incongruities' of the woman's appearance.[37] It is also a novel request and testimony to a shift in photographic practice that occurred by the mid-1920s from one where women appeared in stereotyped 'sloppy pictures' to one where some claimed their right to individual 'character'.

Spurred by the move for women's rights and emancipation and by modern consumer practices, individual identity became increasingly desirable for women. Amateur photography and the services of itinerant photographers did offer the chance for some women to express visually a more individuated self and, indeed, to experiment with visual identity before the 1920s. Posing with a cigarette in a photograph was used by some women as a statement of identity and, more especially, as an articulation of a modern identity. Their modernity was achieved in two ways. The practice of self representation was one way in which women expressed a modern identity. Personal photos have an important role in the modernization of Western culture, as photography is a medium through which

> individuals confirm and explore identity, that sense of self-identity which is an indispensable feature of a modern sensibility – for in Western urban culture it is as *individuals* that people have come to experience themselves, independently of their role as family members or as occupying a recognised social position.[38]

This modern sensibility is made particularly clear when women deliberately posed for the camera in unconventional ways, for instance by smoking. The importance of smoking is heightened by the fact that at this time it was not generally perceived as compatible with a woman's family position or social standing, but was an act associated with individuality and even radicalism for a woman. Women who posed for the camera with cigarettes exemplified the modern practice of individual identity construction.

A second way in which these women expressed a modern identity was through the specific detail of the self portrait. Transgression of the conventions of feminine representation was one aspect of this: these women made spectacles of themselves, albeit for a limited number of viewers. Women who appeared in photographs in anything other than traditional and very contained poses established themselves as unconventional and as defiant of feminine ideals of composure. Smoking, and the posture assumed when doing so, invariably transgressed Victorian conventions. The gender defiance of their composure was heightened by the radical associations of women's tobacco use.

Smoking, particularly of cigarettes, has often been presented as a way in which Western women signalled their modernity and, especially, their emancipation. Schudson, for example, refers to North-American women using smoking to mark their distinctiveness from the past, to express their place in modern times, to 'display their modernity'.[39] But what kind of modernity did smoking help British women construct and convey in photographic portraits? Photographs of Lallie Charles and Muriel de Wend illustrate some of the ways in which women expressed their modernity when they posed for the camera with a cigarette, and these portraits also reveal differences in the ways women utilized cigarettes in the construction of identities.[40]

Around 1910, Lallie Charles (1869–1919) posed with a cigarette for photographer Compton Collier (Fig. 7.1).[41] This was one of several informal photographs and was probably taken in the context of friendship.[42] This photograph is particularly interesting because Charles was an extremely successful photographer. Her portraits of Society women appeared in *The Lady's Realm*, and she also contributed an article on women photographers to *Everywoman's Encyclopaedia*. During the late nineteenth and early twentieth centuries, photography was a growing and respectable profession for middle-class women who were intent on being financially independent and/or who sought an escape from the 'tedium of enforced middle-class unemployment'.[43] Charles was one of these women and, assisted initially by her younger sisters, she opened a photographic studio in 1900. Charles made a speciality of photographing wealthy women. In her London studio, she created an atmosphere of feminine and romantic luxury. Amid rose-coloured silk curtains and pink velvet chairs, Charles 'pictured her subjects as elegant innocents', 'passive and forever girlish'.[44] A typical portrait featured the subject posed 'dressed in lace against a softly lit window and gazing submissively towards the floor'.[45] Charles's penchant for romantic and feminine imagery emerges in Collier's portrait of her, but the similarity ends there. Charles chooses not to appear as ornamental and submissive, and she uses the cigarette and pose to construct a more modern, assertive and active persona.

The photo was taken outdoors with Charles, her back against a wooden post, framed on one side by a clipped tree and ivy and, on the other, by a stone wall. The cigarette, like everything else in the photograph, was quite deliberately included and, along with some golf clubs in the background, signalled that she was a modern and active middle-class woman; the outdoor setting reinforced this impression. Lallie Charles, however, by virtue of her profession and accomplishment, posed a quite visible challenge to Victorian conceptions of domesticated femininity. Perhaps in reference to this status and achievement, Charles stands out, almost luminescent, against the background in the photograph. The direct look into the camera reinforced the impression of a woman with direction. Except where 'disclosure' was important, as in wedding photographs,[46] women usually have their gaze averted; 'frontality' was most often the preserve of men and signified strength, courage and engagement.[47] Crossed legs and a hand in a pocket were also poses typical of men rather than of women. The signifiers of modern, emancipated and independent womanhood were, however, softened by visual reference to Charles's heterosexual attractiveness. This was reinforced by the soft and sensual drapes of her costume which consisted of a light-coloured skirt and long-sleeved jacket open in a deep V-shape at the neck, and a string of beads. This representation of modern womanhood was quite different to that conveyed in photographs of Muriel de Wend in the context of war and its aftermath.

The First World War provided opportunities for some upper-middle- and upper-class women to escape the confines of feminine life and expectations.[48] In this context, as we saw in Chapter 2, it seems likely that many started to smoke or did so more openly. Muriel de Wend trained as a nurse and then in 1916, aged twenty three, she joined the FANY Motor Ambulance Convoy in France, and in 1918 was promoted to Lance Corporal. In letters to her mother, de Wend described how much she enjoyed FANY life and especially the sociability it afforded: 'I love being here. It is rather like being at school again, my four special friends are the nicest girls you could possibly meet.'[49] De Wend, known by her colleagues as 'Wendy', took a number of photographs of her wartime life, many of which portray her and her colleagues and friends smoking.[50] These photographs from 1917 and 1918 were arranged in an album and, along with some loose photographs relating to the FANYs, were eventually passed down to her daughters and then to the Imperial War Museum.

Photographs of de Wend, and also her correspondence, confirm the place of smoking in the routines and rituals of daily life for the FANYs, but they also reveal the importance of smoking for individual and collective identities. Cigarettes are not concealed in photographs of Muriel de Wend and her friends – indeed, the place of smoking in their lives is made explicit. In some photos the cigarette is incidental; importantly, it is not hidden or extinguished. In other photos the cigarette is more self-consciously featured or the significance of smoking is drawn out by de Wend's annotations in her album.

Cigarettes served several, interrelated purposes in Muriel de Wend's visual and textual accounts. Cigarettes paraded de Wend's modernity and emancipation and, especially in her photographs, they convey toughness, independence and knowledge of the ways of the world. The photo of de Wend at her billet in France is illustrative of this (Fig. 7.3).[51] Perched against the door jamb, with her arms in a seemingly uncomfortable position as she tucked both hands in her pockets, de Wend looked directly at the camera with a cigarette drooping from the front of her mouth. There is nothing glamorous about this image, it is quite simply a statement of Muriel de Wend's right to be serving in the war and to smoke. Both of these rights had traditionally been primarily male ones, but women's experiences of the battlefront contributed to the erosion of these traditions. Women at the front 'shared the inconveniences, risks, and dangers of the fighting men', they were exposed to 'the harrowing' sounds, sights and smells of the battlefield, the latter made up of 'putrescent water, stale poison gas, and the effluvia of dead bodies'.[52] Arising from these experiences women 'frequently commented upon the identification they felt with the fighting men'.[53] It is not surprising that some women smoked under these conditions, but de Wend's adoption of a particularly masculine pose – the unsupported cigarette and hands in pockets – suggests a desire to mark visually her equality with men and the equivalence of her contribution to the war.

Figure 7.3   Muriel de Wend. Imperial War Museum, Photograph Archive, HU 87422.
Reproduced by permission of Heather Barthelmas.

In a letter home, de Wend portrays smoking as contributing to a class-specific image of youthful modern womanhood, one that was shaped by the demands and the opportunities afforded some women by the war. In 'slacker time', she recalled, 'many a begrimed and begreased FANY may be seen drinking coffee and smoking a cigarette to the accompaniment of Pelléas and Mélisande or Wagner'.[54] This account combined smoking with signifiers of youth and modernity (the gramophone), the transgression of femininity facilitated by the war ('begrimed and begreased') and social class (classical music).

That this description also located smoking in a collective way of life is confirmed by the content, arrangement and annotation of photographs in her album. One page in the album displays six photos taken of de Wend and friends relaxing on a beach in September 1917; the page was titled '"The calm before the storm". Five hours after these snapshots were taken we were bombed … for five hours.' One of these photos, which depicts seven women sitting together on the rocks, is entitled 'Cigarette stage of the tea'. De Wend's annotation deliberately draws attention to smoking and the communal and ritualistic nature of this practice.

Other group photographs taken on Armistice Day, November 1918, also reveal many women with cigarettes. A photograph that is particularly illustrative of the importance attached to the cigarette in the construction of identity was one taken of Muriel de Wend's corps in August 1921, perhaps at a reunion (Fig. 7.4). The writing

Figure 7.4   Muriel de Wend and friends. Imperial War Museum Documents. Photograph Album. Reproduced by permission of Heather Barthelmas.

on the back of the photograph reveals that it was sent to de Wend by 'Dick and the Dormouse', who may have taken the photograph or organized the distribution of copies produced by someone else, perhaps a commercial photographer. Positioned in front of a tent and attired in full uniform, the women are carefully arranged in a fairly standard format for a formal group portrait, eight women are standing and four are seated in front. However, conventions end there. The seated women cross their legs in a manner that would have scandalized a previous generation. Smiles were also in contradistinction to the formality of Victorian photographic conventions and an assertion of the women's modernity, as were their bold looks into the eye of the camera. Additionally, eight of the women are holding cigarettes in their hands or, in the case of one woman, between her teeth, and one appears to be tapping her cigarette on a cigarette case. The photograph and, in particular, the representation of cigarettes in it, is contrived, but this speaks volumes about the significance of the cigarette in the presentation, not just of individual modern identities, but also of a collective one that was inextricably related to a particular, and shared, experience of serving on the front in the First World War. That this particular photograph was produced just after the war may indicate that the women sought, through the medium of the photograph, to hang on to this identity amid pressures to reintegrate into civilian life.[55] The collective identity may have been transitory, but through possession of copies of this photograph the women had at least one way of holding onto it in the postwar world.

Being photographed smoking was not only about constructing identity in the present – photographs are also tied to the production of memory. With the accessibility of photography from 1900, as advertisements for Kodak cameras made clear, memory now increasingly came in visual form.[56] Keeping photos of oneself, displaying them, organizing them in an album – these are all acts of producing personal history and this, in turn, is key to identity in the modern era. Photographs and photo albums 'both shape and reflect the subject of modernity'.[57] As Maggie Humm explains: 'The popularity of snapshot photography fundamentally altered the ways in which people saw themselves and their worlds ... by encouraging a more creative, active participation in the construction of memory.'[58] Muriel de Wend's album reveals the importance of smoking in the construction of a self which she composed for posterity. Smoking was an important aspect of her identity as a young woman and, moreover, as a woman of a particular historical era; the cigarette located her in biographical and historical time.

The photos of Muriel de Wend and Lallie Charles reveal women experimenting with the visual display of themselves as smokers prior to 1920. Although these pictures suggest that women were prepared to pose with cigarettes outdoors, they were all produced in locations removed from the censorious eyes of the British public and/or in the midst of like-minded people. During the interwar years, being portrayed smoking in a photograph remained a highly meaningful gesture, especially if the photograph was taken by a professional. Nevertheless, more photographs of women smoking circulated both informally, as between friends and family members, and formally, particularly in Society papers and the daily press. The use of smoking in the construction of identity became, at least for some women, a public, even a publicity, exercise as well as a personal one.

For all Eyes to See: Interwar Photographs of Women Smoking

Judging by the photographs in the Documentary Photograph Archive and the Kodak Snapshot Collection, photographs of working-class women smoking are rare and, although middle-class women increasingly took up the smoking habit in the interwar years, it was unusual for them to appear smoking in any type of photograph.[59] Upper-middle-class and upper-class women did appear with cigarettes in amateur photographs, perhaps reflecting both the high incidence of smoking in these social strata and the accessibility of amateur photography.[60] Amateur photographs were, however, for private use and were not generally in the public eye. By contrast, from the mid-1920s professional portraits of literary and artistic women and other public achievers increasingly portrayed them as smokers.[61] These images, produced by notable London photographers such as Bassano, Coster, Freund and Fox Studios, sometimes reached a public audience. These professional portraits were the exception, not the rule.

Technical factors may have discouraged some photographers from portraying clients with lit cigarettes, but these were not insurmountable, as indicated by commercial photographs of glamorous models and actresses smoking, as well as photographic and painted portraits of successful public women.[62] Additionally, cigarettes did not need to be lit. Most portraits did not feature smoking because of the conventions and purposes of female portraiture that were determined as much by sitters as by photographers, and also by concerns about the propriety of both the photographic studio and the sitter. It seems that only the most socially successful photographers and female sitters were prepared to transgress these unwritten rules in the interwar years.

Having a portrait done was a common activity across the social classes by the 1920s, particularly so among the higher social classes and celebrities. Ethel Mannin refers to her album of the interwar years filled with 'studio portraits galore'.[63] Daphne du Maurier had studio photographs but also invited photographers to her Cornwall homes to take photographs of herself and her family.[64] Smoking was not, however, usually a feature of professional portraits of Society women and their middle-class sisters, even if the women were smokers.[65] The cigarette was also invisible in working-class portraiture. The cigarette's invisibility in these contexts

168

can be explained partly by the purpose of the portraits, which most commonly served to locate women in a particular family and social milieu and to record the process of growing up. Markers of gender, age and respectability were key to such portraits.

In the case of the upper classes, portraits also served to launch a debutante into Society and the marriage market. Femininity was central to the presentation of women as respectable family members and as suitable marriage partners. Smoking was incompatible with these objectives, not least because it was still not entirely respectable. Additionally, women's smoking was too strongly associated with the disruption of conventions that were difficult to embrace within the traditional ideal of family life. More specifically, women's smoking signalled new constructions of femininity and gender relations and could be interpreted as evidence of a generation gap within the family.

Similar factors prevented cigarettes appearing in the portraits of women from lower down the social scale. In the 1920s, young and single working-class women often used their 'spends' to augment photographs commissioned by parents with ones for their own purposes – a memento of the first dance and the dress made specially for the occasion, or a record of a new outfit.[66] In these cases, young women visually charted, or produced, personal and consumerist narratives of feminine development. During wartime, women commissioned portraits to give to loved ones serving away from home, a reminder of the 'ties that bind'. Although cigarettes were portrayed as glamorous in cigarette advertisements and in film, this was not the type of femininity celebrated in these portraits. Moreover, as we saw in Chapter 6, glamour was not compatible with working-class feminine respectability.

Interwar Professional Portraiture

Smoking in a professional portrait was radical for an interwar woman, and the appearance of a cigarette was, therefore, highly meaningful. As photographer August Sander once put it: 'In [professional] photography there are no unexplained shadows!'[67] No doubt there were instances where a sitter was unable to relax without a cigarette or where, as in the case of a painting, they were unable or unwilling to forgo smoking for the length of time required.[68] Where this was the case it is still significant that the cigarette or cigar remains visible; both the canvas and also the photographic negative could be modified to remove signs of smoking. In photography, retouching of faces, hair and figures was a common practice – a notable photographer once asked an assistant to put in a window.[69] In professional portrait photography the appearance of a cigarette was never incidental, but who determined its appearance and its particular role in the image? Eric Homberger notes of early twentieth-century photographic practice in the United States that the portrait was a product of 'dynamics' and 'power relations'.[70] In Britain, as in the US, the representation of a smoker was a product of this process.

The changing fortunes of particular studios indicate that by 1900 women were quite discerning about photographic images of themselves and their families. Fashionable studios had to offer a distinctive and recognizable style in both the photographic product and the ambience of the studio, and people chose the one that most suited their needs.[71] Clients also exercised their consumer rights at the proof and print stage. Alice Hughes, a well known and successful photographer at the turn of the century, recounts how the mother of a plain girl complained about the proofs she received of her daughter and responded with a 'list of improvements'.[72] Madame Yevonde recalls that by 1914 the clients of photographer Lallie Charles were routinely complaining:

> They said the photographs were not in the least like them – in the old days the photographs had not been striking as likenesses, but there had been no complaints. There was nothing but grumbles and re-sittings: people did not like their proofs, or if they passed the proofs they did not like the finished prints.[73]

Dorothy Connor, the retoucher for Dorothy Wilding's interwar studios, similarly recalls that clients were vocal: 'I would get very detailed instructions. They want all their character left. Or knock thirty years off!' One actress, Connor remembers, wanted more wrinkles, while Miss Billy Butlin threatened not to order any prints unless her kiss curl was redone.[74] Even in provincial studios, clients exercised some control over the image. Val Williams notes that, 'Even those operating outside the glare of fashionable metropolitan whims and fancies acknowledged how the manner of portraiture must alter as predilections in dress and manner changed with circumstances.'[75]

Facilitated by the expansion of snapshot photography, middle- and upper-class women were also skilled at, and knowledgeable about, image making. In 1897, aged fifteen, Virginia Woolf was already demonstrating considerable flair in using a camera and was producing 'album-like visual narratives'.[76] Photography, Humm observes, 'had a profound effect on the ways in which modernist women chose to present their own identities and those of others',[77] and this undoubtedly had implications for their encounters with professional photographers. Doan refers to '[s]elf imaging, among the financially comfortable and artistically successful' in the interwar years as 'an intensely serious and empowering affair, involving careful negotiations between the photographer and the sitter who activated and animated the creative process'.[78] Radclyffe Hall and Una Troubridge, for example, are described as 'highly skilled and practiced in the staging of their own self-image'.[79] While Doan rightly points to a heightened recognition of the power of visual publicity in elite circles, she presents no evidence of the negotiations involved in the production of their portraits.

Following in the tradition of painters, photographers often expected complete control of the photographic subject. The more expensive portrait photographers prided themselves on a particular style of work and a reputation built around this. Hugh Cecil 'would often turn people away from sittings if neither their looks nor their social standing were up to scratch'.[80] The style of work associated with Wilding, who used a painter in her logo, was akin to 'a Hollywood film director'; even the Duke of Windsor was directed to pose in a particular way for her camera.[81] Clients did exercise some control when choosing the photographers who were most compatible with the image they wished to present, and also at the proof and printing stage, but this amounted to tinkering with an image within a studio's style. Where women were depicted smoking it is not clear whether the image was shaped primarily by the imagination of the photographer or by the sitter. Although it is rare to unravel quite how much control sitters had over the depiction of themselves as smokers, the sitter's subsequent use of a portrait is illuminating. In many cases a portrait would be given to friends or released to the press, suggesting that the sitter regarded the image as a desirable one.

Professional portraits that were released to the press usually linked smoking to public identities and women's successful entry into the public domain on 'equal terms' with men. Often the commission of portraits coincided with the publication of a new book or the exhibition of the artist's work. The occasion that prompted the photographs confirms the place of smoking in the presentation of public achievement. Radclyffe Hall commissioned portraits of herself smoking to coincide with the publication of her books, and photographs of the artist Gluck coincided with her exhibitions. Motor boat racer, Joe (Marion) Carstairs, also smoked in the numerous public portraits that were produced during the 1920s: 'For the camera, she frowned a little, squared her shoulders, held a cigarette in one hand and placed the other in a jacket pocket.'[82] There is a classic photograph taken around 1926 of Carstairs in her motor boat, with a cigarette protruding unsupported from her mouth, wearing a beret, scarf, jacket and trousers; part of this was reproduced in an advertisement for spark plugs.[83]

Portraits of women smoking, whether for public or private use, often made reference to the sitter's public work and achievements, which were signalled within the photograph by the choice of location, props, pose and lighting. The cigarette was often used in specific poses to emphasize the intellectual work of literary women. The association of smoking with contemplation was firmly established in the masculine history of smoking[84], and one that was also promoted in the antics of fictional male characters such as the detective Sherlock Holmes.[85] The use of smoking by women as an aid to thought and writing was less established and visible in popular culture. However, smoking as an aid to cerebral activity and especially to writing was common among women smokers. Vita Sackville-West smoked when she worked and, in more mundane contexts, so too did some Mass-Observation respondents. Gay Taylor recalled that she and her friend 'smoked more when we were trying to concentrate', while Lyn Evans found it helped with writing: 'It's become a habit to have a cigarette burning between my fingers when I write or resting on the edge of the table or on a box of matches. Then when I come to a full stop and pause to think what I shall write next I inhale a lungful. If the next sentence refuses to come I inhale another lungful and eventually the sentence comes.'[86] Modern fiction representations of women writers, perhaps reflecting the practice of the authors, also portrayed smoking in this way. The description of the writer Stephen, in Hall's lesbian classic *The Well of Loneliness*, makes this connection clear: 'the fingers of the hand that slowly emerged from her jacket pocket were heavily stained with nicotine – she was now a voracious smoker'; and when Stephen was unable to write, 'she lit a cigarette and when it was finished found another and kindled it at the stump'.[87]

A photograph taken by Howard Coster in 1934 of writer Sylvia Townsend Warner (1893–1978) illustrates the deployment of smoking to communicate intellectual activity (Fig. 7.5). In this portrait Warner has her legs crossed and leans forward to rest her right elbow on her leg; in her right hand, which is in line with her face, she holds a lit cigarette. The cigarette, hair style and jazzy earrings mark Warner out as a modern woman, but this is not an image of glamorous or youthful modernity but one of modern, intellectual womanhood. Warner is dressed quite simply in a white blouse and skirt although her femininity is accentuated by the prominence of one hand adorned with rings and with a delicate watch at the wrist. Warner is not on display as was typical in commercial glamour photography, but closed in on herself in the style of Rodin's statue 'The Thinker'. She rests her head in her right hand as she holds her lighted cigarette, and her eyes are downcast in thoughtfulness as the smoke from the cigarette trails upward. Warner's intellectuality was reinforced by the attention focused on her head. Aping the style of Victorian painters and photographers of male intellectuals, lighting was used to emphasize her brow.[88] The cigarette she held also helped to frame, and draw attention to, her head while the act of smoking suggested contemplation. The cigarette has burned down to the last inch and is clearly not an aesthetic feature. The stub appears to mark the time that elapses when one is deep in thought and the smoke visibly suggests trails of thought.

Similar techniques appear in other private and public portraits of cerebral women including colour photographs of Virginia Woolf (1882–1941) taken by Gisele Freund in 1939.[89] Smoking small cigars was one of Woolf's pleasures, and was also part of her public as well as private image. The production of these photographs was fraught for Woolf who felt cornered into sitting for Freund: 'I was photographed against my will about 40 times over, which annoyed me.'[90]

Figure 7.5 *Sylvia Townsend Warner by Howard Coster (NPG x3371). National Portrait Gallery, London.*

Her letters reveal her anger at this, and her general dislike of having her portrait taken and used in public display; this is revealing of her knowledge of how the media use and reframe photographs and evidence of her desire to retain control of her self-image.[91] Hermione Lee suggests that Woolf's antipathy is visible in the portraits: 'the photos that resulted from this intrusion ... show up the subject's resistance and dismay'.[92] While this may be the case,[93] some characteristics of these images resonate strongly with features in portraits of other cerebral women. This suggests that, at least at one level, the photographs of Virginia Woolf fit within the visual discourse of intellectual and successful women. Freund's photographs bring together smoking as a sign of intellectual activity with markers of Woolf's relationship to modernism and literature. In one photograph Woolf flicks through a book while, with her elbow resting on the chair arm, she holds a lit cigarette in a holder and looks off, thoughtfully, into the distance. In another photograph in which Freund zooms in on Woolf's face and illuminates her brow, Woolf looks straight into the camera. As if to reintroduce distance between the viewer and sitter, and to signal her status as a critic, Woolf's hand, in which she holds a lit cigarette, comes up between herself and the viewer. The pose, as Lee's interpretation suggests, could also serve to distance Woolf from the photographer.

Portraits of Vita Sackville-West (1892–1962) provide another example of the explicit alignment of smoking with public work and achievement. West started smoking by the time she was eighteen, a habit she continued throughout her life. Although she was a published poet (in 1926 she won the Hawthornden Prize for her poem *The Land*), her notoriety stemmed primarily from her success in developing the Sissinghurst garden and in writing for *The Garden*.[94] Although West did not usually smoke while gardening, a cigarette appeared in the photographic frame whenever she posed for a photograph in her garden. The cigarette, like the garden, her breeches and her dogs, was part of her trademark. The cigarette's significance was, however, more complex. Smoking visibly referred to West's intellectual activity. As her son, Nigel Nicolson, recalls, his mother usually smoked 'about twenty a day while writing, conversing and after meals'.[95] West's smoking style – she favoured paper and quill holders – was also telling. Dressed in breeches and standing amid the fruits of her physical labours at Sissinghurst, West's cigarette holder reminded the viewer of her social class and sophistication. Her smoking practice contributed to the construction of an 'aristocratic individuality',[96] a uniqueness premised on her ability, facilitated in large part by her aristocratic heritage, wealth and success, to engage in manual work and yet remain a lady and, moreover, an intellectual one.

In the early 1930s, just after her second novel *I'll Never be Young Again* was completed, Daphne du Maurier commissioned a portrait of herself smoking (Fig. 7.6). Although Daphne du Maurier frequently appeared smoking in family photographs, this was not usual in professional portraiture. The portrait by Compton Collier depicts her in the kitchen at 'Ferryside', her Cornwall home, against the backdrop of an old painted door, sunlight pouring in behind her. On the ledge behind stands a bowl of shiny apples. Du Maurier sits on a wooden high-backed chair, side on to the camera and with her back to the doorway. Her arms are outstretched and her hands interlocked around one slightly raised knee. This pose is identical to one adopted by her father (the actor Gerard du Maurier who gave his name to du Maurier cigarettes) in a photographic portrait produced in his youth. As suggested by her son, Kits Browning, Daphne du Maurier was probably 'copying'

Figure 7.6   Daphne du Maurier by Compton Collier. Reproduced by permission of the Chichester Partnership.

this pose.[97] But given that her father adopted a range of smoking poses for the camera, the question remains as to why Daphne du Maurier chose to imitate this particular pose and, indeed, what she achieved visually in doing so.

Du Maurier looks serious and a shade defiant as she stares into the camera. Her body is turned sideways, thereby obscuring her female figure, and her clothes contribute to the covering of her body. Dressed simply in a dark jumper, shirt and trousers, du Maurier appears as an active modern woman. Moreover, her clothes emphasize a 'boyish' style. In 1930, trousers were a radical feminine costume, but for du Maurier, who was not greatly into fashion, they were probably chosen for their practicality and their masculine signification. Her biographer Margaret Forster points to du Maurier's pleasure in asserting a 'masculine side'.[98] Distinctive make-up, however, signals her gender, but this type of femininity is one that she has control over – she can put it on, adjust it or leave it off all together. Du Maurier asserts her independence and emancipation, but she retains the right to be feminine if she chooses. Her choice of make-up indicates that she wanted to convey a modern femininity; dark lipstick was at this time a rather risqué choice. As suggested by the lipstick, this photograph resonates with sexual signalling. In this context it is possible that the open door and apples, classic signifiers of sexuality, are not incidental. The complexity of this image is accentuated by the cigarette dangling from the corner of du Maurier's painted mouth.

Cigarettes were usually portrayed supported in the mouth or held in the hand, and both these smoking poses were established in interwar media as feminine ones. Strongly associated with masculine and utilitarian smoking practice, the unsupported cigarette was less commonly seen among women. When this did occur it was usually because the woman was getting a light or was busy with her hands. When this was not the case, the unsupported cigarette suggested that the woman was practised at smoking and able to handle her cigarette like a man; even more than the supported cigarette, this signalled women's equality with men. Whereas a range of smoking styles had been established as feminine by the 1930s, this stance was still quite radical. In 1937 Mass Observation asked its largely middle-class pool of female respondents whether they would talk with a cigarette in their mouth. The general dislike of this practice suggests that a cigarette propped in the mouth was not feminine: 'there is something "unseemly" in the sight of a woman, especially, with a fag sticking out of her FACE.'[99] When a woman sported a cigarette in her mouth it usually jutted straight out at a right angle to her face, and a dangled cigarette was unusual. In the portrait of du Maurier, recourse to the dangling, rather than jutting, cigarette may have been influenced in part by the difficulty of photographing a jutting cigarette in a frontal face shot. (It is noteworthy that Gerald du Maurier sported a jutting cigarette in his portrait.) However, for women the meaning of the dangling cigarette was more slippery than that of the jutting one. Like the jutting cigarette it had strong masculine overtones, but in the absence of signs of refinement it could also suggest slovenliness. Additionally, in potentially sexual contexts and/or when the woman was glamorous, the dangling cigarette could be interpreted as a sign of sexual sophistication and even as sexually suggestive (see Chapter 5). In Daphne du Maurier's case her refinement clearly ruled out any suggestion that her smoking style was a sign of slovenliness. The masculine associations do, however, remain strong, although tempered by her lipstick and obviously feminine face. The cigarette also suggests that she is sexually sophisticated, that she has experience that was denied to most women of her age and class in preceding decades. These meanings are not tempered; Daphne du Maurier stares straight at the viewer, asserting her modernity and her right to be 'worldly wise'. Although this portrait was not used as media publicity, du Maurier did use it for self-publicity and in 1932 gave it to her friend Ethel Mannin who thought it 'charming'.[100]

Photographs of the artist Gluck surrounded by her paintings or the tools of her trade, and smoking a cigarette or cigar, frequently appeared in the press in the interwar years, especially when her work was on exhibition. 'Ultra-modern', declared one newspaper that featured her at work with a cigarette in her mouth at the time of her exhibition at the Fine Art Society Galleries in London. Other photographs of Gluck alongside her exhibits at the Galleries depicted her with a cigar. A studio portrait by Coster also portrayed Gluck dressed in her artist's smock and holding a cigarette.[101] As if to emphasize the masculine domain in which Gluck worked, she often posed in an artist's smock which was, traditionally, a masculine costume. Although it is questionable how much control Gluck had over the content of these photographs, it is significant that the cigarette also featured prominently in Gluck's painted self-portrait. This portrait, which was a clever piece of self-promotion, was completed in 1926 and depicted Gluck in a beret and with a cigarette protruding from the corner of her mouth. It was reproduced in the Society magazine *Eve* in 1926, and then as a Christmas card which Gluck sent to her friends in 1930.[102] Several features of Gluck's modernity were embodied in this painting, including her artistic success, her modern and masculine style, and her public act of smoking.

Earlier in her career, Gluck was also painted smoking a clay pipe. Smoking a clay pipe was a sign that Gluck belonged to a particular community, as early in the twentieth century the clay pipe enjoyed a renaissance in some artistic circles; Gluck's artist friend Ella Naper also smoked one when attired in her 'workmen's corduroy trousers'.[103] The adoption of the clay pipe by this community probably stems from its ability to signal gender and class rebellion. While at this time a few older working-class women smoked clay pipes, this practice was principally engaged in by lower-class men.[104] Although Gluck smoked a clay pipe, the images of herself that she promoted most assiduously in the interwar years were of a woman who smoked cigarettes and the occasional cigar.

In much portraiture of women smoking, heterosexuality is signified in various ways. It is difficult, however, to pinpoint a style of smoking that was exclusively lesbian. In themselves, pipe and cigar smoking, or a masculine style of cigarette smoking, were not indicative of sexuality; a range of smoking styles were fashionable among women.[105] However, masculine smoking practices, in combination with masculine clothes and a lack of feminine signifiers, were significant statements of sexuality for some lesbians including Gluck. Gluck often appeared in photographs with an unsupported cigarette in her mouth – indeed, this was a striking feature of her self-portrait.[106] As we have seen, the dangled cigarette resonated with masculinity, associations that in Gluck's case were reinforced by her fashionable but also masculine attire (shirt, tie, beret) and lack of obvious make-up. The 'worldly wise' association remained strong but, in the absence of signs of glamour, it was not a heterosexual version. Gluck's painting appeared in *Eve* on a page of portraits of women who wore the beret (Fig. 7.7). All were very modern in appearance, but the lesbians Gluck and Carstairs stand out from their heterosexual sisters in their lack of even subtle feminine signifiers; as Rolley explains, 'In a period of fashionable androgeny, signifiers of gender such as earrings became extremely important.'[107] Gluck's public smoking of fairly large cigars also helped her to craft a specifically masculine image and again, in the absence of feminine signifiers, suggested a woman uninterested in asserting femininity or heterosexuality.

Figure 7.7 '*The Beret*', *Eve, 30 June 1926, p. 716. Reproduced by permission of The British Library (shelf mark 184).*

Whereas cigarettes were a very modern smoke and signified engagement with the modern world, cigars emphasized tradition and, being almost exclusively a male smoke, they asserted masculinity. The cigar, especially in the absence of feminine clothes or heterosexual ambition,[108] stressed Gluck's rejection of femininity rather than an assertion of a modern form of femininity. Moreover it confirmed that smoking was not merely a fashion statement for Gluck, but a means of crafting a particular gender identity. Whereas other women may have smoked cigarettes to declare themselves modern women, Gluck used tobacco to visibly distance herself from femininity whether modern or traditional, and the assumed heterosexuality of this gender identity.

Conclusion

Susan Sontag observes that 'photographs ... help people to take possession of space in which they are insecure'.[109] Although referring to the tourist's photographs, this idea has a broader relevance. This chapter has shown how when women posed for photographs with cigarettes or cigars they 'took possession' of several interlinked types of 'space' in which they were insecure. The lack of photographs of lower-class women smoking prior to 1920 could be interpreted as evidence that smoking would not help these women to lay claim to the 'spaces' that mattered to them and in which they were insecure. For working-class women, the photograph can be seen as a means by which they staked their claim to respectable femininities and even modern ones. The compromising associations of tobacco use for lower-class women meant that smoking could not be employed to strengthen their bid for respectable and modern femininities. Lower-middle-class and upper-working-class women were usually motivated to use photographs in similar ways to those of their less affluent sisters, and they too were constrained in their ability to use cigarettes as positive signifiers. However, unlike women lower down the social scale, they could engage in playful ways with the significations of tobacco use in photographs prior to 1920 and, on occasion after this, they appeared smoking in amateur photographs. Secure in their social standing, women of the upper-middle and upper class were less concerned to lay claim to respectability in all their photographs. These women were able to use photography and smoking in combination to take possession of other and gendered spaces in which they were insecure – for instance, professional recognition, wartime individual and collective identities, modernity, the assertion of a masculine style and rejection of femininity. Prior to 1920 this remained a relatively private affair; in the interwar years this also became a public exercise for a minority of publicly successful women.

In a nutshell, when an upper-middle-class or upper-class woman posed for a photograph smoking, it helped her lay claim to a modern identity and, more specifically, modern femininities. This occurred at two levels, first through the practice of being photographed smoking, and second by the specific associations of smoking for women. By being photographed smoking, women demonstrated their willingness and ability to play with identity –this applied also to women lower down the social scale who produced 'joke' photographs – and to lay claim to individual identities not circumscribed by the traditional feminine roles of daughter, wife and mother. Both these elements of the practice of being photographed were evidence of the sitter's modernity. Additionally, where women sought to appear as genuine smokers, their smoking practices visibly asserted their still tenuous claims to new versions of womanhood and equality with men: '"Liberation" was understood by the dominant culture to mean the ability and opportunity to act (and smoke) like men'.[110]

Notes

1. Holland, '"Sweet it is to Scan"', p. 121.
2. Barthes, *Camera Lucida*, p. 89.
3. Ibid., pp. 88, 80.
4. Hirsch, *Family Frames*, p. 5. This has, nevertheless, been an important element in explaining how people feel about photographs of people – see Barthes and Hirsch.
5. Tagg, *Burden of Representation*, p. 100.
6. Ibid., p. 2.
7. Ibid, p. 100.
8. Ibid., p. 119.
9. Ibid., p. 4.
10. Yevonde, *In Camera*, pp. 185–6.
11. Becker, 'Do Photographs Tell the Truth?'
12. Alongside other sources, photographs can be used cautiously as evidence of this sort.
13. Crossick, 'Before the shutters fall', p. 2.
14. Sontag, *On Photography*, p. 23.
15. Holland, '"Sweet it is to Scan"', p. 121. Readings are not static even for the users and owners of photographs – Seabrook, 'My Life is in that Box', p. 176.
16. See Crossick's discussion of photographic postcards of small businesses, 'Before the shutters fall'.
17. Sontag, *On Photography*, p. 71.
18. Doan, *Fashioning Sapphism*, pp. 186–7.
19. Tagg, *Burden of Representation*, p. 37.
20. Linkman, *Victorians*.
21. Although smoking was a masculine practice it was not usual for Victorian men to smoke in professional portraits. This was because smoking was associated with leisure and relaxation which were not the usual themes of professional portraiture. Additionally, in the middle and upper classes, men's smoking was still routinely restricted to specific – and often exclusively masculine – spaces away from the sight of women of their own

social class. There are some professional portraits of men smoking, for example one of the media entrepreneur Alfred Harmsworth, later Lord Northcliffe, 1896 (NPG). Men were also frequently seen smoking in amateur photographs.

22. Crossick, 'Before the shutters fall', p. 4.

23. Speaight, *Memoirs*, p. 122.

24. Linkman, *Victorians*.

25. Holland, 'Sweet it is to scan', p. 145.

26. Linkman, *Victorians*, pp. 173–7.

27. GMCRO, DPA 377/75. This photo was kept by Bessie's mother, Lily Clinton. Although Lily sometimes annotated her photos, this appeared in her collection without comment. There is no evidence that Bessie was a smoker.

28. Cited in Linkman, *Victorians*, p. 46.

29. Ibid.

30. The photograph was taken in the yard of the house where one of the women lived. The chairs that were used and the width of the yard suggest that this was a fairly prosperous upper-working-class household. These women gave the photo to Mrs Robinson who worked at home as a dressmaker while her husband, a skilled-manual worker, was employed as a blacksmith and then as a mechanic.

31. GMCRO, DPA 608/31.

32. Tagg, *Burden of Representation*, p. 37.

33. Linkman, *Victorians*.

34. Ibid., provides fascinating discussion of portraits of eminent men.

35. Roberts, 'Yevonde', p. 9.

36. Portraits by interwar Society photographer Hoppé were clearly differentiated by gender. Beauty and traditional feminine qualities were emphasized in portraits of women, while public involvement was stressed in images of men. See Doan, *Fashioning Sapphism*, p. 178.

37. Ibid., p. 164.

38. Holland, 'Sweet it is to Scan', p. 122.

39. Schudson, *Advertising*, p. 196.

40. A photograph taken between 1903 and 1910 of Sybil Cooper, an upper-middle-class woman, reveals another version of smoking and modern womanhood. See frontispiece in Bland, *Banishing the Beast*. Many thanks to Lucy Bland for information about this photo.

41. Based on Charles's hemline (see other examples of similar skirt length in Rolley and Aish, *Fashion in Photographs*, pp. 79 and 89).

42. The other photographs include two of Charles with female friends and two of her in a group of fifteen sitting with a male companion (NPG x68994–5, x68997–8). Charles is apparently the only woman smoker (NPG x68995).

43. Williams, *Women Photographers,* p. 143.

44. Ibid., p. 145.

45. Ibid., p. 14f; for typical Charles portrait see p. 46.

46. Sontag, *On Photography*, pp. 37–8.

47. Thanks to Linkman for this point.

48. Kent, *Making Peace*.

49. IWM Documents. Letter, Muriel de Wend to her mother, 10 January 1917.

50. IWM Documents. Muriel de Wend Photograph album.

51. IWM Photograph Archive, HU 87422.

52. Kent, *Making Peace,* pp. 65, 59.

53. Ibid., p. 63.

54. IWM Documents. Letter, Muriel de Wend to her mother, 10 January 1917, p. 7.

55. Thanks to Audrey Linkman for this point.

56. Holland, 'Sweet it is to scan', fig. 3.14.

57. Humm, *Modernist Women*, p. 13.

58. Ibid., p. 23.

59. There were exceptions: for example a photograph of Judy Giles' middle-class mother smoking, reproduced in *Parlour and the Suburb.*

60. For example Virginia Woolf's snapshots, discussed in Humm, *Modernist Women.* See also Chapter 2 of the present volume, note 15.

61. Also women not discussed in this chapter such as Vera Brittain, Noel Streatfield, Rosamund Lehmann.

62. As late as the 1940s, photography was not immediate and a time lag occurred between the removal of the cap and the taking of the photo. Cigarette ash would build up in the time it took to take a photograph and smoke would move, which would necessitate substantial retouching of the negative (Marjorie Hughes, communication). Artists encountered similar problems if they attempted to paint smokers (R. Hutchison, communication).

63. Mannin, *Young in the Twenties*, p. 73.

64. Leng, *Daphne du Maurier*, pp. 69, 87.

65. This observation is based on a study of photographs of women from across the social-class spectrum archived in the National Portrait Gallery Heinz Archive and in the Documentary Photography Archive. It is also based on the study of magazines for affluent and Society women such as *Eve, The Sketch* and *Vogue*, all of which routinely featured photographic portraits of notable and/or Society women.

66. GMCRO, DPA 770/1 and 770/4 of Mrs Mapleston; 1121/207 Mrs Malpus.

67. National Portrait Gallery, *August Sander*, title page.

68. Occasionally smoking featured in painted portraits of successful women – see images in NPG Heinz Archive. Even more so than in photography, painting tradition eschewed the representation of women smoking. Paintings, which took considerable time and money to produce, were traditionally conceived of as statements for posterity. Smoking would have been seen as unbecoming and/or as a passing fad not fitting for inclusion. Where painters depicted their subjects smoking this appears to be because they were painting for their own purposes, often depicting friends. In these images, smoking is crucial to the portrayal of character even if inappropriate in traditional painted portraiture. For instance, smoking was a trademark of photographs of Elizabeth Bowen (1899–1973), and a painted portrait of her by Mary Eastman (1945) depicts her with a cigarette; this picture remained in the artist's possession until her death. Similarly, Dorothy Sayers (1893–1957), detective story writer and scholar of European Medieval literature, was represented holding a cigarette in an oil painting produced by Sir William Hutchison 1949/50. Sayers was a close friend of Lord Hutchison and, as his son recalled for me, she sat for this portrait at his request: 'He found

her a fascinating person and asked if he could paint her.' Although the painting was exhibited in Glasgow and possibly London, Hutchison did not choose to sell it and it remained in his possession until his death. Perhaps because she was a friend, Hutchison painted Sayers as he most often encountered her. As his son recalled, my father 'chose to show her in an informal pose as he would have seen her in conversation with her. It suggests to me that D.S. must have been a heavy smoker and that the pose, cigarette in hand, was typical.'

69. de Ville and Haden-Guest, *Society Photography*, p. 22.

70. Homberger, 'J.P. Morgan's Nose', p. 115.

71. Williams, *Women Photographers*, p. 154.

72. Cited in de Ville and Haden-Guest, *Society Photography,* p. 21.

73. Yevonde, *In Camera,* p. 69.

74. de Ville and Haden-Guest, *Society Photography,* p. 22.

75. Williams, *Women Photographers,* p. 147.

76. Humm, *Modernist Women*, pp. 27–8.

77. Ibid., p. 38.

78. Doan, *Fashioning Sapphism,* pp. 166–7.

79. Ibid., p. 185.

80. de Ville and Haden-Guest, *Society Photography*, pp. 17–18.

81. Pepper, *Dorothy Wilding,* pp. 20, 24.

82. Summerscale, *The Queen*, p. 68.

83. Boat photo reproduced in Summerscale, *The Queen*. Spark plug advertisement, *Tatler*, 4 August 1926, p. 11. Thanks to Laura Doan for this image.

84. Schivelbusch*, Tastes of Paradise*, pp. 107–10.

85. Hilton, *Smoking*, pp. 19–20.

86. MOA TC 63: 1/D Taylor; 1/B Evans. See also 1/B Bridgens; 1/D Weaver; 1/C Nelson. It is perhaps also relevant that by 1918 women's smoking was allowed in academic contexts such as Girton College (MOA FR 3192, p. 68).

87. Hall, *The Well*, pp. 210, 215.

88. Linkman, *Victorians*.

89. See also photographs of Vera Brittain, 1936, NPG Heinz Archive.

90. Nicolson and Trautmann, *Leave the Letters*, pp. 342–3. Woolf twice refused to sit for Freund, pp. 342, 351.

91. Woolf refused to be photographed by *The Times* in 1938 (Nicolson and Trautmann, *Leave the Letters*, p. 235) and the NPG in 1934 (Nicolson, *Sickle Side of the Moon*, p. 277).

92. Lee, *Virginia Woolf*, p. 716.

93. Humm, *Modernist Women*, pp. 52–5, argues that Woolf was actually a 'supportive sitter' for Freund, changing her clothing and cooperating so that Freund could use a particular type of film.

94. Studio portraits of West in the 1920s and early 1930s do not portray her with a cigarette. However, from 1932, and following her success as a gardener, she was invariably smoking when photographed in the grounds of Sissinghurst. See photographs in NPG Heinz Archive.

95. Nigel Nicolson, Correspondence.

96. Rolley, 'Cutting a Dash', p. 56.

97. Kits Browning, Communication.

98. Forster, *Daphne du Maurier*, p. 252. 'Daphne as a boy', was the way she described herself on the back of a portrait she gave to her friend Ethel Mannin, *Young in the Twenties*, pp. 140–1.

99. MOA TC 63 1/B Corbett, also 1/B Evans, 1/B M.E.Grant, 1/E Poole.

100. Mannin, *Young in the Twenties*, p. 140.

101. Thanks to Laura Doan for loan of these images.

102. Souhami, *Gluck*, p. 70.

103. Ibid., p. 43.

104. Apperson, *Social History of Smoking*, pp. 215–16.

105. See also Doan, *Fashioning Sapphism*.

106. *Eve*, 30 June 1926, p. 716.

107. Rolley, 'Cutting a Dash', p. 65.

108. Cigars were smoked by some heterosexual women, but straight women, and women who passed as straight, were unlikely to parade this. Cigar smoking would have remained a private practice.

109. Sontag, *On Photography*, p. 9.

110. Greaves, *Smoke Screen*, p. 20.

8

Mixed Messages, 1950–1980

In the postwar decades, smoking was consolidated as a feminine practice: between 1950 and 1975 the proportion of women who smoked in Britain remained fairly stable at just over 40 per cent. This was despite the emergence, and widespread publicity, of scientific evidence that smoking caused cancer and other health problems. So what was keeping women smoking, and indeed encouraging them to start smoking? Why, after 1960, were an increasing proportion of working-class women smoking? And why, by 1980, was smoking most common among the working classes, whereas pre-1939 it was most common among the middle and upper classes? Why were increasing numbers of teenage girls attracted to smoking? Hilton argues that smoking cessation rates were not as high as health campaigners would have liked because of a '"dissonance" of culture that saw advertising images, film representations, social and economic realities, and the survival of a liberal smoking tradition juxtaposed with the promotion of the dangers of smoking by established medical bodies'.[1] Hilton is right to highlight 'dissonance' in the decades after the Second World War, but he tends to assume that men and women had the same relationship to smoking and smoking culture.[2] Smoking patterns were gendered. Most notably, women were slower to quit smoking than men – indeed, men's smoking started to decline at least fifteen years before women's. In order to explain women's smoking and account for the differences between male and female smoking patterns, we need to address the gender dimensions of 'dissonance' and, moreover, to focus on women's experiences of anti-smoking campaigns, smoking practices and visual culture.[3]

This chapter begins by introducing the female smoking population between 1950 and 1980. It then outlines the emergence of anti-smoking initiatives and the implications of these for women. Following this, an exploration of images of women smokers reveals the continued promotion of smoking as a feminine practice. While image was key to women's experience of cultural 'dissonance', the final section of this chapter considers evidence of gendered needs and smoking practices and the limits of image.

Female Smokers

Cigarette smoking was common among women across the social classes and age groups in the postwar decades. The proportion of women who smoked remained consistently high until the late 1970s: in 1949, 41 per cent of women aged 16 years and over smoked manufactured cigarettes, 45 per cent in 1966 when women's smoking peaked, and 43 per cent in 1975.[4] The *amount* that women smoked did, however, increase. In 1950, women smokers consumed on average about fifty-five cigarettes a week, in 1975 over a hundred.[5] After 1975 the prevalence of women's smoking slowly declined and by 1980 it was down to 39 per cent.[6] By this time the percentage of men who smoked manufactured cigarettes had been falling steadily for twenty years: it was 63 per cent in 1949, 60 per cent in 1959, 54 per cent in 1969 and 42 per cent in 1980.[7] Due to the faster rate of decline of smoking among men than among women, and fewer boys than girls starting to smoke, by 1984 the percentage of women and men who smoked manufactured cigarettes was almost equal, 34 and 35 per cent respectively. Nevertheless, male smokers still outnumbered women smokers because a minority of men consumed pipe tobacco, cigars and roll-your-own cigarettes.[8] Taking into account all types of tobacco products, in 1990 there were 38 per cent of men compared with 31 per cent of women who smoked.[9]

Although the prevalence of women's smoking remained fairly stable between 1950 and 1975, the postwar decades witnessed two key changes in the profile of the woman smoker. First there was a shift in the proportions of women smoking within specific social classes; whereas the proportion of working-class women smoking rose, the proportion of women smoking in the higher social classes fell. In 1948, similar proportions of women smoked within most income groups (39 to 43 per cent) although smokers were slightly more common among the most affluent (46 per cent).[10] For most of the 1950s, however, women in the poorest households were least likely to smoke. In 1958, for example, the proportion of women smoking among the lowest of the Registrar General's social-class categories (SC VI) was 23 per cent, significantly lower than the average of 39 per cent for all social classes.[11] Although during the 1960s the prevalence of smoking remained low among women at the bottom of the social scale, it was usual for a greater proportion of women to smoke in the other working-class and the lower-middle-class groups (SC III, IV and V) than in the professional and managerial classes (SC I and II). By 1971, 34 per cent of women in SC I smoked, and 37 per cent in SC II, compared to roughly 47 per cent of women in SC III, IV and V, and 24 per cent in SC VI. During the 1970s, while the proportion of women smokers in the highest social class fell, a process begun in the 1960s, those in the lowest social class began to increase dramatically. Whereas in 1971, 34 per cent of SC I smoked compared to 24 per cent of SC VI (with the average across all classes of 42 per cent), in 1979 only

23 per cent of women in SC I smoked compared to 39 per cent of women in SC VI (with the average across all classes of 39 per cent). The 1980s confirmed the shift toward the equation of smoking with the lower social classes.[12]

The second shift in the profile of women smokers related to age.[13] Between 1949 and 1980 a significant proportion of women of all ages smoked, although smoking was most common among women under 60 years of age. From 1949 to 1959, women in the 25–34 age group were more likely to be smokers (55 per cent) than younger or older women. Smoking was still common among younger women – indeed, 45 per cent of 16–24-year-olds smoked in 1949 and 41 per cent in 1959. *Woman's Own,* a magazine with a largely upper-working-class and lower-middle-class readership, reported in 1955 on a survey to which 'thousands responded' which revealed that a third of young women aged 15–25 years smoked.[14] The probable exclusion of the higher social classes from this survey explains why the figure is not greater. Other surveys of the period reinforced the prevalence of smoking among the young. Expenditure on cigarettes by single people aged 15 to 25 years was sufficiently high for Abrams to include it in his 1959 survey of 'teenage' expenditure.[15] Throughout the 1960s almost half of all 16–24-year-old women smoked, putting them roughly on par with women in both the 25–34 and 35–59 year age groups.

A trend toward smoking in adolescence became increasingly apparent in the postwar decades. An advertisement for chewing gum in schoolgirl magazine *Jackie* reveals commercial recognition of smoking as a teenage practice: 'You can have clean teeth, but strongly-flavoured foods, cigarettes and so on, leave a clinging, tell-tale hint that spoils the nicest kiss'.[16] Roughly a third of girls aged 16–19 were smokers in both 1949 and 1959, and this proportion increased dramatically to 45 per cent during 1960; after slipping slightly in the mid-1960s, it rose to 53 per cent by 1969 before dropping back to 46 per cent in 1975.[17] The increased importance of the teenage years for the onset of smoking is confirmed by statistics based on the recalled age at which women started to smoke. In 1965, 25 per cent of women recalled starting to smoke in their teens, 33 per cent in 1975 (this compares to 65 per cent of men in 1965, 61 per cent in 1975).[18]

The consolidation of feminine smoking, and within this, shifts in the age and social-class profile of the woman smoker, occurred in a context of increased knowledge about the health risks of smoking. So what did science have to say about women's smoking and did women get the message?

Women Smokers at Risk?

Claims that smoking damaged health were not unusual prior to the Second World War. However, in 1950 an article by Richard Doll and Austin Bradford Hill, published in the *British Medical Journal,* presented evidence that smoking was an important factor in causing lung cancer. Doll and Hill's tentative conclusions, and the case against smoking, was consolidated by further research during the 1950s. Initially their conclusions were challenged and it was not until 1957 that the Medical Research Council (MRC) accepted a causal link between smoking and lung cancer and that this link was publicly acknowledged in the House of Commons.

In 1962 the report of the Royal College of Physicians (RCP), *Smoking and Health*, stated that 'heavy cigarette smokers may have thirty times the death rate of non-smokers'.[19] The 1962 report's findings were widely reported in the press, although responses varied from 'the *Guardian's* comprehensiveness' and '*The Times*' "rational" qualifications' to 'the *Mirror's* short-lived melodramatics' and 'the almost oblivious attitude of the *Daily Express*'.[20] The government responded to the report with health-education initiatives and the regulation of tobacco advertising. By 1963 the Ministry of Health had issued one million posters and several health films.[21] A code of advertising practice was set up to regulate how smoking could be represented in the press and on TV and then, following the 1964 Television Act, a blanket ban on TV advertising was introduced in 1965. These initiatives aimed to discourage children from smoking but, consistent with a liberal respect for the rights of the individual, adults were expected to decide for themselves whether or not to smoke.

The second RCP report, *Smoking and Health Now*, published in 1971, confirmed that smoking caused lung cancer as well as bronchitis and heart disease. Additionally, it reaffirmed the 1962 report's findings about smoking-related mortalities.

> It is estimated that over 20,000 deaths in men between the ages of 35 and 64 are caused every year by smoking in the United Kingdom. The chances are that two out of every five heavy cigarette smokers, but only one out of every five non-smokers, will die before the age of 65. The man of 35 who is an average cigarette smoker is likely on average to lose 5½ years of life compared to a non-smoker.[22]

Newspapers provided 'exhaustive' coverage of the report,[23] and the government were spurred on to further health initiatives characterized by risk reduction (although there was also a strong vein in support of abstention) and voluntary regulation of the tobacco industry[24]. In 1971 the tobacco industry agreed to print health warnings on cigarette packets and to publish detail of the tar and nicotine yield of cigarettes. Smokers were advised to stop smoking or to switch to low-tar brands.[25] Action on Smoking and Health (ASH) was set up with government funding as a lobbying and campaigning organization. But the £100,000 spent annually by the government on anti-smoking initiatives was paltry compared to the £52 million that the tobacco industry had spent on sales promotions in 1968.[26]

The reasons why action against smoking was slow and piecemeal are various. Virginia Berridge identifies several factors that contributed to the government's reluctance in the 1950s to act on Doll and Hill's findings. One set of factors related to vested interest: many senior politicians and advisors smoked, and the government relied heavily on the revenue from tobacco sales. Other factors related to the perceived legitimacy of the epidemiological evidence which depended on statistical proof, rather than results generated from laboratory experiments. There were also issues about appropriate forms of intervention. Public health had traditionally been concerned with 'the containment of epidemics of infectious, not chronic, disease' and policy-makers were 'very wary of intervening in matters of individual habit', especially those of men.[27] Some of these factors account for the continued reticence of governments to tackle smoking over the next twenty years. The interlinked interests of the tobacco industry, government and the national press were, as Peter Taylor demonstrated, a major factor.[28] Additionally, as Hilton argues, the government persistently opposed attempts to regulate personal habits because of the hold of 'the culture of the independent, liberal individual'.[29] These explanations do not, however, explain adequately the treatment of smoking among girls and women. There was also a gender agenda.

Hilton argues that, as a result of extensive media coverage and radio reportage of smoking and health issues, the dangers of smoking were widely known about as early as the 1950s and definitely by the 1960s, although smokers were 'adept at finding loopholes in the anti-smoking message' and using this to justify their habit.[30] But were women smokers aware that smoking posed a danger to *their* health?

A 'conspicuous absence' was how Bobbie Jacobson described the position of women in anti-smoking initiatives prior to 1981.[31] Although cigarette smoking was common among women between 1950 and 1980, the medical profession and government were slow to acknowledge that women's smoking was a problem. In 1983 the RCP admitted that women's needs had only recently been acknowledged because of the 'mistaken impression' that women were 'relatively immune to the effects of smoking'.[32] Even in 1983, the RCP concluded, 'most research and anti-smoking propaganda is still aimed at and produced by men'.[33]

Anti-smoking campaigns of the 1950s sometimes acknowledged that women smoked, but they were targeted principally at children, especially boys, and their fathers.[34] Reaction to the MRC Report in 1957 from Amy Dixon in the *Marlton Gazette & Herald* is illustrative of how women were commonly reasoned to be at little risk of harm from smoking.[35] Women, she claimed, are unlikely to give up smoking as a result of the MRC report as it is 'directed chiefly against the lifelong heavy smoker who inhales', in other words the hardened male smoker. Most women, Dixon notes, 'merely puff' rather than inhale, and so there 'is not much here to be given up'. Dixon's response was also revealing of the widespread belief in the social value of smoking. Assuming that only cigarettes were dangerous to health, Dixon asked why these dangers could not now be eliminated to produce a 'safe cigarette' because 'the social effects of tobacco are simply incalculable'. Reference to the harm caused by smoking featured only occasionally in the women's press. Steps were rarely taken to discourage readers from smoking even when opportunities presented themselves. For instance, in a feature on dental care in 1960, *Woman* acknowledged that smoking discoloured women's teeth. The solution proffered was not for women to give up smoking but to use a cigarette holder and, ideally, a filter.

Twenty thousand men, and three thousand women, died from lung cancer in 1959 according to the 1962 report of the RCP. Deaths among women were mentioned in the media's response to the report, but they were overshadowed by the death toll among men;[36] the endangered smoker was still widely presented as male. By the 1960s, teenage girls and young women were a growing group of smokers. Although addressed in one Ministry of Health survey by McKennell and Thomas, they were excluded from another by Bynner. The decision to focus on boys in Bynner's study was rationalized by pilot research which suggested that they were 'the group in which smoking begins', but girls smoked less and usually when 'encouraged' by boys.[37] Girls' smoking was not perceived as sufficiently distinctive or urgent to warrant specific research.

After 1962, young women's magazines, probably encouraged by the Ministry of Health, did print occasional features discouraging their readers from smoking. *Honey*, for example, urged its readers to quit smoking: 'If you feel sophisticated when you smoke ... If you feel superior when you take a puff ... If you can't face people without a cigarette ... Read on.'[38] Two-thirds of this double-page feature was dominated by a photograph of a pretty young woman with a cigarette in her mouth with a young man, standing behind her, leaning forward to cut it off (Fig. 8.1). 'Facts' that were presented included that smoking was not a sign of maturity, that it was going out of fashion, that 'boys do not like their girlfriends to smoke' and that it was 'not pretty': 'Very few girls can smoke gracefully ... most of them look plain messy. A drooping cigarette downgrades a swinging outfit, ruins the effect of a careful make-up. Smoking on the streets and in buses is just about as unfeminine as anything you can do. There's nothing fetching about nicotine-stained fingers and yellow teeth.' Other 'facts' were that smoking was 'expensive', 'ridiculously extravagant' and 'dangerous'. Although the dangers of smoking came seventh in the list of nine 'facts', the article did stress that smoking caused lung cancer. Indicative of the masculine image of the victim of smoking, the feature specifically mentioned the then recent death of male singer and smoker, Nat King Cole. Though the health risks of smoking were acknowledged, the

Figure 8.1   A quit smoking article. Honey, May 1965, p. 75. Thanks to photographer Francis Ray Hoff. Reproduced by permission of The British Library (shelf mark pp 6014 bd).

anti-smoking message was delivered primarily through appeals to the young reader's assumed desire to be heterosexually attractive. The beauty risks posed by smoking – 'smoker's fur', stained fingers and teeth – had long been recognized, and products were available to tackle these,[39] but beauty problems were presented as avoidable and invariably played down because of the dominant discourse which equated women's smoking with feminine attraction. After decades during which the tobacco industry in particular had worked successfully to feminize the image of smoking, anti-smoking initiatives sought to challenge the idea that smoking was consistent with feminine attractiveness. *Honey*'s feature did not, however, move beyond presenting the beauty risks as superficial, and its strategy of describing smoking as unattractive did not challenge visually the concept of the pretty woman smoker. Additionally, *Honey* was reluctant to condemn all women smokers as ungraceful, perhaps because some well-respected women still smoked. Such an explicit and feminized anti-smoking feature was unusual but it was weak and, moreover, merely a drop in the ocean compared to the high-profile media promotion of women's smoking.

Women's magazines usually gave less publicity to the dangers for women of smoking. The risks associated with smoking were ignored, or relegated to the sidelines and, frequently, contradicted by the messages of cigarette advertisements which appeared almost side by side with health features, as the following examples illustrate. After pages of discussion in *Woman* on 'How to be a healthy woman', the feature concluded with a few 'cautionary tales' – 'Don't smoke, don't become overweight, and don't fail to see a doctor when it's sensible'.[40] The importance of the rather brief 'cautionary' note about smoking was further undermined not just by the inclusion of two full-page cigarette advertisements in this issue, but by the placing of one of these advertisements opposite a page of this health feature. When a reader wrote to *Woman* about a child nearly eating a cigarette, she was told that cigarettes, matches and ashtrays containing stubs should be kept well away from children.[41] There was no mention that smoking damaged the health of women (the dangers of passive smoking not being acknowledged until the 1980s) or that giving up was a sensible option. Moreover, the back page of this issue carried an advertisement for cigarettes which presented smoking as 'healthy' and linked to 'nature'. Unattractive and negative ways of understanding smoking have often been suppressed by threats from the tobacco industry to deprive the media of advertising revenue.[42] This perhaps explains why the BBC 4 radio programme *Woman's Hour* regularly and critically discussed smoking in the 1950s and 1960s,[43] whereas women's magazines were less responsive. Although advertising interests contributed to the specific way in which smoking was presented in magazines in the 1950s and 1960s, even magazines that were not reliant on revenue from cigarette advertising did not usually stress the dangers of smoking for women. Women's smoking remained low-profile, in part because women were assumed to smoke more safely. In the 1950s and 1960s the image of the 'at-risk' smoker was a male one, and this image was slow to change.

In the 1970s women smokers did achieve visibility, but government attention focused on mothers-to-be. Since the late 1960s evidence had been accumulating that a pregnant woman harmed her foetus by smoking, and this was recognized in the 1971 RCP report. As Berridge explains, the case against pregnant women smoking was seemingly consolidated by the results of the National Child Development [NCD] Study, published in 1972, in which it was argued that there was a *connection* between smoking and low birth weight. The media subsequently publicized the report's findings but inaccurately reported that smoking *caused* low birth rate and the deaths of 1,500 babies a year.[44] Although causality was not established, the results of the NCD study contributed to the case against smoking during pregnancy, and this was incorporated into the Health Education Council's position on smoking. Concerns about infant mortality since the 1960s, and the increased acceptability of epidemiological evidence, provided a context in which the report's findings were accepted and acted on. Mothers became the focus of a new anti-smoking advertising campaign from 1973. Graphic images, including a photograph of a naked pregnant woman smoking, publicized the danger to unborn children of expectant mothers' smoking. Television advertisements in 1974/75 warned women that smoking in pregnancy produced under-sized babies that were 'undernourished with thin arms and wasted flesh', and that it 'may even threaten his [*sic*] life'.[45] Appealing to the mother's sense of responsibility, one television commercial asked 'Is it fair to your baby to smoke cigarettes?', while another slogan asked 'Do you want a cigarette more than you want a baby?'[46] The message was reiterated in popular magazines and books on pregnancy.[47]

Although pregnant smokers were in the limelight, it was not women who were perceived to be at risk but their unborn children. The risks of smoking to women, whether pregnant or not, remained obscured. Those who sought advice found that there was 'little information available' about women.[48] While health-education initiatives encouraged children and young women to abstain from smoking and later, from around 1970, extended such advice to pregnant women, the dominant view was that women were usually low-risk smokers and that safe smoking was an option. Ironically, the feminization of safer smoking practices may have encouraged women to believe they were immune from harm. As evident in the advice presented by the 1972 Standing Liaison Committee on the Scientific Aspects of Smoking and Health, 'safer' smoking was remarkably consistent with the dominant representation of feminine smoking practices: 'Stop smoking. If you cannot, then smoke a lower tar cigarette, take fewer puffs, do not inhale, leave a longer stub and take the cigarette out of your mouth between puffs.'[49]

There is insufficient evidence to map precisely women's knowledge of the risks that smoking posed to them between 1950 and 1980. Drawing on the smoking experiences of fathers and husbands, some of the Scottish women interviewed by Rosemary Elliot claimed always to have known that smoking was bad for health but not that it was life-threatening. Jess, born in 1916, told Elliot: 'I can't remember when they [anti-smoking publicity] started, but I always knew that there was a certain amount of risk where cigarette smoke was concerned. But I used to think it was just you know chest troubles, coughs and bronchitis and things like that – it never went any deeper'.[50] Though vague about timing, women referred to becoming aware of the health risks of smoking through anti-smoking campaigns and the appearance of health warnings on cigarette packets. One woman claimed ignorance of the health risks until her own father became ill and died of lung cancer in the 1980s. Recalling their pregnancies, some women offered a precise time-frame to the publicity about smoking while pregnant. Alice and her friends were not encouraged to stop smoking when they were carrying children in the 1960s. Maggie, in contrast, noted that while she was not aware of the risks when carrying her first child in 1962, she was aware when carrying her second child in 1964 that smoking made 'children much smaller and weedier'.[51] Graham's interviews with expectant mothers in the mid-1970s confirm that by this time most women were aware of the medical arguments against smoking while pregnant, but that such knowledge did not translate automatically into acceptance.[52] Graham found that some women doubted the validity of scientific arguments because they were inconsistent with their own experiences and those of family, friends and neighbours. Other women with whom Graham spoke accepted the scientific argument but felt unable to act on this for reasons I will discuss later. Being aware of risks to the foetus did not mean that women were fully aware of the risks of smoking to their own health. In light of the widespread presentation in the 1950s and 1960s of men as the smokers at risk of health problems, it is significant that Maggie, interviewed by Elliot, recalled that while the view was that 'pregnant women shouldn't smoke ... ordinary women could go on smoking'.[53]

Health education and the media, including the women's press, did not make the risks to women explicit or high-profile. Indeed, it was not until 1983 that women's smoking was specifically considered by the RCP, and even then women were sidelined in the report's introduction. Not all women were unaware of the risks prior to the 1970s, but access to available information was undoubtedly shaped by social class. It was mainly middle-class women who listened to *Woman's Hour*, read the *Guardian* or studied medical reports in the 1950s and 1960s. This explains, in part, why smoking began to decline among women from the higher social classes during the 1960s. However, irrespective of whether women were aware of the risks that smoking posed to their health they still encountered plenty of encouragement to smoke.

Images of Women Smokers

Between 1950 and 1980, the tobacco industry increased its efforts to promote smoking, and a proliferation of new brands vied for public attention. Between 1962 and 1969, UK manufacturers launched seventy new cigarette brands, especially filter cigarettes which, by 1969, accounted for almost 75 per cent of total sales.[54] Television provided smoking with a new media profile. Wills showed their first TV commercials in September 1955 with fifteen-second spots for Woodbine and Capstan cigarettes,[55] and by 1960 the tobacco industry relied heavily on TV advertising; whereas in 1956 it spent £0.4 million, this increased to £4.2 million by 1960, and £8.1 million by 1964.[56] Extensive press advertising cost the tobacco industry £1.7 million in 1955 and a staggering £11 million by 1968.[57] Promotion of smoking was also achieved through media coverage of high-profile events sponsored by the tobacco industry.

Image had been important to the promotion of smoking culture throughout the first half of the twentieth century, and it continued to be the linchpin of the tobacco industry's efforts to sell cigarettes and other tobacco products. As anti-smoking campaigns gained ground in the 1960s, the visual emerged as the key terrain on which the battle over smoking was fought. Health-education poster campaigns in the late 1950s, even those aimed at children, had not been visual and had relied on statements about the dangers of smoking to health.[58] After the 1962 report, however, 'there was a move towards a more visually arresting and aggressive type of message' targeted at adults and children through poster campaigns and health education films.[59] The anti-smoking lobby was, as Berridge and Loughlin observe, adopting the visual strategies of the tobacco advertisers.[60] At the same time, the anti-smoking lobby also campaigned – successfully in some cases – for constraints on the promotion of images of smoking. Television advertising was banned by 1965. Bold health warnings appeared on cigarette packets from 1971. While these informed smokers directly about health risks, they also had important implications for image. As Chapman notes, image was key to the differentiation of brands, and the cigarette packet played a crucial part in this.[61] The appearance of a cigarette packet contributed to the image of the cigarette and the person who smoked them. Health warnings disrupted the image of cigarettes in general and, more specifically, the image of the brand and that of the smoker. The images used in cigarette advertisements were also curtailed. In 1962 the tobacco industry adopted a voluntary code to exclude advertisements that 'over-emphasised the pleasures of smoking; featured conventional heroes of the young; appealed to manliness, romance or social success'.[62] Similar guidelines were incorporated in 1975 into the Advertising Standards Agency's (ASA) Code of Advertising Practice which specified that cigarette advertisements should not suggest that smoking or particular cigarette brands were 'a sign or proof of manliness, courage or daring'.[63] Indicative of the lower priority attached to female relative to male smoking, it was two years before the 'virility clause' was matched by a 'femininity clause' which disallowed advertisements from suggesting that 'female smokers are more glamorous or independent than non-smokers' or that 'smoking enhances feminine charm'.[64] In response to restrictions on tobacco advertising and widespread publicity about the health risks of smoking, the tobacco industry became more creative with image. Advertising was 'designed to blind consumers to the true nature of what they were buying';[65] increasingly this had to be achieved through the use of symbolism rather than images of actual people.

Given the status of women's magazines as a source of information and guidance for women, it is significant that many carried cigarette advertisements. The withdrawal of cigarette advertisements from women's magazines during the Second World War as a result of paper shortages was only slowly reversed. Throughout the 1950s few advertisements appeared in the weekly service magazine *Woman*, which catered for the lower-middle and working classes, and in 1950 only occasional advertisements featured in the elite (bi-)monthly magazine *Vogue*, although by 1955 cigarette advertising in *Vogue* returned to the pre-1939 level of one advertisement per issue. By the 1960s, cigarette advertisements were again commonplace in both

Vogue and *Woman*, and placed prominently on the back cover or opposite popular features such as horoscopes or problem pages. After cigarette advertisements were banned from television in 1965, there was a further increase in the number of advertisements in women's magazines. In 1965, *Woman* featured usually one cigarette advertisement every two issues, by 1970 this had risen to one or two per issue. Two years later as many as five cigarette advertisements appeared in a single issue of *Woman*, although one to three was more usual at this time.[66] Research undertaken by Jacobson and Amos in the mid 1980s suggests that while magazine editors may not have directly promoted smoking, they were nevertheless prepared to carry cigarette advertisements. Often this was because of the revenue from advertising, although some editors rationalized the decision in terms of the principles of liberal individualism. Cigarette advertisements, they pointed out, complied with advertising standards, and cigarette packets and advertisements made clear that smoking endangered health. These editors refused to 'act as censors for intelligent readers in what they saw as a free society'; they insisted that it was up to the individual to decide what was best for her.[67]

Cigarette advertising did not feature in magazines for schoolgirls such as *Jackie*, or in magazine for older, working teenagers such as *Valentine*, *Roxy* and *Mayfair*. Even more sophisticated magazines like *Petticoat* and *Honey*, which catered for young women in their late teens and early twenties, often did not carry cigarette advertisements. There was not, however, a universal reluctance to feature cigarette advertisements in magazines for young women. Often the only explanation for the absence of cigarette advertisements was that the magazine was not rated by advertisers as a medium for promotions. *Vanity Fair*, an up-market paper for the 'younger, smarter woman' under twenty-five, did attract tobacco advertising, and it sporadically featured cigarette advertisements throughout the 1950s and 1960s.[68]

Positive images of smoking culture were not restricted to cigarette advertising in girls' and women's magazines of the 1950s and 1960s. Celebrity smokers were another way in which glamorous images of smoking remained in focus even in magazines for schoolgirls or older teen readers.[69] In women's magazines, smokers featured in fashion promotions and in advertisements for products other than cigarettes. Fiction also presented central female characters as smokers. In the first quarter of 1968, for instance, a central female character smoked her way through a story at least once a month in *Petticoat*.[70] Presenting a businesslike image, *Woman*'s agony aunt Marj Proops appeared at the top of her problem page in 1970 with a cigarette in a holder.

By the 1970s, women smokers were rarely visible in women's magazines outside the context of cigarette advertisements. Smoking also had a lower television profile. The BBC had come under pressure since the 1960s to cut down the frequency with which smoking appeared, particularly in programmes such as *Z-Cars* which, it was believed, encouraged hero worship.[71] Nevertheless, in the

1970s shows still featured guests who smoked and smokers continued to appear in a range of series, soaps and films, including the weekend matinees. The visibility of smokers was much reduced by the mid-1980s as leading British TV serials such as *Crossroads* and *Coronation Street* 'specifically avoid showing their characters smoking, while new series such as *Brookside* … and *EastEnders*, take a firm anti-smoking stance'.[72] At the cinema, smoking continued to figure prominently between 1960 and 1990, although there was a decline in smoking by major characters.[73] Product placement also ensured that cigarettes were high-profile in box office hits. Phillip Morris paid $42,000 to ensure that Marlboro cigarettes were well publicized in *Superman II*; Lois Lane puffed on Marlboro while 'Superman fought the Evil Three against a backdrop of Marlboro vans'.[74]

Girls and women encountered positive images of female smokers in all areas of visual media. They certainly made an impression on Christine and Gail, both born in the 1950s and interviewed by Elliot in 2000.[75] Cigarettes appeared as the adjunct to a range of attractive femininities and lifestyles, and were linked to glamorous women in the 1950s and 1960s and to lithe and liberated young women in the 1970s. Smoking was portrayed as the accessory of successful socialites, home-lovers and women in pursuit of romance. Each of these feminine attractions will now be examined more closely.

Feminine Attractions

Glamorous women regularly appeared in cigarette advertisements of the 1950s. Affluent beauties in evening dress, actresses and pretty television presenters all extolled the virtues of their favoured cigarette brand.[76] The association of smoking with sophistication and glamour was consolidated throughout the 1950s and early 1960s in representations of feminine fashion in glossy women's magazines.[77] In an advertisement for Brenner fashions, for instance, a beautiful woman stands facing the camera with a cigarette in a holder (Fig. 8.2).[78] Smoking contributed to the elegance of this woman, and also accentuated her sexuality by highlighting her parted, ruby-red lips. The sexual overtones were further enhanced by the woman's closed eyes and a glimmer of a smile which suggested that she was lost in pleasant and romantic daydreams.

Smokers were portrayed as sensual, elegant and beautiful – on occasions, so too were cigarettes and cigarette smoke. A *Vogue* feature on evening dress, which featured a pretty young woman smoking, described her white organdie stole that she wore draped across her shoulders, as 'soft as cigarette smoke curling into a summer dusk'.[79] The importance of the cigarette for the well-dressed woman was heightened by the place of the cigarette holder in 1950s fashion. As described by *Vogue,* the look of 1950 required 'big sleeves … a short skirt that narrows from a slight peg top … The hair is short; the cigarette holder long'.[80]

*Figure 8.2   Brenner fashion advertisement. Vogue, March 1954, p. 46. Thanks to Condé
Nast. Reproduced by permission of The British Library (shelf mark LD 89).*

On-screen, smoking and glamour remained synonymous. In *Breakfast at
Tiffany's*, released in 1961, Holly Golightly, played by Audrey Hepburn, rarely
appeared without a cigarette. Publicity stills for the film portrayed Hepburn looking
chic and beautiful in a black dress and strings of pearls as she gazed at the viewer
over her extended cigarette holder. Off-screen, images of celebrities reinforced the
association of smoking with glamorous femininities as when actors Ava Gardner
and Janet Leigh appeared smoking with partners Frank Sinatra and Tony Curtis in
a double-page spread in *Valentine*.[81] The association of smoking with a specifically
British style of feminine glamour was assured by media photographs of Princess
Margaret. With her cigarette in a holder, the Princess regularly graced the pages of
women's magazines.[82]

In the 'swinging sixties' the cigarette transformed into an accessory for the lithe
and liberated young woman. The place of smoking in contemporary youth culture,
which was heavily influenced by the pop industry, contributed to this. All of the
Beatles, for example, were heavy smokers in the 1960s and 1970s; the cigarette
appeared in media coverage of their activities and on the record cover of Abbey
Road.[83]

Although female models were uncommon in cigarette advertisements of the 1960s and 1970s, they still appeared in advertisements for brands specifically targeted at women. The liberated smokers who featured in these advertisements were conspicuously slim, a point exaggerated by clothes, pose, props and camera angle. Thinness was not only the feminine-body ideal of this period but also, increasingly, a defining feature of cigarettes, and even cigars, sold to women. Toledo cigars were, the advertisement explained, made for men but ideal for women because they were 'long, slender, golden, mild – so smooth, in every way, that they *belong* in a girl's smoking wardrobe'.[84] Dunhill Slims were, as their name suggests, a thin version of the Dunhill cigarette.[85] The advertisement (Fig. 8.3)

Figure 8.3   Dunhill Slims cigarette advertisement. Woman, 15 August 1970, p. 57. Thanks to British American Tobacco. Reproduced by permission of The British Library (shelf mark 1723).

featured a tall and thin female with slightly wild hair, dressed in a slinky, long black dress which accentuated her length and slimness. She was portrayed reclining on a gently curved long seat with a cigarette poised between her long and slender fingers. The woman in this advertisement was the embodiment of the cigarette and, conversely, the cigarette was, by transference of meaning, endowed with the qualities of the model.

Slimness and liberation were synonymous for women. Cigarette advertisements implied that smoking was a sign of women's liberation, while the brand names aligned this liberation with being, and becoming, thin. Virginia Slims, a cigarette for women that was launched in Britain in 1976, made this link explicit when it told women, 'You've come a long, long way'.[86] The liberation that Virginia Slims most obviously heralded was, however, only the freedom to smoke. This consumerist version of liberation had been employed in advertisements addressed to women since the 1960s. Cigarettes targeted at women, such as Olivier in 1963, or designed for them, such as Dunhill Slims in 1970, often drew on the discourse of women's rights and aligned this with a notion of consumer equality. Olivier advertisements explained that: 'Women like us like our very own things. Like fashion. Like Olivier. So beautifully cool and smooth. So elegantly packed. So sensibly priced. Our very own Olivier'.[87] Expressing a similar sentiment, but more succinctly, advertisements for Dunhill Slims stated 'Let him light it – but this one's yours'.[88] Reclining, with her leg bent and one arm on her hip, the Dunhill woman stared confidently at the viewer (see Fig. 8.3). Alongside her status as a smoker and consumer she was also sexually liberated.

Women smokers of the late 1960s and 1970s, unlike their counterparts of the 1950s and early 1960s, were often more sexual than sensual. Jane Birkin, a British girl who became a French 'sex symbol', posed with a cigarette in her mouth for *Vanity Fair*.[89] The association of smoking with sexually liberated young women was often implicit. In a fashion spread in *Honey*, entitled 'The cold grey light of dawn', a young woman in evening dress, but with tousled just-got-out-of-bed-hair, sucks honey from her finger as she is embraced gently by her lover.[90] Cigarettes with long stubs of cold ash sit in an ashtray on the table beside them, suggesting that a few hours earlier smoking had been abandoned for other pleasures.

Partygoers and other sociable women were often smokers. Lifestyle advertisements continued to place the woman smoker central to social activities well into the 1960s. Chic women, dressed in black, with a cigarette in one hand and a glass of liqueur in the other, were the centre of attention at sophisticated parties.[91] Smoking also featured in the party life of younger women. With a cigarette in one hand and a champagne glass in the other a young woman modelled a 'princess dress' for Richard Shops, while a cigarette in a holder was the accessory highlighted in a dressmaking pattern for a 'party two-piece'.[92] The social value of smoking was reinforced in magazine features such as an article in *Honey* on parties. Readers were advised: 'If you can't think of a question, ASK FOR SOMETHING: a cigarette (even if you have your own). A light. An ashtray. Or to pass the peanuts because you're starved.'[93] Although food and drink were mentioned as conversation openers, smoking practices were presented as particularly useful. The author also proffered advice on being witty, again using smoking as an example: 'Would you mind holding my cigarette while I have a puff? I promised my mother not to touch a cigarette.' It is unclear whether the mother's opposition to her daughter smoking was supposed to be because she: thought her daughter too young to smoke, disapproved of women smoking, or believed smoking to be a harmful practice. Whatever the reason, it was apparently quite legitimate for the party girl to smoke even in defiance of her mother's wishes. Aside from the effervescence of parties, smoking was also compatible with quieter social pleasures. Aboard a small boat with her male partner and another couple, a woman smokes while chatting and drinking hot chocolate.[94] Women were told that a good hostess needed 'Ronson home lighters for your dining room and sitting room, for your cocktail and dinner parties'.[95]

While cigarettes were portrayed as aids to sociability, they were located at the heart of romance. The place of smoking in specifically heterosexual romantic encounters was well established prior to 1950 and it remained so in the second half of the twentieth century. Film provided graphic celebration of the romantic and sexual role of women's smoking but so too did advertising and print media. Cigarettes were presented as facilitating relaxed conversation which was a necessary prelude to romance. In 'A Man for Judith', a short story in *Woman*, a young widow, Judith, meets a handsome young widower, Paul, at a dinner party hosted by mutual friends. Paul is just the sort of man with whom Judith thinks she could fall in love but, when sat next to him at the dinner table, she becomes self-conscious and unsure of herself: 'She was furious with herself for being tongue-tied, for needing something to do with her hands. She dug into her bag for her cigarettes, but he was already offering his.'[96] A witty comment from Paul breaks the ice as they light their cigarettes. The full-page illustration depicts this moment with Judith laughing gaily, a cigarette in her hand. Romantic smoking scenes were also common in magazine fiction. In 'Night of the Party', for example, Maggie was being courted by Roger, an attentive male admirer. Although there was no reference to her smoking, the full-page illustration depicted Maggie holding a cigarette packet in one hand and a cigarette in the other as, tucked under Roger's arm, she lit her cigarette from the light he offered.[97] Although advertisers were increasingly restricted after 1962 in how they could promote cigarettes, the romantic twosome remained a staple ingredient, even if only by suggestion. Prominently placed on the back cover of *Woman* a typical Benson & Hedges advertisement promoted smoking as the ideal accompaniment to romance.[98] The photograph shows a rowing boat moored at the side of stream in the fading light of a summer's day. An open picnic basket is in the foreground, in which there are two sets of silver cutlery and a cigarette packet. On the small jetty, two plates and two glasses of wine stand abandoned. The presence of the couple is almost tangible, but they are not visible in the advertisement, and the viewer is left wondering where they are and what they are doing.

After 1950, and consistent with other commercial advertising, smoking was increasingly presented in a domestic context.[99] Most often it was men puffing on pipes who dominated representations of home life, but the cigarette-smoking woman also had her place. An advertisement for gas fires, for example, portrayed a woman sitting by the fireside smoking and chatting to her male companion.[100] People were, however, unusual in representations of domesticity in cigarette advertisements of the 1960s and 1970s. This was in stark contrast to the representation of couples characteristic of 1950s advertisements,[101] and a deliberate response to restrictions on how people could be portrayed in cigarette advertisements. Full-page advertisements were dominated by photographs of cigarette packets surrounded by various props. Fancy ashtrays or a silver platter signified an affluent home life, while a cup of coffee with cream, brandy glasses, and a bowl of exotic fruits suggested domestic comforts.[102] In advertisements for low-tar and menthol brands, which were targeted mainly at women, the props were usually specifically feminine or feminized: a looking mirror; small candlesticks suitable for a dressing table; and dainty china ornaments.[103]

The domestication of the woman smoker was highlighted in advertisements for coupon cigarette brands. Following the example of Embassy in 1962, and spurred on by the ban on television advertising from 1965, coupon or stamp schemes were introduced for most of the mainstream cigarette brands and, in particular, those targeted at working-class consumers. Investment in gift-coupon schemes increased from £8 million in 1965 to £50 million by 1975, although from the mid-1970s, as a result of tax changes, these schemes became unprofitable and folded.[104] Advertisements for coupon cigarettes, especially when they appeared in the women's press, attempted to embrace women within a domesticated smoking culture. These advertisements suggested to women that by purchasing cigarettes, either for themselves or for their male partners, they could collect coupons that would enable them to acquire a range of gifts for their families and their home. Indeed, many of the domestic and feminine props that appeared in the advertisements could be 'purchased' with cigarette coupons. The glossy all-colour gift catalogue central to the launch of Embassy's coupon scheme was such a novelty that it made front-page news, the *Daily Mirror* even listing items from the catalogue.[105] By the time that the second Embassy catalogue was issued in September 1963, there were 1.5 million applicants on the mailing list.[106] One Embassy advertisement actually masqueraded as information about the gift catalogue: 'Just Out! ... Embassy Gift Catalogue fourth edition. Over 600 personal and household gifts illustrated in 60 full-colour pages.'[107] By the 1970s, the domestic side of smoking was accentuated as companies competed with one another to offer better gifts more quickly: 'you can get a top quality gift in half the time it takes with other 5/2 cigarettes'.[108]

The Unattractive Female Smoker

The cigarette was the accessory of glamorous, as well as young and liberated, women. It was smoked by partygoers, by women falling in love, and by those who revelled in domesticity.

However, not all images of women smokers were positive. In anti-smoking campaigns, women smokers were portrayed as irresponsible, foolish or ignorant. Sometimes anti-smoking imagery suggested the incompatibility of smoking and specific feminine roles, most notably that of mother and mother-to-be. In magazines, young and glamorous working-class women smokers were often portrayed on the knife-edge of respectability for the same reasons as had their pre-1950s counterparts – that is, the sexual connotations of working-class glamour. By the 1950s, working-class women's smoking was no longer associated with loose sexual morals, but the sexual sophistication suggested by certain kinds of smoking practice ensured that it was still problematic for the sexual reputation of a young working-class woman. Not surprisingly, magazines for working-class teenagers warned that the combination of smoking and glamour spelt trouble for the 'ordinary girl', although this did not rule out all forms of smoking as unacceptable.[109] Although not all female smoking was approved of, even those who met with disapproval were usually portrayed as visibly attractive, as in the *Honey* feature discussed earlier (Fig. 8.1).

A few physically unattractive female smokers were visible in film, television and print media from the 1950s but these were always in the minority. Significantly, after more than 50 years of representing women smokers as visibly middle or upper class, it was in this context that the working-class woman smoker came to the fore. An advertisement for Wisdom toothbrushes, featured in *Woman*, provides one of the first visibly negative images of a woman smoking to appear in a modern woman's magazine (Fig. 8.4).[110] In many ways she was similar to the minority of unattractive women smokers who appeared on television, most famously the charwoman Hilda Ogden who smoked her way through several decades of *Coronation Street*. The Wisdom woman smoker was portrayed as old, physically unattractive and working class – the latter indicated by her overall and head scarf which together symbolized paid or unpaid domestic drudgery. Significantly the markers of age, gender and class were particularly negative ones; alternative and more attractive signifiers of age could have been employed, as was usual in magazines at this time, but they were not.[111] The Wisdom woman was also portrayed as a habitual smoker; she was dressed for work but had a cigarette drooping from the corner of her mouth as if it were a permanent feature. The Wisdom woman differed markedly from

Figure 8.4   Wisdom toothbrush advertisement. Woman, 11 July 1970, p. 64. Thanks to Wisdom Ltd. Reproduced by permission of The British Library (shelf mark 1723).

the usual images of women smoking because she lacked refinement. As we saw in Chapter 6, refinement required attention to the finer details of appearance and depended on careful maintenance and control/containment of the female body. Aside from appearance, refinement also required a certain posture (elegant and contained) and behaviour (polite, not coarse). Refinement was key to the visual representation of the attractive and respectable woman smoker – its absence was central to the unattractive and negative connotations of the Wisdom image. In the

Wisdom advertisement the woman smoker was unkempt; her hair protruded at all angles from her headscarf, her overall was rumpled, the pocket sat untidily. Further, this woman wore no make-up although she lacked the fresh look of youth. This woman's body was also out of control: her skin was wrinkled and sagging, she was over weight and her hair was dishevelled. Although this woman crossed her arms in a defensive gesture, her posture suggests that she was also, quite literally, holding herself and her overall together. The image implies that this unruliness was partly caused by age and, more importantly, by gender and class. The delicate bracelet on the woman's wrist merely serves to remind us of a more refined femininity and, if anything, it strengthens the impression that this woman has 'let herself go'. The Wisdom woman represented the unrespectable working class; she was the 'real' working-class woman that young women, interviewed in the 1990s, described as 'scruffy', 'common', 'greasy', 'fat', and as always having 'a fag in their mouths'.[112]

Although negative and unattractive images of women smokers were more common after 1950 than before, smoking was still primarily associated with positive and attractive images of womanhood. As was the case pre-1950, in the postwar decades there was little space in visual culture for the unattractive woman, whether she smoked or not. Not surprisingly, representations of unattractive women smokers did little to counter the dominant image of the feminine smoker – because they were in the minority and because they were not the types of smokers that most girls or women related to, they were invariably 'Other'. However, aside from the plethora of positive images of women smoking, there were other reasons why cigarettes remained attractive to women.

The Limits of Image? Coping with Disadvantage

The anti-smoking lobby and public-health officials were concerned about the influence of positive images of smoking, especially on young people. Other factors were also deemed important, notably the influence of parents and siblings who smoked and the example of peers; a concern to be slim was also identified.[113] But the factors which encouraged girls to try cigarettes and those which encouraged adults to continue smoking were often different; as one woman put it, 'I used to smoke because I wanted to, now I smoke because I need to'.[114]

Feminist research of the 1970s and 1980s pointed to gender-specific factors that kept women smoking and which made it particularly hard for them to give up despite their knowledge of the health risks involved. Women, it was argued, used smoking as a 'safety valve', a means of coping with anger and frustration for which, unlike their male peers, they had few legitimate outlets.[115] Graham found that while many expectant mothers accepted that smoking endangered the health of the foetus, some continued to smoke after weighing up the needs of their unborn child and those of their partners, themselves and their existing children. As one woman explained: 'They say it can be born dead if you smoke, through coming on early. I've cut down, and I'm to 10 a day. If I cut down any more, I take it out on him [her son] which isn't fair on him. So it's one bairn or the other.'[116] For these women smoking was a means of coping with stress, of mitigating the boredom and monotony of being housebound and, on a practical level, of managing childcare responsibilities and delineating time for relaxation. Although some observers suggested that women's smoking was a result of their emancipation,[117] research in Britain suggested otherwise. Smoking, Jacobson argued, was a response to continuing inequalities that blighted the lives of many women, including full-time housewives and mothers, independent career women and women who combined paid work and family responsibilities. According to Jacobson, women often felt dependent on cigarettes to help them manage the stresses they experienced and, because of gender factors, they often lacked the confidence to quit.[118] Hilton claims that the fictional experience of James Bond is 'illustrative of both male and female smokers'.[119] While it can be safely assumed that lack of confidence was never a problem for Bond, there are points of similarity. As for Bond, individual need was an important reason why women could not or did not want to quit smoking, but these included gendered needs. Identity issues were another factor, but these too were gendered in significant ways. Bond smoked to 'posit his individuality', but women often smoked to escape one identity – that of 'mother' – and to temporarily regain a more individualized one. By 1990, when prevalence of smoking was twice as high among women in the lowest social groups as among women in the highest, it became clear that inequalities were classed as well as gendered. After interviewing 905 mothers with young children in working-class households, Graham concluded that disadvantaged women smoked when 'life's a drag'.[120] Other research confirmed the links between smoking and gendered disadvantage for young women: 'while the transition to adulthood is often associated with notions of independence, the lives of young women are often constrained, both by the structures of the labour market and by familial expectations'.[121]

Many women felt dependent on tobacco to cope. Unlike men, they were presented with no alternative to the cigarette if they tried to quit. Pipes and cigars, though misguidedly presented until the late 1970s by the RCP and the press as relatively safe forms of smoking, were not options for most women because they were defined as masculine.[122] While there were material dimensions to women's smoking needs and practices, these were increasingly interwoven with visual culture in at least two ways. First, the fact that pipes and cigars were not usually perceived as alternative smoking practices for women suggests the notion that image remained powerful: while the cigarette had been visually feminized, cigars and pipes had not. Second, when women talked about their smoking practice they frequently drew on discourses about the properties of tobacco. The idea that a cigarette helped women to manage stress, boredom and danger had been legitimized by wartime discourse on smoking and persistently and visually reinforced in film through the smoking practices not just of women, but of men, both the good guys and the bad. How women, and indeed men, conceptualized the cigarette and the comforts it afforded was inextricably related to visual culture.

Conclusion

Girls and women received mixed messages about smoking in the period 1950 to 1980. From the 1950s, scientific evidence brought the dangers of smoking to the fore, but the risks of smoking for women were only gradually acknowledged and communicated to women. Meanwhile, a proliferation of positive images of smokers encouraged women to smoke. Negative images of women smokers did appear, but typically, even in anti-smoking campaigns, these did not portray the smoker as visibly unattractive. On the occasions where physically unattractive women were portrayed smoking, they were not the kinds of women that most smokers identified with, since they were invariably presented as members of the unrespectable working class. On their own, these mixed messages are not enough to explain why cigarette smoking continued to appeal to girls and women, but they do go a long way toward explaining why anti-smoking campaigns had only limited success in 'beating the ladykillers'.[123]

Notes

1. Hilton, *Smoking*, p. 235.
2. Men and male examples form the principle focus of Hilton's discussion and he does not comment on the male subjects of many of the sources he uses, such as references to 'smokers' in the popular press, the medical journal *The Lancet* and several contemporary surveys; see also Hilton's comment on Bond, p. 226.
3. Aspects of the gender dimensions of smoking 1950–1980 are addressed in studies by Virginia Berridge, Rosemary Elliot, Hilary Graham, Bobbie Jacobson.
4. Wald et al., *UK Smoking Statistics*, p. 35, Table 4.1.2.
5. Ibid., pp. 16–17, Table 2.3.
6. Ibid., p. 35, Table 4.1.2.
7. Ibid., p. 34, Table 4.1.1.
8. Ibid., pp. 14–15.
9. Graham, *When Life's a Drag*, pp. 12–13.

10. Ibid., p. 60, Table 5.1.

11. Ibid., p. 62, Table 5.2.

12. Ibid., for figures 1960s–1980s. For men too, the social-class distribution of smokers shifted after 1958 with the percentage of smokers falling dramatically among men of Social Class I (p. 61, Table 5.2).

13. Wald et al., UK Smoking Statistics, p. 35, Table 4.1.2.

14. *Woman's Own*, 1 March 1956, pp. 20–1.

15. Abrams, *Teenage Consumer*.

16. *Jackie*, 30 January 1965, p. 15.

17. Wald et al., *Smoking Statistics*, p. 35, Table 4.1.2.

18. Ibid., p. 91, Table 7.1.

19. RCP, *Smoking and Health*, p. S3.

20. Hilton, *Smoking*, p. 203.

21. Ibid., p. 186.

22. RCP, *Smoking and Health Now,* p. 2.

23. Hilton, *Smoking*, p. 207.

24. Berridge, 'Post-war Smoking Policy'.

25. Elliot, 'Destructive but Sweet', p. 269.

26. RCP, *Smoking and Health Now*, p. 2.

27. Berridge, 'Post-war Smoking Policy', pp. 66–7.

28. Taylor, *Smoke Ring*.

29. Hilton, *Smoking*, p. 189.

30. Ibid., p. 230.

31. Jacobson, *The Ladykillers,* p. 74.

32. RCP, *Health or Smoking?*, p. 61.

33. Ibid., p. 69.

34. See examples cited in Berridge, 'Constructing Women and Smoking', p. 331, and Hilton, *Smoking*, p. 191.

35. Player, DD PL 7/19/3 *Marlton Gazette & Herald,* 19 July 1957.

36. Elliot, 'Destructive but Sweet', pp. 247–8.

37. McKennell and Thomas, *Adults' and Adolescents' Smoking Habits*; Bynner, *Young Smoker,* p. 17.

38. *Honey*, May 1965, pp. 74–5.

39. For example *Woman*, 13 March 1943, p. 16; *Woman and Home*, February 1935, p. 75.

40. *Woman*, 24 January 1970, pp. 24–5, 47–8; advertisement on p. 46.

41. Ibid., 12 September 1970, p. 41.

42. Taylor, *Smoke Ring*; Jacobson and Amos, *When Smoke Gets In Your Eyes*.

43. Hilton, *Smoking*, p. 213.

44. Berridge, 'Constructing Women and Smoking', p. 334.

45. Cited in Graham, 'Smoking in Pregnancy', p. 399.

46. Ibid., p. 400.

47. Ibid.

48. RCP, *Health or Smoking?*, p. 61.

49. Cited in Elliot, 'Destructive but Sweet', p. 269.

50. Ibid., p. 340.

51. Ibid., p. 337.

52. Graham, *Smoking in Pregnancy*.

53. Elliot, 'Destructive but Sweet', p. 337.

54. Alford, *Wills*, p. 454.

55. Ibid., p. 425.

56. RCP, *Smoking and Health Now*, p. 17.

57. Ibid., p. 17.

58. Hilton, *Smoking*, p. 190.

59. Ibid., p. 191.

60. Berridge and Loughlin, 'Smoking and the New Health Education in Britain'.

61. Chapman, *Great Expectorations*.

62. RCP, *Smoking and Health Now*, p. 18.

63. Cited in Jacobson, *Beating the Ladykillers*, p. 52.

64. Ibid., p. 59.

65. Taylor, *Smoke Ring*, p. 38.

66. *Woman*, 20 May 1972. In the 1980s, cigarette advertisements continued to be commonplace in magazines such as *Woman, Vogue, Good Housekeeping*, although some editors refused advertisements specifically targeted at women or those for high-tar brands (Jacobson and Amos, *When Smoke Gets in Your Eyes*, p. 11).

67. Jacobson and Amos, *When Smoke Gets in Your Eyes*, p. 12.

68. For example *Vanity Fair*: June 1950, p. 4; November 1959, p. 129; October 1969, p. 105. Jacobson and Amos, *When Smoke Gets in Your Eyes*, discovered that while 1980s magazines aimed at schoolgirls continued to reject cigarette advertisements (*Jackie, Smash Hits, Just 17, My Guy, Blue Jeans*), those which targeted women in their late teens and young twenties (*Honey, 19, Company*) did take advertisements.

69. For example *Jackie*, 3 February 1965, pp. 12, 18; *Valentine*, 1 June 1957, pp. 8–9.

70. *Petticoat*, 20 January 1968; 24 February 1968; 16 March 1968.

71. Hilton, *Smoking*, p. 233.

72. Jacobson, *Beating the Ladykillers*, p. 79.

73. Stockwell and Glantz, 'Tobacco Use'.

74. Parr, 'S for Smoking'; Jacobson, *Beating the Ladykillers*, p. 80.

75. Elliot, 'Destructive but Sweet', pp. 350, 352.

76. *Woman*, 28 May 1955, p. 59; 5 November 1955, p. 48. *Vogue,* November 1955, p. 193.

77. For example *Vogue*: March 1954, p. 163; February 1960, pp. 55, 57; 1 March 1965, pp. 93–4.

78. *Vogue*, March 1954, p. 46.

79. *Vogue*, May 1954, p. 101.

80. *Vogue*, January 1950, p. 34.

81. *Valentine,* 1 June 1957, pp. 8–9.

82. For example *Woman*: 14 May 1955, p. 19; 21 May 1955, pp. 20–1; 22 August 1970, p. 33.

83. *Valentine*, 20 July 1968, p. 7.

84. *Vogue*, August 1964, p. 24.

85. *Woman*, 15 August 1970, p. 57.

86. Jacobson, *Beating the Ladykillers*, p. 58.

87. *Woman,* 15 June 1963, p. 50.

88. *Woman*, 15 August 1970, p. 57.

89. *Vanity Fair*, January 1970, p. 39.

90. *Honey*, November 1970, pp. 102–3.

91. *Vogue*, January 1964, p. 16; *Vanity Fair*, October (I) 1960, p. 15.

92. *Vanity Fair,* November 1959, p. 21; October (I), 1960, p. 122.

93. *Honey*, April 1960, p. 64.

94. *Honey*, April 1960, p. 98.

95. *Vogue*, April 1954, p. 217.

96. *Woman*, 5 March 1960, pp. 24–5.

97. *Woman*, 16 January 1960, p. 13.

98. *Woman*, 7 June 1975.

99. Holland, 'Sweet it is to Scan', p. 148.

100. *Woman*, 28 August 1965, p. 14.

101. For example *Woman*, 11 June 1955, p. 42. See also Warsh and Tinkler, 'In Vogue'.

102. *Woman*, 21 August 1965, p. 34; 1 August 1970, p. 64; *Woman's Own,* 14 June 1975, p. 58; *Woman*, 4 July 1970, p. 32; 17 May 1975, back page.

103. *Woman*, 13 May 1972, pp. 54, 65, 89.

104. Jacobson, *Beating the Ladykillers*, p. 50.

105. Alford, *Wills*, p. 452.

106. Ibid.

107. *Woman*, 11 September 1965, p. 67.

108. *Woman*, 4 July 1970, p. 32.

109. *Valentine*, 27 January 1962, pp. 16–18.

110. *Woman*, 11 July 1970, p. 64.

111. Positive images of older women from the middle and working classes were common in advertisements, see *Woman,* 10 January 1970, p. 6; 14 February 1970, p. 41.

112. Skeggs, *Formations,* pp. 75, 83.

113. Jacobson, *Ladykillers*.

114. Jacobson, *Beating the Ladykillers*, p. 98.

115. Ibid., p. 89.

116. Graham, 'Smoking in Pregnancy', p. 403.

117. Cited in Jacobson, *Ladykillers*, p. 40.

118. Jacobson, *Beating the Ladykillers*, p. 98.

119. Hilton, *Smoking*, p. 226.

120. Graham, *Life's a Drag*, p. xi.

121. Daykin, 'Young Women and Smoking', p. 95.

122. Pipes and cigars were widely regarded as safe in the period 1950 to early 1970s because they were smoked in different ways to that for cigarettes. By the 1980s it was clear that ex-cigarette smokers smoked pipes and cigars in the same way they had smoked cigarettes and therefore put themselves at risk (RCP, *Health or Smoking?*).

123. Jacobson, *Beating the Ladykillers*.

Conclusion

Young and fresh-faced, she wears a touch of make-up, a turquoise beaded top and dangly earrings – the sort of outfit available from any high-street fashion store for young women. In most respects she is like all the other pretty young women appearing in glossy teen magazines. In one respect, however, she is startlingly different. She holds a cigarette, and this is unusual in print media, especially since the demise of cigarette advertising. It is not the cigarette, however, that catches – or rather offends – the eye. It is the brown-stained teeth and gums revealed by the young woman's smile. The text reinforces what is apparent from the image: 'teeth getting a bit minging?'[1]

This anti-smoking image is shocking, and intentionally so. It is shocking because it is such an unpleasant and unattractive picture produced through the juxtaposition of youth and freshness with staining and decay. New possibilities for creating images have mushroomed since 1980 with the advent of digital technology but, even so, in mainstream media it is still uncommon to see unattractive images of women: the pretty girl still reigns supreme. More specifically, it is still unusual to see unattractive images of women smokers. There have been fewer images of smokers in the print media and on television since the 1960s, arising from the suppression of tobacco advertising, pressure on television producers not to promote smoking and a widespread, but by no means universal, dislike of the cigarette habit. But attractive smokers still achieve visibility. Celebrity smokers occasionally grace the pages of glossy magazines exhibiting 'nicotine chic' even though often condemned.[2] The cigarette has continued to have a starring role in many recent films. Research suggests it is most common in the hands of the 'bad guys', but as the researchers admit, it can be 'cool to be bad'.[3] While Catherine Tramell may have been suspected of murder in *Basic Instinct*, there is nothing unattractive about Sharon Stone's depiction of how this woman smokes throughout her interview with the police. Moreover, the continued association of smoking with the management of stress, loneliness and other emotions – graphically conveyed in film especially by the smoking habits of lower-class and 'less attractive' characters – contributes to a discourse on tobacco's role in comfort and coping. Attractive images of women smokers also appear on the margins of mainstream visual culture, especially in the context of sexual fetish. The increased condemnation of smoking has, some argue, even enhanced the eroticization of the woman smoker. The visibility of attractive women smokers is, however, not only the result of the production and display of new images but also the recycling of old ones. Retro-chic has provided a means for glamorous images of women smokers from the 1950s and 1960s to resurface. Audrey Hepburn, as Holly Golightly, displays her cigarette in its long holder as she looks enticingly at us from the window of an art gallery, a display of gift cards and even a young woman's handbag. The recycling of this image not only ensures that women smokers are widely visible, but the contexts in which it appears ensures that the glamorous and sophisticated credentials of the smoker are reaffirmed.

That Holly Golightly features in contemporary visual culture is testimony to this society's continued addiction to the smoking image. It is also evidence of how deeply ingrained is the association of smoking with attractive femininities. As this book has demonstrated, this process began around 1880 and escalated after 1920 with the growth of a mass media that was increasingly dependent on visual imagery. Drawing upon the long-established association of smoking with men and masculinities, and a marginal discourse on smoking and female sexuality, the cigarette became a symbol of women's rights, emancipation and modernity. In the interwar years smoking came to represent – and indeed constitute – the modern woman in terms of her appearance, her use of space and her relationships with men. Initially some advertisers played on the sexual associations of smoking, but from the late 1920s the main tobacco manufacturers preferred a more conservative approach in their bid to establish smoking as a respectable feminine practice. The sexual connotations of smoking nevertheless remained an important element in the construction of feminine modernity and, more generally, feminine attraction. Indeed the feminization of smoking was inextricably related to its heterosexualization. Smoking became aligned with heterosexual attraction, glamour, sex and seduction. The unruly and 'other' heterosexualities associated in Victorian and Edwardian times with women smoking, and the continued association of smoking with the sexual availability of working-class women, nevertheless contributed a certain tension to representations of women smoking. Initially only visibly middle- and upper-class women could smoke without risk to their sexual reputations. The modernity, glamour and respectability of smoking were the privilege of class, and this did not change until the Second World War. By the 1940s, and facilitated by the belief that tobacco helped people cope with stress, cigarette smoking emerged as a legitimate and quite respectable feminine practice for women from all social classes. While by 1950 smoking was acknowledged to be an aid to managing the demands of modern female life, the glamour of smoking reached new heights with 1950s fashions. Harping back to earlier associations with women's rights and female emancipation, in the 1960s and 1970s smoking also became the accessory of lithe young women who demanded consumer equality as well as sexual liberation. While the sociability of female smoking was affirmed in the postwar decades, so too was its place in heterosexual intimacy and domestic bliss.

The deep-seated association of smoking with respectable femininities was not only a matter of image: for more than a century, women have smoked and, since the 1920s, visibly so. Though, with few exceptions, smokers were usually men in the 1880s, by 1920 women smokers were increasingly evident in upper- and certain middle-class social circles, and they were even acknowledged by government. By the late 1930s, smokers predominated among the middle-class women who responded to a Mass-Observation directive on smoking; most of those who were non-smokers admitted that they had tried to develop a taste for cigarettes.[4] Prompted by the Second World War, smoking increased among women from across the social classes and, by 1949, there were 47 per cent of women under 60 years old who smoked, and 41 per cent of all women.[5] Women smokers remained commonplace in all walks of life in the 1950s, 1960s and 1970s – princesses enjoyed a cigarette, so too did idols of the stage and screen, professional women, suburban housewives, exhausted mothers, even teenaged girls. It was not until the mid-1970s that the prevalence of female smoking began to decline. At this point the proportion of men who smoked, especially cigarette smokers, had been falling for 15 years; by the 1980s roughly equal proportions of women and men were smokers of cigarettes.[6]

There has always been some opposition to women's smoking, and criticism was rife prior to the First World War. According to critics, smoking damaged women's reproductive health and their nerves; cigarettes also undermined a woman's femininity and destroyed her beauty. Between 1920 and 1950 these objections were muted: in a culture where smoking was increasingly celebrated as safe, sensible and sociable and where women were ostensibly liberated from Victorian conventions, objections to women's smoking appeared old-fashioned and constraining. In the 1950s, scientific evidence emerged that reinforced the arguments of the anti-smoking lobby. Lung cancer, heart disease and bronchitis were the main risks identified by research, but this new knowledge did little to disrupt discourses on the attractiveness and respectability of women's smoking. This was not surprising. On the one hand, it was not until the 1970s that the at-risk smoker emerged as a feminine one. Until then public-health campaigns and initiatives had focused principally on men. Women, it was assumed, smoked less and more safely than men. On the other hand, women still received plenty of encouragement to smoke. The cigarette had become firmly established as a convenient means to manage the demands of life, particularly so for disadvantaged women, especially mothers confined to the home. The notion that a cigarette was a 'friend' to the stressed, bored and lonely was visibly reinforced in popular culture. Additionally, it was only gradually that positive images of women smokers, including those in cigarette promotions, were removed from circulation. This, as we have seen, has by no means been completely successful.

The gradual establishment of smoking as a female and feminine practice since the late 1800s resulted from a range of factors. Important preconditions for the growth of women's smoking included technological developments that resulted in the modern, manufactured cigarette and, related to this, the increased availability of affordable cigarettes. Changes in women's lives, shifts in male smoking practices and, after 1920, the pervasiveness of cigarette-smoking culture also provided increased opportunities for women to smoke. But opportunities do not explain motivations. Why women should want to smoke, and the ways in which they engaged in the smoking habit, need to be understood in the context of the ascendancy of the visual in modern life.

The history of women's smoking is related to changes in women's lives, experiences and expectations and the prominence of the visual in these. 'The modern world is very much a "seen" phenomenon'[7] and information, pleasure, communication and identity have become increasingly dependent on the visual. In this context, smoking practices were perceived and utilized by an increasing number of women as visible signs in the presentation of self and in the 'reading' of others. In making identity statements women drew on the discourse of smoking and masculinity which, after 1920, was increasingly given visual expression in the media. After 1920 they could also draw upon a burgeoning, and highly visual, discourse on women and smoking. Some women were motivated to start smoking, and encouraged to continue, for reasons other than image. Tobacco was experienced by many as a comfort and/or as a stimulant, but these effects were inseparable from the visual significance of smoking. Women's understandings of smoking were inextricably related to the visual representation of smoking, particularly after 1920 with the proliferation of images of smokers in the mass media. Even prior to the emergence of women's smoking as a media spectacle, women were still aware of the meanings attached to smoking and the significance of being seen to smoke.

The history of women's smoking is bound up with issues of visibility. Issues relating to being seen to smoke were often important for whether women did smoke and, if they did, how and where. Some women defiantly chose to smoke in public even when female smoking was a minority practice and frowned upon in respectable society. For others, social censure encouraged smoking as a private pleasure. After 1920 it became increasingly acceptable for middle- and upper-class women to be seen smoking, but for many working-class women the public face of their smoking practice was still problematic. The visibility of the smoker was not solely a matter of face-to-face contact. After 1860 it was also increasingly dependent on media, most notably the photograph.

The significance of being seen to smoke had important implications for constructions of femininity, modernity and respectability. Smoking challenged Victorian constructions of feminine appearance and, as the practice increased among women, new conceptions of femininity emerged that embraced this practice.

Given the challenge that smoking posed to Victorian feminine demeanour, it is no surprise that it became key to interwar feminine modernity. Prior to the normalization of women's smoking, the practice was symbolically radical; it also visually disrupted traditional notions of feminine appearance – it altered how women looked, moved and occupied space. Women's smoking also created a spectacle and this deliberate focusing of attention on oneself was antithetical to notions of feminine modesty. Not surprisingly, it took some time before women's smoking was redefined as respectable. Respectable smoking was, however, always a matter of appearances and this served to exclude some women from the community of respectable smokers. Respectable women smokers had to visually distance themselves from the association of smoking with the sexually immoral, and often synonymous with this, the unrespectable working-class woman. The look of the middle and upper classes was partial guarantor of this. Refinement was also critical to feminine respectability, and this required attention to the finer details of appearance – respectable smokers had to ensure that they took meticulous care of their appearance and that they looked like members of the respectable classes. No lipstick marks on cigarette ends, no threads of tobacco stuck to their lips and no tobacco stains on fingers, nails and teeth.

Such strictures remain the essence of feminine smoking today, although there is far less certainty about the compatibility of femininity, respectability and smoking than there was fifty years ago. Indeed, girls and women from all social classes and age groups are frequently criticized for smoking. But whereas in the early stages of women's smoking history the woman smoker was singled out for criticism, today she stands alongside the male smoker, almost equals in the social and moral disapproval which their practice now attracts. They are only 'almost' equal because the greatest social censure is reserved for women who smoke when pregnant or breastfeeding. Gendered concerns still play an important part in defining reactions toward people who smoke. In the anti-smoking image, the young woman with stained teeth and fingers transgresses the rules of femininity and feminine respectability which are inextricably related to appearance. Her image graphically conveys some of the risks of smoking, albeit the more superficial ones. Whether such an image can discourage women from smoking, or persuade them to quit if they are already smokers, is another matter. Is it possible to combat the deep-seated and continually reinforced association of smoking and feminine attraction with an image that is a travesty of youthful femininity? Can young women actually identify with such an 'ugly' figure? Indeed, can the feminine attractions of smoking be countered by images of women smokers, however presented? In a society which has become increasingly dependent on the visual and where schoolchildren are often savvy about the construction of images, is this smoker credible? Perhaps it is only a lack of attractive images of women smokers that will really lay the feminine attractions of smoking to rest – at the moment this is inconceivable.

Notes

1. 'Dump the Fags', NHS advertisement, August 2005.
2. Boseley, 'Make Young Smokers a Burning Issue', p. 17. For example, 'Celebrity Smokers', *Heat*, 3–9 November 2001, pp. 74–5.
3. Omidvari et al., 'Smoking in Contemporary American Cinema'; Laurance, 'The Burning Issue', p. 3.
4. MOA, TC63, Box 1.
5. Wald et al., UK Smoking Statistics, p. 65, Table 4.1.2.
6. Ibid., pp. 34–5, Tables 4.1.1 and 4.1.2.
7. Jenks, 'The Centrality of the Eye', p. 2.

Bibliography

Archival Sources

Bridgeman Art Library, London.
British Film Institute (BFI) National Library, London.
Documentary Photograph Archive (DPA), Greater Manchester County Record Office.
Elizabeth Roberts Archive (ERA), Centre for North-West Regional Studies, Lancaster University.
Hulton Archive
Imperial War Museum (IWM), Department of Documents, London.
Imperial War Museum (IWM), Photograph Archive, London.
National Museum of Photography, Film and Television, Bradford. Kodak Photography Archive.
Mass-Observation Archives (MOA), University of Sussex.
   Topic Collection (TC) 63 Smoking Habits 1937–65. Boxes 1–2.
   File Report 979 *Smoking*, 1941.
   File Report 3192 *Man and his Cigarette*, December 1949.
National Archive (formerly, Public Record Office), Kew.
National Portrait Gallery (NPG), Heinz Archive & Library.
Pankhurst Centre, Manchester.
Player's Archive, Nottingham Record Office, Nottingham.
Wills Archive, Bristol Record Office, Bristol.

Magazines and Periodicals (consulted at Colindale Newspaper Library unless otherwise stated)

Englishwoman (Manchester Central Library)
Eve
Everywoman's Yearbook (Manchester Central Library)
Girls' Favourite
Girls' Friend
Girls' Reader
Glamour (British Library)
The Guider (Girlguiding UK Archives, London)
Honey (British Library)

Jackie
Lucky Star
Mabs Weekly
Mandy
Mayfair (British Library)
Men Only (British Library)
Miss Modern
Modern Woman
My Weekly
Our Girls
Pam's Paper (British Library)
Peg's Paper (British Library)
Petticoat
Poppy's Paper (British Library)
The Princess
Punch (Manchester John Rylands Library, University of Manchester)
School-Days (British Library)
The Schoolgirl (British Library)
The Sketch
Suffragette News Sheet (Manchester Central Library)
Time & Tide (Manchester Central Library)
Tobacco Trade Review (TTR)
Valentine
Vanity Fair (British Library)
Vogue (British Library, formerly at Colindale)
Votes for Women (Women's Library, London)
War Budget
Woman
Woman and Home
Woman's Own

Newspapers (pre-1920 consulted at Colindale Newspaper Library, London; 1920–1980 consulted at Manchester Central Library)

Daily Express
Daily Mail
Daily Mirror
Evening News (London)
Manchester Evening News
Manchester Guardian
News of the World
Sunday Express
The Times
Westminster Gazette

Personal Communications (quoted)

Rosemary Betterton, email, 20 September 2005
Lucy Bland, email, 27 January 2005
Kits Browning, phone conversation, 8 September 2005
Marjorie Hughes, letter, 8 August 2002; phone conversation, 11 September 2002
Richard Hutchison, letter, 18 August 2002
Nigel Nicolson, letter, 18 May 2004
Doug Rendell, letter, 6 August 2002; phone conversation, 11 September 2002
Mary P. Shuttleworth, communication, August 2005
Lisa Z. Sigel, email, 7 April 2004

Websites

Dry Drunk Exhibition. The New York Public Library http://www.nypl.org/research/chss/ spe/art/print/exhibits/drydrunk/intro.htm (accessed 16 June 2004)
Female Celebrity Smoking List. http://www.smokingsides.com (accessed 18 July 2002)
Hulton Archive. http://creative.getyimages.com

Books, Articles, Papers and Theses

Abrams, M., *Teenage Consumer Spending in 1959: Middle Class and Working Class Boys and Girls*, London: London Press Exchange, 1961.
Alexander, S., 'Becoming a Woman in London in the 1920s and 1930s', in D. Feldman and D. Stedman Jones (eds), *Metropolis, London: Histories and Representations since 1800*, London: Routledge, 1989.
Alexandra, Queen, *Queen Alexandra's Christmas Giftbook: Photographs from my Camera*, London: *Daily Telegraph*, 1908.
Alford, B.W.E., *W.D. & H.O. Wills and the Development of the U.K. Tobacco Industry 1786–1965*, London: Methuen, 1973.
Allen, G., *The Woman who Did*, London: Virago, 1994 [1895].
Alloula, M., *The Colonial Harem*, London: University of Minnesota Press, 1986.
Apperson, G.L., *The Social History of Smoking*, London: Martin Secker, Ballantyne Press, 1914.
Atkinson, D. *The Suffragettes in Pictures*, Stroud: Sutton, 1996.
Avery, V., *London Morning*. Exeter: Arnold-Wheaton, 1984.
Ballaster, R., Beetham, M., Frazer, E. and Hebron, S., *Women's Worlds: Ideology, Femininity and the Women's Magazine*, London, Macmillan, 1991.
Barthes, R., *Camera Lucida: Reflections on Photography*, trans R. Howard, New York: Hill and Wang, 1981.
Becker, H., 'Do Photographs Tell the Truth?', in T.D. Cook and C.S. Reichardt (eds), *Qualitative and Quantitative Methods in Evaluation Research*, London: Sage, 1979.

Bell, D., *The Cultural Contradictions of Capitalism*, 2nd edn, London: Heinemann, 1979.

Berridge, V., 'Constructing Women and Smoking as a Public Health Problem in Britain 1950–1990s', *Gender & History* 13 (2001), pp. 328–48.

——, 'Post-war Smoking Policy in the UK and the Redefinition of Public Health', *Twentieth-Century British History* 14 (2003), pp. 61–82.

—— and Loughlin, K. 'Smoking and the New Health Education in Britain, 1950s–1970s', *American Journal of Public Health* 95 (2005), pp. 956–64.

Bingham, A., *Gender, Modernity and the Popular Press in Inter-War Britain*, Oxford: Oxford University Press, 2004.

Bland, L., *Banishing the Beast: English Feminism & Sexual Morality 1885–1914*, Harmondsworth: Penguin, 1995.

Boseley, S., 'Make Young Smokers a Burning Issue', *The Guardian*, 7 October 1997, p. 17.

Brandt, A.M., 'Recruiting Women Smokers: The Engineering of Consent', *Journal of the American Women's Association* 51 (1996), pp. 63–6.

Brandt, B., *The English at Home*, London: Batsford, 1936.

——, *London in the Thirties: Bill Brandt*, London: Gordon Fraser Gallery, 1983.

Braybon, G. and Summerfield, P., *Out of the Cage: Women's Experiences in Two World Wars*, London: Pandora, 1987.

Breward, C., *The Culture of Fashion. A New History of Fashionable Dress*, Manchester: Manchester University Press, 1995.

Brittain, V., *Testament of Youth*, London: Virago, 1978.

Buckley, C. and Fawcett, H., *Fashioning the Feminine: Representation and Women's Fashion from the Fin de Siècle to the Present*, London: I.B.Tauris, 2002.

Burt, C., *The Young Delinquent,* Bickley: University of London Press, 1944 [1925].

Bynner, J.M., *The Young Smoker: A Study of Smoking among Schoolboys...*, London: HMSO, 1969.

Cadogan, M., *Richmal Crompton: The Woman Behind William*, London: Allen & Unwin, 1986.

Campbell, C., 'A Plea for Tobacco', *The English Illustrated Magazine* II (1893), pp. 81–4.

Chapman, S., *Great Expectorations: Advertising and the Tobacco Industry,* London: Comedia Publishing Group, 1986.

Charlton, A., 'Galsworthy's Images of Smoking in the Forsyte Chronicles', *Social Science & Medicine* 15A (1981), pp. 633–8.

Clyde, I., *Eve's Sour Apples*, London: Eric Partridge, 1934.

Collins, M., *Modern Love: An Intimate History of Men and Women in Twentieth-century Britain*, London: Atlantic Books, 2003.

Cooper, S., 'Snoek Piquante', in M. Sissons and P. French (eds), *Age of Austerity*, Oxford: Oxford University Press, 1986.

Corner, J., 'General Introduction: Television and British Society in the 1950s', in J. Corner (ed.), *Popular Television in Britain: Studies in Cultural History*, London; British Film Institute, 1991.

Cox, P., *Gender, Justice and Welfare: Bad Girls in Britain, 1900–1950*, Basingstoke: Palgrave Macmillan, 2003.

Crossick, G., 'Before the Shutters Fall: Shopkeepers and Photography in Britain and France in the Early Twentieth Century', paper presented at North American Conference on British Studies, Toronto, 2–4 November 2001.

Crow, D., *The Victorian Woman*, London: George Allen & Unwin, 1971.

Dale, E., *The Content of Motion Pictures*, New York: Macmillan, 1935.

Davies, A., *Leisure, Gender and Poverty: Working-class Culture in Salford and Manchester, 1900–1939*, Buckingham: Open University Press, 1992.

——, 'Cinema and Broadcasting', in P. Johnson (ed.), *Twentieth-Century Britain: Economic, Social and Cultural Change*, London: Longman, 1994.

Daykin, N., 'Young Women and Smoking: Towards a Sociological Account', *Health Promotion International* 8 (1993), pp. 95–102.

Dayus, K., *Where There's Life*, London: Virago, 1985.

De Ville, N. and Haden-Guest, A., *Lenare, the Art of Society Photography 1924–1977*, London: Allen Lane, 1981.

Doan, L., *Fashioning Sapphism: The Origins of a Modern English Lesbian Culture*, New York: Columbia University Press, 2001.

Docherty, T., *Pre-Code Hollywood: Sex, Immorality, and Insurrection in American Cinema 1930–1934*, New York: Columbia University Press, 1999.

Dunhill, M., *Our Family Business*, London: The Bodley Head, 1979.

Durant, H., *The Problem of Leisure*, London: G. Routledge & Sons, 1938.

Dyhouse, C., *Girls Growing Up in Late Victorian and Edwardian England*, London: Routledge & Kegan Paul, 1981.

Elliot, R., 'Destructive but Sweet': Cigarette Smoking among Women 1890–1990, Unpublished PhD thesis, University of Glasgow, 2001.

——, '"Everybody did it" – or Did they?: the Use of Oral History in Researching Women's Experiences of Smoking in Britain, 1930–1970', *Women's History Review* 15 (2006), pp. 297–322.

Ernster, V., 'Mixed Messages for Women, a Social History of Cigarette Smoking and Advertising', *New York State Journal of Medicine* (July 1985), pp. 335–40.

Felski, R., *The Gender of Modernity*, London: Harvard University Press, 1995.

Flint, K., *The Victorians and the Visual Imagination*, Cambridge: Cambridge University Press, 2000.

Forster, M., *Daphne du Maurier*, London: Arrow, 1994.

Gardiner, J., *From the Closet to the Screen: Women at the Gateways Club, 1945–85*, London: Pandora, 2003.

Giddens, A., *Modernity and Self-Identity: Self and Society in the Late Modern Age*, London: Polity, 1991.

Giles, J., '"Playing Hard to Get": Working-class Women, Sexuality and Respectability in Britain, 1918–40', *Women's History Review* 1 (1992), pp. 239–55.

——, *Women, Identity and Private Life in Britain, 1900–50*, London: Macmillan, 1995.

——, *The Parlour and the Suburb: Domestic Identities, Class, Femininity and Modernity*, Oxford: Berg, 2004.

Gilman, S.L. and Xun, Z. (eds), *Smoke: A Global History of Smoking*, London: Reaktion, 2004.

Glendinning, V., *Vita: The Life of V. Sackville-West*, Harmondsworth: Penguin, 1984.

Goffman, E., *The Presentation of Self in Everyday Life*, Harmondsworth: Penguin, 1990.

——, *Gender Advertisements*, New York: Harper and Row, 1979.

Goodman, J., *Tobacco in History: The Cultures of Dependence*, London: Routledge, 1994.

Gordan, P. and Doughan, D., *Dictionary of British Women's Organisations 1825–1960*, London: Woburn Press, 2001.

Graham, H., 'Smoking in Pregnancy: The Attitudes of Expectant Mothers', *Social Science & Medicine* 10 (1976), pp. 399–405.

——, *When Life's A Drag: Women, Smoking and Disadvantage*, London: Department of Health, 1993.

Graves, R. and Hodge, A., *The Long Weekend: A Social History of Great Britain 1918–1939*, London: Sphere, 1991 [1940].

Greaves, L., *Smoke Screen: Women's Smoking and Social Control*, London: Scarlet Press, 1996.

Greenfield, J., O'Connell, S. and Reid, C., 'Fashioning Masculinity: *Men Only*, Consumption and the Development of Marketing in the 1930s', *Twentieth Century British History* 10 (1999), pp. 457–76.

Gregory, I., *In Memory of Burlington Street: An Appreciation of the Manchester University Unions 1861–1957*, Manchester: Manchester University Union, *c.*1957.

Haggis, J. 'Gendering Colonialism or Colonising Gender? Recent Women's Studies Approaches to White Women and the History of British Colonialism', *Women's Studies International Forum* 13 (1990), pp. 105–15.

Hall, L.A., *Sex, Gender and Social Change in Britain since 1880*, London: Macmillan, 2000.

Hall, R., *The Well of Loneliness*, London: Virago, 1982.

Hall, S., 'Encoding/Decoding', in S. Hall, D. Hobson, A. Lowe and P. Willis (eds), *Culture, Media, Language: Working Papers in Cultural Studies 1972–79*, London: Hutchison, 1980.

Hartley, J. (ed.), *Hearts Undefeated: Women's Writing of the Second World War*, London: Virago, 1995.

Haskell, M., *From Reverence to Rape: The Treatment of Women in the Movies*, London: New English library, 1975.

Higgs, M., *Three Nights in Women's Lodging Houses*, private circulation from author, 1905.

Hilton, M., *Smoking in British Popular Culture 1800–2000*, Manchester: Manchester University Press, 2000.

——, 'Advertising the Modernist Aesthetic of the Marketplace? The Cultural Relationship Between the Tobacco Manufacturer and the "Mass" of Consumers in Britain, 1870–1940', in M. Daunton and B. Rieger (eds) *Meanings of Modernity: Britain from the Late-Victorian Era to World War II*, Oxford: Berg, 2001.

Hindley, D. and Hindley, G., *Advertising in Victorian England, 1837–1901*, London: Wayland, 1972.

Hirsch, M., *Family Frames, Photography, Narrative and Postmemory*, London: Harvard University Press, 1997.

Holland, P., '"Sweet it is to Scan...": Personal Photographs and Popular Photography', in L. Wells (ed.), *Photography: A Critical Introduction*, 2nd edn, London: Routledge, 2000.

Homberger, E., 'J.P. Morgan's Nose: Photographer and Subject in American Portrait Photography ', in G. Clarke (ed.), *The Portrait in Photography*, London: Reaktion, 1992.

Hoole, J. and Sato, T. (eds), *Alphonse Mucha*, London: Lund Humphries in association with Barbican Art Gallery, 1993.

Horwood, C., *Keeping Up Appearances: Fashion and Class between the Wars*, Stroud: Sutton, 2005.

Hughes, C., *Women's Contemporary Lives: Within and Beyond the Mirror*, London: Routledge, 2002.

Humm, M., *Modernist Women and Visual Cultures: Virginia Woolf, Vanessa Bell, Photography and Cinema*, Edinburgh: Edinburgh University Press, 2002.

Hunting, J.D., 'Women and Tobacco', *National Review* 14 (1889), pp. 218–28.

Hutcheon, L. and Hutcheon, M., 'Smoking in Opera', in S.L. Gilman and Z. Xun (eds), *Smoke: A Global History of Smoking*, London: Reaktion, 2004.

Isenberg, N., 'Cinematic Smoke: From Weimar to Hollywood', in S.L. Gilman and Z. Xun (eds), *Smoke: A Global History of Smoking*, London: Reaktion, 2004.

Jackson, A.A., *The Middle Classes, 1900–1950*, Nairn: David St John Thomas, *c.*1991.

Jackson, C. and Tinkler, P., '"Ladettes" and "Modern Girls": "Troublesome" Young Femininities', *Sociological Review*, forthcoming.

Jacobs, L., *The Wages of Sin: Censorship and the Fallen Woman Film, 1928–1942*, London: University of California Press, 1997.

Jacobson, B., *The Ladykillers: Why Smoking is a Feminist Issue*, London: Pluto, 1981.

——, *Beating the Ladykillers: Woman and Smoking,* London: Pluto, 1986.

—— and Amos, A., *When Smoke Gets in Your Eyes*, British Medical Association Professional Division, Health Education Council, 1985.

Jeffreys, S., *The Spinster and Her Enemies: Feminism and Sexuality 1880–1930,* London: Pandora, 1985.

Jenks, C., 'The Centrality of the Eye in Western Culture: An Introduction', in C. Jenks (ed.), *Visual Culture*, London: Routledge, 1995.

Jephcott, P., *Girls Growing Up*, London: Faber & Faber, 1942.

——, *Rising Twenty: Notes on Some Ordinary Girls*, London: Faber, 1948.

Kalmar, I.D., 'The Houkah in the Harem: On Smoking and Orientalist Art', in S.L. Gilman and Z. Xun (eds), *Smoke: A Global History of Smoking*, London: Reaktion, 2004.

Kent, S.K., *Making Peace: The Reconstruction of Gender in Interwar Britain*, Princeton: Princeton University Press, 1993.

Klein, R., *Cigarettes are Sublime*, London: Duke University Press, 1993.

Kobal, J., *The Art of the Great Hollywood Portrait Photographers*, London: Pavilion, 1988.

Koetzle, M., *Feu d'Amour, Seductive Smoke*, Cologne: Benedikt Taschen, 1994.

Laermans, R., 'Learning to Consume: Early Department Stores and the Shaping of the Modern Consumer Culture (1860–1914)', *Theory, Culture & Society* 10 (1993), pp. 79–102.

Laurance, J., 'The Burning Issue: Only Villains Smoke in Hollywood', *The Independent*, 9 August 2005, p. 3.

Laver, J., *The Age of Optimism: Manners and Morals 1848–1914*, London: Weidenfeld & Nicolson, 1966.

Law, G., 'New Woman Novels in Newspapers', *Media History* 7 (2001), pp. 17–31.

Lee, H., *Virginia Woolf*, London: Chatto & Windus, 1996.

Leiss, W., Kline, S., and Jhally, S., *Social Communication in Advertising: Persons, Products and Images of Well-being*, London: Methuen, 1986.

Leng, F., *Daphne du Maurier: A Daughter's Memoir*, Edinburgh: Mainstream, 1995.

Lewis, R. and Maude, A., *The English Middle Classes*, London: Penguin, 1953.

Light, A., *Forever England: Femininity, Literature and Conservatism between the Wars*, London: Routledge, 1991.

Linkman, A., *The Victorians: Photographic Portraits*, London: I.B. Tauris, 1993.

Linton, E.L., 'The Wild Women as Social Insurgents', *The Nineteenth Century* 30 (1891), pp. 596–605.

——, 'A counterblaste', *English Illustrated Magazine* 11 (1893), pp. 84–9.

Lister, M., and Wells, L., 'Seeing Beyond Belief: Cultural Studies as an Approach to Analysing the Visual', in T. van Leeuwen and C. Jewitt (eds), *Handbook of Visual Analysis*, London: Sage, 2001.

MacKinnon, K. and Owen, L., *Smoking in Films: A Review*, London: HEA, 1997.

Maitland, S., *Vesta Tilley*, London: Virago, 1986.

Mannin, E., *Young in the Twenties*, London: Hutchinson, 1971.

Marchand, R., *Advertising the American Dream: Making Way for Modernity, 1920–1940*, London: University of California Press, 1986.

Mayhew, H., *London Labour and the London Poor*, Vol. IV, London: Frank Cass, 1967 [1st edn 1851].

McDowell, C. *Forties Fashion and the New Look*, London: Bloomsbury, 1997.

McKennell, A.C., and Thomas, R.K., *Adults' and Adolescents' Smoking Habits and Attitudes: A Report on a Survey carried out for the Ministry of Health*, London: HMSO, 1967.

McKibbin, R., *Classes and Cultures: England 1918–1951*, Oxford: Oxford University Press, 2000.

Melman, B., *Women and the Popular Imagination in the Twenties: Flappers and Nymphs*, London: Macmillan, 1988.

Mitchell, D., 'The "New Woman" as Prometheus: Women Artists Depict Women Smoking', *Woman's Art Journal* 12 (1991), pp. 3–9.

——, 'Images of Exotic Women in Turn-of-the-century Tobacco Art', *Feminist Studies* 18 (1992), pp. 327–50.

Nava, M., 'Modernity's Disavowal. Women, the City and the Department Store', in M. Nava and A. O'Shea (eds), *Modern Times: Reflections on a Century of English Modernity*, London and New York: Routledge, 1996.

—— and O'Shea, A., (eds) *Modern Times: Reflections on a Century of English Modernity*, London and New York: Routledge, 1996.

Nead, L., *Myths of Sexuality: Representations of Women in Victorian Britain*, Oxford: Blackwell, 1988.

Nicolson, N., *Portrait of a Marriage: Illustrated Edition,* London: Weidenfeld & Nicolson, 1990.

——, *Portrait of a Marriage,* London: Phoenix, 1996.

Nicolson, N. and Trautmann, J. (eds), *The Question of Things Happening: The Letters of Virginia Woolf. Vol II: 1912–1922,* London: Hogarth, 1976.

—— (eds), *A Change in Perspective: The Letters of Virginia Woolf. Vol III: 1923–1928,* London: Hogarth, 1977.

—— (eds), *A Reflection of the Other Person: The Letters of Viriginia Woolf. Vol IV: 1929–1931,* London: Hogarth, 1978.

—— (eds), *The Sickle Side of the Moon: The Letters of Virginia Woolf. Vol V: 1932–1935,* London: Hogarth, 1979.

—— (eds), *Leave the Letters till We're Dead: The Letters of Virginia Woolf. Vol VI: 1936–1941,* London: Hogarth, 1980.

Omidvari, K. et al., 'Smoking in Contemporary American Cinema', *Chest* 128 (2005), pp. 746–54.

Oram, A. and Turnball, A., *The Lesbian History Sourcebook: Love and Sex between Women in Britain from 1780 to 1970,* London: Routledge, 2001.

O'Shea, A., 'English Subjects of Modernity', in M. Nava and A. O'Shea (eds), *Modern Times: Reflections on a Century of English Modernity,* London and New York: Routledge, 1996.

O'Sullivan, T., 'Television Memories and Cultures of Viewing, 1950–65', in J. Corner (ed), *Popular Television in Britain: Studies in Cultural History,* London: British Film Institute, 1991.

Parr, G., 'S for Smoking', *Sight and Sound* (December 1997), pp. 30–3.

Peiss, K., 'Making Faces: The Cosmetics Industry and the Cultural Construction of Gender, 1890–1930', *Genders* 7 (1990), pp. 143–69.

——, *Hope in a Jar: The Making of America's Beauty Culture,* New York: Henry Holt, 1998.

Pepper, T., *Dorothy Wilding: The Pursuit of Perfection,* London: National Portrait Gallery, 1991.

Priestley, J.B., *English Journey,* London: Heinemann, 1984 [1934].

Rappaport, E.D., *Shopping for Pleasure. Women in the Making of London's West End,* Princeton and Oxford: Princeton University Press, 2001.

——, 'Travelling in the Lady Guides' London: Consumption, Modernity, and the Fin-de-siècle Metropolis', in M. Daunton and B. Rieger (eds), *Meanings of Modernity: Britain from the Late Victorian Era to World War II,* Oxford: Berg, 2001.

Rice, M. Spring, *Working-Class Wives, their Health and Condition,* London: Virago, 1981 [1939].

Richards, J., *The Age of the Dream Palace: Cinema and Society in Britain, 1930–39,* London: Routledge, 1984.

Richards, T., *The Commodity Culture of Victorian England: Advertising and Spectacle, 1851–1914,* London: Verso, 1991.

Richardson, D., *Pilgrimage,* Vol. 1, London: Dent & Sons, 1967.

Rieger, B. and Daunton, M., 'Introduction', in M. Daunton and B. Rieger (eds), *Meanings of Modernity: Britain from the Late Victorian Era to World War II*, Oxford: Berg, 2001.

Roberts, P., 'Yevonde: "Be Original or Die"', in R. Gibson and P. Roberts, *Madame Yevonde: Colour, Fantasy and Myth*, London: National Portrait Gallery, 1990.

Rodaway, A., *A London Childhood*, London: Virago, 1985.

Rolley, K., 'Cutting a Dash: The Dress of Radclyffe Hall and Una Troubridge', *Feminist Review* 35 (1990), pp. 54–66.

—— and Aish, C., *Fashion in Photographs 1900–1920*, in association with the National Portrait Gallery, London: Batsford, 1992.

Rose, G., *Visual Methodologies: An Introduction to the Interpretation of Visual Materials*, London: Sage, 2001.

Rosen, M., *Popcorn Venus: Women, Movies and the American Dream*, New York: Avon, 1973.

Rowntree, B.S. and Lavers, G.R., *English Life and Leisure: A Social Study*, London: Longmans, Green and Co, 1951.

Royal College of Physicians, *Smoking and Health*, London: Pitman, 1962.

——, *Smoking and Health Now*, London: Pitman, 1971.

——, *Health or Smoking?*, London: Pitman, 1983.

Ryan, L., 'Negotiating Modernity and Tradition: Newspaper Debates on the "Modern Girl" in the Irish Free State', *Journal of Gender Studies* 7 (1988), pp. 181–97.

Samuel, R., 'Suburbs under Siege: The Middle Class between the Wars PART III', *New Socialist* 11 (1983), pp. 28–30.

Schivelbusch, W., *Tastes of Paradise: A Social History of Spices, Stimulants & Intoxicants*, New York: Pantheon, 1992.

Schudson, M., *Advertising, the Uneasy Persuasion: its Dubious Impact on American Society*, New York: Basic, 1985.

Seabrook, J., 'My Life is in that Box', in J. Spence and P. Holland (eds), *Family Snaps: The Meanings of Domestic Photography*, London: Virago, 1991.

Shackell, D., *Modern Fashion Drawing*, London: Pitman & Sons, 1934.

Shilling, C., *The Body and Social Theory*, 2nd edn, London: Sage, 2003.

Sigel, L.Z., *Governing Pleasures: Pornography and Social Change in England, 1815–1914*, London: Rutgers University Press, 2002.

Skeggs, B., *Formations of Class and Gender: Becoming Respectable*, London: Sage, 1997.

Sontag, S., *On Photography*, Harmondsworth: Penguin, 1979.

Souhami, D., *Gluck: Her Biography*, London: Pandora, 1989.

Speaight, R., *Memoirs of a Court Photographer*, London: Hurst & Blackett, 1926.

Stacey, J., *Star Gazing: Hollywood Cinema and Female Spectatorship*, London: Routledge, 1994.

Steele, V., *Fashion and Eroticism: Ideals of Feminine Beauty from the Victorian Era to the Jazz Age*, Oxford: Oxford University Press, 1985.

Stein, S., 'The Graphic Ordering of Desire: Modernization of a Middle-class Women's Magazine, 1919–1939', in R. Bolton (ed.), *The Contest of Meaning: Critical Histories of Photography*, Cambridge MA: MIT Press, 1989.

Stevenson, J., *British Society 1914–45*, Harmondsworth: Penguin, 1984.

Stocks, M., *Eleanor Rathbone: a Biography*, London: Gollancz, 1949.

Stockwell, T.F. and Glantz, S.A., 'Tobacco Use is Increasing in Popular Films', *Tobacco Control* 6 (1997), pp. 282–4.

Storey, J., *Our Joyce, 1917–1939: Joyce Storey: Her Early Years*, London: Virago, 1992.

Summers, A., *What's Wrong with England*, London: Robert Hayes, 1928.

Summerscale, K., *The Queen of Whale Cay*, London: Fourth Estate, 1998.

Tagg, J., *The Burden of Representation: Essays in Photographies and Histories*, Basingstoke: Macmillan, 1988.

Tate, C., *Cigarette Wars: The Triumph of 'The Little White Slaver'*, Oxford: Oxford University Press, 1999.

Taylor, P., *Smoke Ring: The Politics of Tobacco*, London: Bodley Head, 1984.

Tickner, L., *The Spectacle of Women: Imagery of the Suffrage Campaign, 1907–14*, London: Chatto & Windus, 1987.

Tinkler, P., *Constructing Girlhood: Popular Magazines for Girls Growing Up in England, 1920–1950*, London: Taylor & Francis, 1995.

——, '"Red Tips for Hot Lips": Advertising Cigarettes for Young Women in Britain, 1920–70', *Women's History Review* 10 (2001a), pp. 249–72.

——, 'Rebellion, Modernity and Romance: Smoking as a Gendered Practice in Popular Young Women's Magazines, Britain 1918–1939', *Women's Studies International Forum* 24 (2001), pp. 1–12.

——, 'Refinement and Respectable Consumption: the Acceptable Face of Women's Smoking in Britain, 1918–1970', *Gender & History* 15 (2003), pp. 342–60.

——, 'Smoking and Sapphic Modernities', in L. Doan and J. Garrity (eds) *Sapphic Modernities: Sexuality, Women and English Culture*, London: Palgrave, 2006.

—— and Warsh, C., 'Feminine Modernity in Inter-war Britain and North America: Corsets, Cars and Cigarettes', *Journal of Women's History*, forthcoming.

Tyau, M-C. T.Z., *London Through Chinese Eyes or My Seven and a Half Years in London*, London: Swarthmore Press, 1920.

Tyrrell, I., 'The Limits of Persuasion: Advertising, Gender and the Culture of Australian Smoking', *Australian Historical Studies* 114 (2000), pp. 27–48.

——, *Deadly Enemies: Tobacco and its Opponents in Australia*, Sydney: UNSW Press, 1999.

Valverde, M., 'The Love of Finery: Fashion and the Fallen Woman in Nineteenth-century Social Discourse', *Victorian Studies* 32 (1989), pp. 169–88.

Wald, N., et al., *UK Smoking Statistics*, Oxford: Oxford University Press, 1988.

Walker, J.A. and Chaplin, S., *Visual Culture: An Introduction*, Manchester: Manchester University Press, 1997.

Walkerdine, V., 'Dreams from an Ordinary Childhood', in *Schoolgirl Fictions*, London: Verso, 1990.

Warsh, C.K., 'Smoke and Mirrors: Gender Representation in North American Tobacco and Alcohol Advertisements before 1950', *Social History* 31 (1998), pp. 183–222.

—— and Tinkler, P., 'In Vogue: North American and British Representations of Women Smokers in *Vogue*, 1920s–1960s', *Canadian Bulletin of Medical History/Bulletin Canadien d'histoire de la médecine*, forthcoming.

Webb-Johnson, C., 'Women's Clubs', in B. Braithwaite, N. Walsh and G. Davies (eds), *Ragtime to Wartime: the Book of Good Housekeeping, 1922–1939*, London: Ebury Press, 1986.

Wells, H.G., *Ann Veronica*, London: Virago, 1980 [1909].

White, C.L., *Women's Magazines 1693–1968*, London: Michael Joseph, 1970.

Williams, V., *Women Photographers: The Other Observers 1900 to the Present*, London: Virago, 1986.

Wilson, E., *Adorned in Dreams: Fashion and Modernity*, London: Virago, 1985.

—— and Taylor, L., *Through the Looking Glass: a History of Dress from 1860 to the Present Day*, London: BBC Books, 1989.

Winship, J., 'New Disciplines for Women and the Rise of the Chain Store in the 1930s', in M. Andrews and M. Talbot (eds), *All the World and Her Husband: Women in Twentieth-Century Consumer Culture*, London: Cassell, 2000.

Wood, C., *Victorian Panorama: Paintings of Victorian Life*, London: Faber & Faber, 1990.

Yevonde, M., *In Camera*, London: John Gifford, 1940.

Zweig, F., *Women's Life and Labour*, London: Gollancz, 1952.

Index